Guest Management

Dr. Raj Kumar Singh
D.H.C.T. Mangt. (W.B.)
P.G.D.B. Mangt. (U.P.)
C.F.N. (Delhi)
MHCIMA (London)
Ph.D. (Management)
Director
'SAMS' Institute of Hotel Management,
Varanasi

AMAN PUBLICATIONS
NEW DELHI

Published by :
Rajiv Jain for Aman Publications
LG-4A, Ganpati Bhawan, 4675-B/21, Ansari Road,
Darya Ganj, New Delhi-110002
Ph. : 23255012, 23282127
E-mail: sshjbs@yahoo.com

Published 2018

ISBN–81–8204–005-1

Sole Distributor :
Jindal Book Services
LG-4A, Ganpati Bhawan,
4675-B/21, Ansari Road,
Darya Ganj, New Delhi-110002

Laser Typesetting by :
Deep Printers, New Delhi-110002

Printed by :
Tarun Offset, Delhi, India

Preface

The oriental world conceived the radical Philosophy of Hospitality with the broadest possible openness of heart and mind by stating 'Udar Charitanamtu, Vashudhaiwa Kutumbkam.' Vedas inculcated the doctrine of human ethics–'Athithi Devo Bhava'. In both above teaching it was a process of evolution in the broadness of life.

In the course of time, things changed a lot, though the basic principles of Atithi Seva–i.e. Guest Management remained the same but the practical aspect has rolled down to a new dimension due to growing aspirations of global guest influx. Since our ancient idea of guest management had been more emotional and Metaphysical, we got our self a bit uncomfortable in the arena of Guest Management in the world of Physics, but with the help of my first hand knowledge and understanding I tried to draw a synthesis of guest management in this book from the contrast and realities of thesis and antithesis.

Journey of this book is actually a walk on the line of doubledged sword with the expansion of mind and reduction of Geography; a guest may come from fag end of the poles.

One who would serve need to know desires, the expectations and mental states of the guest with the right earnest in a freak of the moment, with my comprehensive experiences tried to reduce this colossal science of art—Guest Management in this book which is firstly worth reading, secondly worth keeping and thirdly worth for reference for the professionals of Hospitality Industry, students and faculties of Catering Colleges of India and Abroad.

Contents

1

Understanding Customer Choices

Hospitality customers usually make purchases by simultaneously evaluating several criteria. A typical buying decision might take into account service quality, delivery speed, price, and any special buying incentives, for instance. It is imperative that businesses take into account customer preferences and choices when making decisions regarding product and service attributes. Managers need to understand how customers integrate, value, and trade off different product and service attributes. By the same token, information about customer demands and preferences must be incorporated into the design and day-to-day management of service-delivery processes.

DESCRETE CHOICE ANALYSIS

The discretechoice analysis (DCA) approach provides a robust and systematic way to identify the implied relative weights and attribute trade-offs revealed by decision makers' choices (whether customers or managers). To be sure, DCA is not the only approach that has been used to understand and model consumer decision making, but it has proved particularly valuable in many hundreds of applications since its introduction by Daniel L. McFadden (winner of the Nobel Prize for economics in 2000).

More important, DCA is one of only a few modeling approaches based on a sound, welltested, and relatively comprehensive behavioral theory (known as random-utility theory-RUT) that leads to a wide variety of testable and tractable models of choice behavior. Indeed, RUT provides a sound theoretical link between behavior observed in experiments, surveys, or other forms of stated preferences and the behavior observed in real-life situations.

As a disclaimer, we must note that all models are abstractions of reality, and the applicability of a particular choice model depends on the assumptions, theoretical foundations, and scientific methods used in modeling, data collection, and analysis, as well as one's understanding of customer demands and firms' resources by the managerial decision makers.Close, but not conjoint. DCA is often compared to and confused with another (strategic) marketing-research method known as conjoint analysis.The two bear superficial resemblance to each other insofar as they both analyze customer responses to experimentally designed profiles of products or services.

Conjoint-analysis data are obtained in the form of ratings or rankings based on comparisons of experimentally designed product-and-service descriptions or profiles (that is, customers do not select particular alternatives, but instead rate or rank them). More rarely, conjoint analysis involves binary responses (yes or no) regarding particular attribute packages. DCA distinguished. In contrast, DCA places a respondent in simulated choice-making situations derived from realistic variations of the product and service offerings that one might find in the market.

DCA is used to identify the relative weights that customers accord to product or service features and attributes. The weights are derived from consumers' responses to experimentally designed descriptions of product and service options. DCA results can lead to many managerially useful conclusions, such as identification of optimum product-and-service bundles, identification of market segments, measurement of brand equity, and development of processimprovement action plans.

META-CHOICE

The purpose of meta-choice is to assess and challenge management preconceptions of business and market conditions and to uncover customers' decision-making patterns using available market information. The first step in this framework-building process is to identify the relevant choice drivers, using qualitative market assessment, in-depth interviews, case studies, focus groups, and analysis of secondary information. Great care must be taken to ensure that all (or at least as many as possible) of the determinant demand-choice drivers are identified and expressed in terms understood by customers.

One should consider the following two questions when building a list of market-choice drivers:

1. Is it necessary to include an exhaustive list of all salient product and service drivers?; and
2. How can product and service attributes be configured so that the critical choice drivers are identified while the choice experiment is at once realistic and small enough to be tractable?

The next step is to identify the range of variability, or the levels of the demand-choice drivers. Although the range of variability should span the actual values of product attributes observed in the market and encompass the entire range of possible options, it should also be small enough to keep the experiment to a realistic and practical size, so as not to overwhelm the respondents with too many scenarios from which to choose. Once the range is determined, it must be divided into two or more discrete levels for experimentaldesign purposes.

Two levels are sufficient to estimate the linear effect that the attributes have on choice, but more than two levels are needed to estimate non-linear effects for quantitative attributes. As well, several levels of qualitative demand drivers like check-in times or room color are often required. Constructing a choice-driver list can be an intensive process. It requires consensus building and using both creative and analytical techniques. Depending on the exact nature of the study, the process of finalizing the list of choice drivers may take a few days or several weeks of fact finding, discussions, and profile iterations.

After identifying the demand-choice drivers, a systematic procedure is used to construct the choice experiments. A typical choice experiment consists of a series of choice exercises in which respondents are asked to choose a bundle of product and service attributes from a set of options. One can frame choice exercises in any of several ways. For example, one can show the respondents two restaurant profiles and ask them to choose restaurant number one, restaurant number two, or neither one. A second approach is to show respondents one restaurant profile at a time and ask them either to accept or reject the restaurant represented by each profile.

A third option is to ask respondents to identify the most desirable and the least desirable features for each of the restaurants presented. Yet a fourth approach would be to ask respondents to indicate how often (say, in a six-month period) they might choose to visit each establishment presented in a profile. However the DCA exercise is designed, researchers should strive for realistic descriptions of products or services. The nature of each customer-choice exercise depends on the choice drivers and their possible values.

To successfully assess each choice driver's effect on customer preferences, respondents are presented with several different choice scenarios generated by means of sophisticated experimental-design procedures. Such design procedures typically generate many possible alternatives. Once the experimental design is implemented in the form of a set of choice scenarios, response data are collected from a sample that represents the population of interest. Discrete-choice responses are categorical, because respondents choose one option from each set of options. As a consequence, several hundred observations are needed to satisfy the asymptotic conditions specified for estimating the model's parameters and obtaining reliable statistical tests.

Hence, responses from multiple individuals are aggregated in estimating the choice model. However, more recently, advanced statistical methods have been used to estimate distributions of individualpreference effects or segment-level choice models (e.g., latent-market segmentation; Bayesian estimation methods). It is important to note that when one combines the responses of many individuals to estimate choice models, differences in individual preferences become an issue (i.e., socalled "preference heterogeneity"). Both choice sets and respondents in choice experiments are randomly assigned to blocks, with the purpose of that randomization being to ensure that the resulting data are orthogonal (that is, mutually exclusive or mathematically independent).

Estimated-choice models include the following information:

— Relative weights for each choice-driver (e.g. price, speed) on individual, segment, or aggregate choices stated in the experiment.

— Relative weights for interactions among choice-drivers-as specified in the estimated model.

— Several statistical goodness-of-fit measures for the estimated model(s).

Customer-choice Modeling

By understanding consumer choices, senior managers can effectively develop and position product and service offerings to better suit their customers' needs. In addition, mathematical models representing customer choice can be linked to operating decisions (e.g., budgets, labor scheduling, special-activities planning, service offerings), and optimal service configurations can be identified for further improvement. The statistical models developed from discrete-choice experiments can be easily incorporated in spreadsheet-based decision-support systems (DSSs)to create a model for strategy development.

Although designing choice experiments and estimating models requires sophisticated training and skills, implementing the estimated model(s) in a spreadsheet-based DSS fairly straightforward. Once the DSS is set up, manager has only to input the attributes of the desired product-service offering and the available competitors' products to predict expected market shares for all. The DSS captures the dynamic nature of the market, allowing managers to evaluate multiple businesses, operating and marketing strategies, and the effects of changing strategies in the competitive marketplace. In addition, the predictive power of DCA-based models can be further improved by market- segmentation techniques such as latent-segment analysis.

Relative weights of various choice drivers (âs, or utility estimates) can be used to identify the similarities in a firm's user base and assess how those commonalities affect the current and future value of firm offerings. Choice models also can identify key features that drive market share in different customer-preference clusters. The group labeled Gourmet Buyers, for example, carries relatively high utilities for all choice drivers except price. Members of the Tough Sells group, on the other hand, consider each of the four choice drivers to be of roughly equal importance, whereas the Bargain Hunters seem by nature to be the most price sensitive.

Identifying such preference differences across customer groups can help a firm improve the effectiveness of its marketing campaign for each cluster. In addition to identifying the overall relative effects of customer preferences, choicemodeling results can also be used to assess the implications for overall market share resulting from changes in the value of one or more choice drivers. For example, choice models can be used to assess how the market share of one firm will be affected by a competitor's change in one or more choice drivers.

By assessing the relative weights of various market drivers to identify order-winning features, firms can further optimize product and service offerings. This analysis allows firms to focus on a few selected choice drivers when developing new products and services or when changing selected features of existing offerings.

Education and training

Choice models and associated decision-support spreadsheets also can be used as education and training tools and to help managers better align their decisions with what customers want and are willing to pay for. Often managers of large service organizations (including hotels and resorts) are busy managing day-to-day operations, so that gaps may exist between customers' needs and managers' perceptions of those needs. Comparing two choice models-one representing customer choices and another one representing the managers' beliefs about customer choices-can identify such perception-choice gaps.

Furthermore, customer-choice information obtained from DCA can be used to design services and improve management of operating processes. For example, assume that customers of a particular quick-service restaurant place more weight on (short) waiting time than they do on the number of food items on the menu. In that case, managers should focus their attention on the back-end processes that would result in reduced waiting times, including some or all of the following: efficient scheduling of the appropriate labor force, streamlining operations and minimizing redundancies, and limiting the number of menu items to speed up the orderpreparation cycle.

Chef's Table

Bread is the most universal and versatile of foods. Hailed throughout history as a secular mainstay and a sacred symbol, this fundamental fare appears in as many forms as there are cultures around the world. Bread has almost always been a part of the human diet, but over the centuries the world's bakers have made many improvements and variations. In fact, today's breads scarcely resemble the earliest versions of the food.

Paleontologists working in the Nile Valley have discovered mortars and pestles used for grinding grain and other evidence that suggest the production of primitive bread over 17,000 years ago. Using stones in open fires to cook a gluey dough of water and wild grain, wandering hunter-gatherers became the first bakers. This ancient bread making predated civilization, but may have activated it as well. The desire for a stable food supply spurred the subsequent cultivation of grain which lay the foundation for civilized life.

The earliest breads were simple, flat cakes, a form still popular in many cuisines today. Yeast breads made their debut about 9,000 years ago in Sumaria and were probably created by accident when dough was left unattended long enough to allow the fermentation caused by yeast to begin. The process of leavening was perfected when centuries later the oven was invented in Egypt, giving rise to a whole new world of texture and flavor.

Records reveal over thirty kinds of bread were baked by Egyptians who enjoyed them in this life and apparently the hereafter as they supplied deceased loved ones with loaves in burial tombs. The demand for bread was met in part with the invention in the early Roman Empire of the first rotary mill powered by slaves or animals. Another Roman device was a mechanical system to mix and knead dough. By the time of Christ, Rome had 250 bakeries which were selling more than half a million loaves every day. It was such a key element in the Roman diet, their very word for bread was synonymous for food of all kinds.

Roman legions were responsible for spreading the art of bread making across the European continent, but heartier grains than the wheat from Rome had to be adapted to areas with colder climates and rocky soil. After the fall of Rome, fine bread in Europe was scarce for centuries until colonists found the fertile soil in America perfect for wheat production and began a healthy export business. By the time of the Revolutionary War, wheat was America's leading crop, and in 1776, seventy-five tons of wheat from George Washington's farm alone were shipped overseas. Given the nature of politics at that time, one can only assume that he was driving a hard bargain.

Bread is a synonym for money, a religious icon and the basis of many rituals. Even "toasting" with drinks is derived from the medieval custom of floating crusts of bread in festive brew. Breaking bread seals friendships and alliances. A newfangled invention is the best thing since sliced bread. Breadwinning secures families, and the breadbasket in our country is the "land of plenty." To be on the safe side, we know on what side our bread is buttered, and we cast our bread upon the waters to ensure a fair share for all. What began as the first civilized sustenance continues to play an integral part of our cultural fabric with meanings and metaphors as numerous as its flavors. Nutritious to be sure; but every time we break our daily bread, we are enjoying a slice of history.

The Super Chef Phenomenon

Of all the trends in the restaurant industry over the last decade, the 90's have perhaps been most noted as the "Decade of the Chef". In the past, the Chef was for the most part an obscure position, with those in the field relatively unknown by the public, underpaid and often unappreciated. Then the public relations experts figured that by marketing the Chef, the independents would have a leg up on the chains that couldn't market specific personnel. This ploy worked so well that some of these media darlings became SuperChefs, and grew their newfound fame into chains and even retail food lines.

The result of all this is that the public now seems more interested in the movement of known Chefs than in new restaurants. Restaurateurs are all vying for the same known Chefs, and committing huge free agent dollars to acquire these superstars. Hotels and casinos are paying dollars well out of proportion to economics just to gain affiliations with a Chef who will not only drive restaurant revenue, but hotel occupancy and casino handle as well. So how does a restaurateur compete? How does an independent restaurant with a single 150-seat upscale take advantage of this trend?

Some of you probably don't care to compete on this basis, and there are lots of reasons to avoid making your Chef the centerpiece of your restaurant. But if you do, you have two basic choices: Hire the Name or Grow Your Own. Before we explore these options, we must first determine the proper ingredients for a SuperChef. To become a SuperChef, an individual must of course have the culinary and management skills, but must also have creativity and personality.

Creativity goes beyond presentation skills, to a willingness, desire and ability to innovate in preparation, flavors and textures. And to be attractive to the media a SuperChef candidate must have a distinguishable personality and be relatively well spoken. So that's the basic recipe. To make it happen, you can:

Hire the Name. Chefs can of course be bought. Such a move can bring instant acclaim and hordes of new patrons to your door. However, aside from the expense, this type is prone to leaving for a better offer at any time, or spreading him or herself too thin over several projects. Best advice here: Make the Chef a partner in the business and have an ironclad employment agreement.

Grow Your Own. This is the preferred route if you can do it. You can usually get someone who is more loyal and besides, it should cost less. If you have a Chef who could grow into a SuperChef, then go for it. Do the following:

— Hire a PR firm to get the Chef in the media as often as possible
— Internally market the Chef at every opportunity (name on menu, presence on the floor, showcasing original specials).
— Enter (and win) food competitions
— Get James Beard Foundation recognition
— Volunteer food items prepared by the Chef at hi-profile charity events
— Contribute recipes to the media whenever possible
— If you plan do the above, get an employment agreement first and consider making the Chef a partner in your business

Some restaurateurs get a chill going down their spine when they think of affiliating with or creating a SuperChef. With very good reason. As an example, consider the plight of a restaurant that hires a Chef, puts his name on the front door, builds their entire marketing campaign around him, and then watches him leave. Or the restaurant that develops a menu around a chef's capabilities only to see him walk out the door with the kitchen staff and all hope of recreating special menu items.

However, despite many restaurateurs' distaste for such a SuperChef, the public loves them. They will flock to their restaurants on Tuesday nights, and gladly wait an hour on Thursdays. Best of all, the named Chef is an independent restaurants best offense against a chain's clout.

Opportunities and Resources for Green Hotels

The term "green hotels" describes hotels that strive to be more environmentally friendly through the efficient use of energy, water, and materials while providing quality services. Green hotels conserve and preserve by saving water, reducing energy use, and reducing solid waste. They have seen benefits such as reduced costs and liabilities, high return and low-risk investments, increased profits, and positive cash flows.

Identifying these benefits and incentives has allowed the popularity of green hotels to grow. Hotels are consistently becoming greener. The most costly and wasteful use of resources in hotels are usually in the consumption of nonrenewable energy, excessive water use, and the generation of waste.

A Zero Waste Approach

The goal of being a green hotel is to eliminate as much as possible your negative impacts on the environment both by reducing your consumption of resources and by changing your practices so that the waste you do produce can be used as raw material by someone else. Some of the examples listed are programs that resulted in savings through increased efficiency or reduced cost. While recognizing that an incremental improvement may be the first step in the process of greening a hotel, it is important to keep in mind the ultimate goal of zero waste.

The Zero Waste Alliance, a non-profit organization that provides a forum for those interested in zero waste strategies, shows that a zero waste approach can increase efficiency, provide cost savings, reduce the burden of extraction from and waste to nature, and allow more resources to be available. This philosophy and strategy can be incorporated by small businesses, governments, schools, and communities, and is recommended to hotels for consideration in developing their green programs.

Becoming a zero-waste hotel does not necessarily mean the elimination of all by-products. It means using resources efficiently, using renewable resources, and when generation of by-products is unavoidable, using those by-products as the raw material for other processes. The biological by-products of hotel activities should be able to be safely assimilated into natural systems by bacterial processes in soil or water. These materials are biological nutrients. Substances that can be recycled and are not biological nutrients can be reused as technical "nutrients" and recycled with ongoing value. You can find more information on this "cradle-to-cradle" approach, from one of the pioneers of zero-waste chemistry, McDonough, Braungart Design Chemistry.

Energy Efficiency

Tourist accommodations can have large, expensive energy requirements, especially for space heating and cooling systems. However, there are many options for conserving energy. Strategies from designing for passive solar heating to something as simple as providing good insulation can help reduce or eliminate the need for costly heating and cooling. Simply changing thermostat settings can make a big difference.

Hotels worldwide are recognizing opportunities to implement energy-efficient projects in space heating and cooling systems. For example, The Hyatt Regency International Hotel in New Zealand understood that guests often left appliances and heating and cooling systems on when they were out of their rooms. The hotel developed a project to link energy use with room occupancy. Now when a guest leaves the room, all energy appliances shut down, with the exception of refrigerators, alarm clocks, and other essential appliances. The project costs were $16,000, while the payback period was only 14 months, with savings of $14,000 annually.

In another case, the Sheraton Auckland Hotel and Towers realized that the daily washing of sheets, towels, flannels, tablecloths, and other linens accounted for 35% of the energy consumed in the laundry process, while drying consumed 65%. The hotel simply changed the temperature of the wash from 85 degrees Celsius to 65 degrees Celsius. This change saved $2,000 in energy costs in the first 3 months alone, and the linens came out just as clean. This project, in addition to reducing energy costs, reduced the use of washing chemicals and decreased pollution of the hotel wastewater. Also, allowing the hotel guests the option of having linens washed every other day rather than daily can significantly assist in energy and water conservation.

Lighting is the second largest energy-using system in a hotel, and is probably the easiest and most cost-effective area for reducing energy costs. According to the Alliance to Save Energy, fluorescent lamps produce four times as much light per watt than incandescent lamps, and they can last eight to ten times longer. A compact fluorescent light used in place of an incandescent light that is left on continuously for 12 months, all 8,760 hours of the year, will pay for itself in less than one year.

The Sheraton Tacoma Hotel developed a project to transition to compact fluorescent light fixtures. The staff replaced 2,000 incandescent light fixtures with quadruple-tube compact fluorescent light bulbs in various areas of the hotel such as the guest rooms and the lobby. The cost saving was calculated at up to $15,000 with a payback rate of 18 months.

Solar power is being recognized more and more commonly as a limitless natural resource with economic and environmental benefits. In contrast, gas and oil are non-renewable resources and contribute emissions of greenhouse gases. Today solar power is being harnessed in many new systems providing thermal and light power to hotels in innovative ways. For example, the Sanga Saby Hotel in Sweden installed solar panels on the roof of the sauna area, which supplement heat for the pool and sauna. These natural power supplies are becoming a popular means of saving energy and, consequently, money.

One of the most common ways of harnessing solar power is to use photovoltaic panels. Photovoltaics assist facilities in getting off the power grid, with the resulting decrease in both utility costs and vulnerability to market fluctuations in energy prices. Architectural solar panel at the Aurum Lodge in Alberta, Canada. The panels provide shade during summer months and heat during the winter season. At the Aurum Lodge photovoltaics produce more than 50% of the electricity. The lodge also has solar collectors for heating and cooling the hotel.

Water Conservation

Water-efficient practices use improved technologies that deliver equal or better service using less water. Water conservation encourages hotels to better manage how and when water is being used, addressing both the technical and human side of water management issues. It is estimated that by 2010, water use will increase to approximately 475 gallons per day for each room in high luxury facilities. However, in other accommodations, water use is still a cost and an important stress on the local environment.

In many cases water conservation can be a matter of purchasing and using the proper systems and tools. Choose products that have standardized replaceable components for the best long-term performance. Factors to include when considering water sources may include renewability, potential impacts on the environment and water supplies as well as the economic benefit. In many developing countries hotel water use may impact the water supplies of the local people.

Identifying where water use is excessive is important to luxury hotels and hotels in developing areas. In one case a study completed on tourism in Palawan, Philippines, it was estimated that in the early stages of tourism development in Busuanga West, the amount of water required for a single high-standard hotel-room would be 396 gallons per day. This was enough water to support 14 local people at their current standard of living. Low-flow shower heads and faucet aerators are some options for water conservation, which are becoming common among hotel facilities. The payback period for their use can be 3-4 years depending on the extent of the project.

In one example, the Houston-based Green Hotels Association observed water use in the San Antonio-based La Quinta Inn. Through a one-month period, the hotel showed an average of 100 gallons of water being used per guest per billing period. The chain totaled more than a billion gallons in the first nine months in 1996. La Quinta Inn then installed low-flow shower heads and aerating faucets in each room, resulting in a saving of $1.50 per room per month. Replacing all toilets with ultra-flow toilets at a cost of $3,250 showed a payback in 2.1 years and annual water saving of 180,000 gallons per year.

In many water assessments, urinals and automatic flushing toilets are found to consume a great deal of water. The THC Rotorua Hotel in New Zealand had urinals that flushed automatically every nine minutes. Each flush used 10 liters of water. This added up to 66 liters per hour, or 1,580 liters per day, regardless of whether the urinals had been used or not. The total consumption for three urinals was 4,740 daily.

The hotel then installed detectors that sense when the urinals are being used and allow flushing to occur at a specified time after use. This program reduced water consumption in the three urinals from 66 liters per hour to 40 liters during the day and 20 liters in the evening. In addition to installing the urinal sensors the hotel installed low-flow shower heads at a cost of $3,060. The annual cost savings for the water conservation came to $5,244, with a payback of only seven months.

As toilets and urinals are being recognized as high consumers of water, options are becoming available that have lower flush volumes, and systems are being introduced that separate solids from the fluids. This is an example of a water filtration unit from Ecolab that can operate in hotel facilities. Filtration systems are expected to filter out solids and oils from sources such as laundry waste water and allow the water to be reused.

Another target for hotels is water consumption in washing machines and air-cooling systems. The Saunders Hotel Group, for example, had to reduce water use due to high water rates and use restrictions. The hotel chain includes the Boston Park Plaza Hotel, the Copley Square Hotel, and the Lenox Hotel.

The hotel group's S.H.I.N.E. program annually saves four million gallons of drinking water, 225,000 kilowatts of electricity, and more. They installed new and efficient laundry systems, switched from water-cooled to air-cooled ice machines, and eliminated water-cooled air conditioning equipment. These projects saved the hotel 1.5 million gallons of water annually.

Solid Waste

Solid waste in hotels has many components, including paper, food, various metals, plastics, aluminum, and glass. In a recent waste generation study, wastes from 25 hotels were examined. The statistics showed that from 1991-1993 the hotel waste consisted of 46% food waste, 25.3% paper, 11.7% cardboard, 6.7% plastics, 5.6% glass, and 4.5% metals. This gives a picture of the variety of waste that can be produced by only a small number of hotels in a city. When looked at with a zero-waste attitude, these figures show the opportunities for both resource recovery and waste reduction.

Implementing a solid waste reduction program in a hotel can create significant cost savings in waste hauling fees while creating a more environmentally friendly hotel. This is especially true as solid waste becomes a more significant environmental issue and landfill fees increase. Often hotels hesitate to establish programs in solid waste management because of the coordination and cooperation needed among management, employees, and guests. However, the cost benefit is an incentive.

The Westin San Francisco Airport Hotel implemented their recycling program in 1994. The hotel practices such waste-reducing steps as purchasing recycled content products, providing environmental education to their employees, donating their excess food to local food banks, and recycling paper, aluminum, and plastics. The hotel has been recognized for its waste reducing efforts, and it participates in organizations with others who share an interest in green practices.

The hotel is a member of the Recycled Paper Coalition and the Sustainable San Mateo County Business Council, and received an award from the Waste Reduction Awards Program in 2000. Annually, they recycle 22 tons of materials and save $6,000. Another aspect of a solid waste reduction program is dealing with food waste, which can frequently be a large portion of the waste produced in hotels and lodging facilities.

Overpreparation, table scraps, cooking losses, and packaging failures lead to accumulation of food waste. Because spoiled food and even leftover plate scrapings can be composted, hotels are increasingly recognizing that composting is a better use of organic materials than trucking them to landfills. Creating a food waste reduction program may involve several steps. The Totem Pole Restaurant at the Thunderbird Hotel in Bloomington, Minnesota began a food waste reduction program by having the head chef monitor the food inventory, the amount of food per meal, and the percent of waste per meal. This did not eliminate food waste completely, but it reduced the quantity.

The head chef also reduced food waste by regularly checking the amount and type of food commonly disposed in the recycling containers. By doing this, the chef determined what foods were reusable and helped to decide how to revise the food preparation procedures to reduce food waste. This resulted in a 20% reduction in food waste. The cost saving of $451.25 per month was offset by the $128.00 per month cost to have these materials picked up for recycling, resulting in a total saving of $323.25.

Certification and Benchmarking Recommendations

So how do you know when you have become a green hotel? How will you know how you rank among other hotels? There are green hotel certification opportunities and benchmarking tools available to help chart your progress in becoming a green hotel.

International Hotel Environmental Initiative (IHEI)

The IHEI promotes improvements in the hotel industry. It provides a benchmarking tool and a has a variety of suggestions from recommended products to environmental hotel magazines.

CERES Green Hotel Initiative

This organization provides an online best practice survey checklist. This is a great way to assess or monitor your progress in becoming a green hotel. Questions vary from water conservation and energy efficiency practices. And, like the IHEI, they provide suggestions for product purchasing and a step-by-step process in starting a green hotel.

Green Hotel Association

The Green Hotels Association provides more information on green hotels and some general steps for greening your hotel. It also provides suggestions for less-toxic product substitutions. It provides the hotelier with an opportunity to receive a catalog on greening lodging facilities, and become a member.

Green Leaf Program

The Hotel Association of Canada's Green Leaf Eco-Rating Program uses a 1-5 scale to help a hotel track its progress toward becoming green.

Cool Companies

This organization offers tools for looking into energy efficiency in everything from your hotel to your home. It offers case studies, policy information on energy, a "how-to" guide on saving energy, and much more.

2

Value Oriented Customer Care

The concept of perceived value has recently gained its importance and wide popularity in the business environment because of its effect on consumer behavior and providing strategic implications for the success of companies. It is recommended that products offering value for money not only influence customers' choice behavior at the pre purchase phase but also affect their satisfaction, intention to recommend and return behavior at the post purchase phase. Hence, perceived value is claimed to be a major tool to help the service provider to gain a better competitive position in the market. However, despite its strategic importance for marketing, perceived value did not receive enough investigation in the literature. In particular, very few efforts have been made to measure this construct in the hospitality industry. Although the conceptualization of perceived value goes back to late 70's, researchers recently began to give reasonable attention to its operationalization.

The existing efforts have been hampered by various difficulties mainly arising from inadequate conceptualization and the wide spectrum of other constructs involved in the formation of value judgement. Perceived benefits, perceived price, monetary price, psychological price, and behavioral price are all concepts that are associated with conceptualization of perceived value. Furthermore, perception of value is recommended to be affected by stimulus and personal response factors such as characteristics of product, interest in product, different needs, motives, expectations, personality and social status.

Therefore, evaluation of this construct is claimed to vary among individuals and this has made the process of perceived value measurement a complicated and challenging task. Despite the presence of the above-mentioned issues, there have been some attempts for the assessment of perceived value through a variety of techniques. For example, if the objective of the research is to explore the concept of value, focus group interviews are used. If the study aims to decompose the overall value judgement into various benefits sought in consumption, conjoint analysis is recommended. In the recent literature perceived value is usually operationalized using a single item scale which aims to capture customers' overall value judgement on a statement (e.g. the hotel is good/bad value for money). However, such practice suffers from two apparent shortcomings.

Firstly, that approach fails to reflect the widely accepted theoretical definition of perceived value which states that it is the consumer's overall assessment of the utility of a product based on perceptions of what is received and what is given. By implication, perceived value is a trade-off between two components; benefits and sacrifices. The former is known as get component (what customers get from a product) and the latter is known as give component (what customers give in order to get a product; usually refers to the money paid).

Secondly, the concept of perceived value is proposed to be multi-dimensional and therefore the use of a single item scale would not capture dimensions of this construct adequately. In accordance with the recent argument, perceived value is consisted of two dimensions called acquisition value and transaction value. Acquisition value is perceived net gains associated with the products or services acquired in consumption. Acquisition value has a close relationship with the perceived benefits as well as perceived sacrifices. Hence, it is positively influenced by the product benefits and negatively influenced by the money given up to obtain the product. Scholars argue that the most important element of this "get" component is perceived quality. Transaction value is defined as the difference between consumers' internal reference price and the price offered within the context of a special price deal. From the customer point of view, a deal is assessed by comparing the selling price to the customer internal reference price.

Therefore, a buyer, on examining the financial terms of the price offer, might perceive additional value beyond that provided by acquisition value. Thus, transaction value can be conceptualized as the psychological satisfaction or pleasure obtained from taking advantage of the financial terms of the price deal. This distinction between acquisition value and transaction value is particularly important when considering the impact of perceived value on consumers' willingness to buy, information seeking behavior and/or comparing alternatives. Although it is the acquisition value that is usually meant when addressing perceived value, transaction value has also been claimed to have a profound effect on the consumer perception of value. This is especially relevant in purchasing situations when customers take advantage of a special price deal. Some argue that the influence of transaction value on behavioral intentions is mediated by acquisition value. The likelihood that the buyer intends to purchase the product is positively related to overall perceptions of acquisition and transaction value.

A few efforts have been done for measuring the perceived value construct. Therefore they made an effort to test the validity of these two dimensions with two empirical studies. Their research was experimental and concerned with perceived product value and customers' choice behavior in the pre-purchase phase. The perceived value construct was operationalized by a twelve-item scale split into two dimensions. As a result, these two dimensions were found to be valid and reliable. However, despite of their pioneering effort, the research was experimental and applied to product evaluation rather than services at the pre-consumption stage. Goods contain more search quality attributes whilst services contain more experience quality attributes, which can only be recognized during or after consumption phase. In line with this view, perception of benefits and sacrifices (the two components of perceived value) associated with a product or service consumption during or after use situations might be different from the pre-purchase.

The purpose of this education is to test the dimensionality of perceived value of hospitality services and explore the nature of the relationship between this construct and other theoretically related constructs at the post-consumption stage. At the mean time, an effort is made to investigate whether the two-dimensional scale developed by Grewal et al. would maintain its validity and reliability for the evaluation of hospitality services.

The investigates the validity and reliability of the two perceived value dimensions with two empirical studies applied in hotels and restaurants. To do that, the 12 item perceived value scale developed by Grewal et al. was adapted to the evaluation of hotel and restaurant services. The following section illustrates the scale adaptation and questionnaire development procedures.

MEASUREMENT OF PERCEIVED VALUE

Grewal et al. used nine statements to measure acquisition value and three statements to measure transaction value. The scale was accompanied by a seven-point Likert type rating scale marked strongly disagree (1) and strongly agree (7). The two empirical applications concerned with two different samples, undergraduate students and employees of a university. According to the factor analysis results the scale is found to be valid. The internal consistency measured by Cronbach Alpha statistics indicates that the scale is reliable (alpha coefficient was .95 for the acquisition value scale and .85 for the transaction value scale). As Grewal et al. applied this instrument for the evaluation of a product (bicycle) in pre-purchase setting, modifications were needed to regulate this instrument so that it can be applied on hotels and restaurants in post-purchase evaluation. Using Grewal et al.'s instrument for the measurement of perceived value, their definitions of both perceived acquisition value and perceived transaction value were also accepted and adopted as the operational definitions for this study. According to Grewal et al. perceived acquisition value is "..the perceived net gains associated with the products or services acquired. That is the perceived acquisition value of a product will be positively influenced by the benefits buyers believe they are getting by acquiring and using the product and negatively influenced by the money given up to acquire the product."

Grewal et al. also defined perceived transaction value as "the perception of psychological satisfaction or pleasure obtained from taking advantage of the financial terms of the price deal." The scale items' modifications included changing the tense of the statements from present to past to capture post-consumption evaluation and rewording some of the statements so as to suit the attributes of hotels and restaurants. In accordance with the definition of the acquisition value, all of the nine statements exemplify the process of trade-off between a 'get' component or a product benefit (e.g. good quality) and a 'give' component or a sacrifice (e.g. money paid).

In accordance with the definition of transaction value, the three statements used for its measurement embodied the pleasure associated with taking advantage of a price deal. These are:

(1) reflecting on the price paid, feel that got a good deal,
(2) it added to pleasure knowing that we got a good deal on the price,
(3) beyond saving money, there was a good feeling attached to making a good deal – as was the case here.

The first part included respondents' profile. Since the study did not target any specific market segment, both questionnaires started with an attempt to draw a profile of the respondents as hotel/restaurant customers. This included questions about the frequency of purchase, the last service experience, the type of hotel/restaurant visited, the purpose of travelling/meal occasion, in addition to whether or not the respondent took advantage of any kind of price deal. The questionnaire also ended with the personal demographic data to help complete the respondents' profile. Demographic data included gender, age, nationality, occupation, and income.

Second part included the perceived value scale. As mentioned before, perceived acquisition value was measured using nine Likert statements modified from the scale presented by Grewal et al.. Respondents were asked to rate the attributes on a 7-point scale marked "strongly disagree" and "strongly agree". Similarly, using the same 7-point Likert scale, transaction value was measured by three statements. The acquisition value statements used in the Restaurant Study were virtually the same as those used in the Hotel Study. Just the word hotel was replaced with the word restaurant, in addition to some other limited changes in the wording to suit the nature of the product investigated. For example, the statement "This hotel met specific needs (e.g. comfortable accommodation, convenient location) at a reasonable price" was reworded as "This restaurant met specific needs (e.g. tasty food, convenient location) at a reasonable price." On the other hand, the three transaction value statements were exactly the same in both studies.

Third part included the measurement of related constructs. As value is claimed to be a higher-order construct that is dependent on other lower-order independent latent constructs (price and quality), we also measured other variables to establish the scale validity. These were overall value, behavioral intentions, overall customer satisfaction, overall quality, and perceived price.

Overall value: Respondents were asked to rate their evaluation of the overall value of their last hotel stay or meal experience for the price they paid. A 7-point bipolar rating scale was used ranging from "extremely bad value" to "extremely good value." The purpose of this question is to test the concurrent validity of the perceived value scale.

Behavioral intentions: According to theory, perceived value is correlated to behavioral intentions. Hence, behavioral intentions were detected using two questions asking about the return and recommendation intentions. Overall customer satisfaction and overall quality. Value has been argued to play a mediating role between quality and satisfaction, that is the higher the quality the higher the value, and the higher the value the higher the satisfaction. Additionally, to majority of scholars in this domain, quality is the most important, if not the only, constituent of the get component of perceived value. However, despite the expected positive correlation between perceived value and both customer satisfaction and perceived quality, an extremely high correlation will pose some doubts on the discriminant validity of the perceived value scale.

Perceived price: As monetary price represents the major sacrifice of the perceived value equation, two questions were used to assess the respondents' perception of the "fairness" of the price paid, based on both their internal feeling and their knowledge about other alternatives in the market place. In the first instance, respondents were offered three choices to pick the one that best describes their feeling about the price they paid. Each respondent was asked to choose whether s/he thinks the price was a fair price, more than the fair price, or less than the fair price. Then, respondents were asked to rate the price they paid for that hotel compared to other alternatives in the market place. Three options were offered to pick one, indicating the price was around, higher, or lower than the average market price. Before sending the questionnaire to sample, it was tested on a group of university employees and postgraduate students. The clarity of questions and scale items was explicitly discussed with the respondents. The scale was applied on two different samples; hotel customers, and restaurant customers.

Hotels Customers

Hotel customers whose last hotel stay was less than six months before. 400 questionnaires were distributed through a hotel reservation company that offers its services within the UK. The questionnaires were sent to customers who contact the company for a future reservation along with the reservation confirmation letter. Subjects were instructed to fill in the questionnaire based on their last actual hotel stay. 120 questionnaires were received back with a response rate of 30%. Four questionnaires were excluded due to excessive missing values. The respondents were 28% females and 72% males. Most of them had their last hotel stay in hotels located in a city center (38%) or a city suburb (25%).

Reliability of the scale

Cronbach coefficient alpha is "the most commonly accepted formula for assessing the reliability of a measurement scale with multi-point items". Although both acquisition value and transaction value scales were highly reliable, one statement – if we had stayed in that hotel at a price lower than the price paid, we would have got money's worth – was excluded from the acquisition value scale because of its low correlation magnitude with the other scale items. This increased the alpha score of the acquisition value scale (Alpha = .97). As for the transaction value scale, it was also found to be reliable (Alpha = .93).

Validity of the scale

Validity refers to how well the scale measures what it sets out to measure. Construct validity is the most important type of validity. It refers to "how well the measure conforms with theoretical expectations". Two types of validity were essential in order to establish the construct validity; concurrent validity and discriminant validity.

Firstly, the concurrent validity was established as the correlation between overall value and both the perceived acquisition value and perceived transaction value was extremely high (.91 and .82 respectively) which indicates that both measures seem to measure the same construct.

Secondly, the discriminant validity of both scales was tested using principal components analysis. According to theory, the two perceived value dimensions should emerge from this analysis. According to the latent root criterion technique regarding the number of factors to extract, only factors with eigenvalue greater than 1 are considered significant. In this case, only one factor was extracted. This single component explained almost 79% of the total variance. This result lays doubts on the discriminant validity of the scale, and leads us to questioning the multi dimensionality of perceived value and whether acquisition value and transaction value are two distinguished dimensions as theorized or the same thing as the findings indicate.

A series of calculations was conducted to further investigate the validity of the scale by looking at the correlation between the two scales. This resulted in some significant findings. The correlation between the total acquisition value and total transaction value scores was .86. This is quite a high correlation that supports the argument made on the results of the principal components analysis. On the other hand, the correlation between both of the perceived value scales on the one side, and repurchase intention and recommendation intention on the other side is strong as was suggested in the literature (.71 and .83 for acquisition value, and .58 and .79 for transaction value respectively). This means that behavioral intentions can be predicted by measuring perceived value. This supports the predictive validity of the scale. In addition to that, it can be noticed that the correlation between acquisition value and transaction value on one side and the internal reference price and market reference price on the other side is moderately strong (.54 and .48 for acquisition value, and .51 and .43 for transaction value respectively). It is not an extremely strong correlation as the correlation between acquisition value and transaction value. By considering this fact, and recalling the role of the price deal in creating a perception of transaction value, we suggest that comparing actual price to both the internal and external reference prices may be a more appropriate measure for the dimension of transaction value that could not be captured using Grewal et al.'s technique.

Restaurants Customers

The study was conducted on fast food customers. The questionnaire was distributed by hand on customers of the food court of a town-center shopping mall and a university coffee shop. A total of 130 questionnaires were distributed. Subjects were instructed to fill in the questionnaire based on their last in-store fast food experience. A total of 122 questionnaires were received back. Two questionnaires were excluded due to excessive missing values. The respondents were 72% females and 28% males. Most of them had their last fast food meal experience in a burger, pizza, or chicken restaurant with percentages of 41%, 28%, and 15% respectively.

Reliability of the scale

Moving to the perceived value scale, the reliability score was calculated for both of the acquisition and transaction value scales. Both scales were highly reliable (Alpha = .93 and .86 respectively). It is worth mentioning here that the statement that was excluded from the acquisition value scale in the Hotel Study was also excluded in this study for the same reason, that is low correlation magnitude with the other statements of the scale. Again, this increased the Alpha score of the scale.

Validity of the scale

Like the Hotel study, the multi dimensionality of perceived value was reinvestigated using principal components analysis. Similarly, only one component that had an eigenvalue of greater than one was extracted. This single component explained almost 66% of the total variance. These support that all the eleven items in the perceived value scale are measuring one construct rather than two. It was also found that the correlation between acquisition value and transaction value was almost as high as it was in the Hotel Study (.87). All these results are consistent with the results of the Hotel Study. Furthermore, the moderate to weak correlation between acquisition value and transaction value on one side and internal and external reference prices on the other side (.41 and .13 for acquisition value, and .41 and .12 for transaction value respectively) supports our suggestion that the missing dimension of transaction value can possibly be captured by comparing the price paid to the customer reference price. All the other findings were consistent with the findings of the Hotel Study and in turn support all the arguments made earlier.

To summarize, the most significant finding of the two empirical studies is that despite the fact that the refined perceived value measurement scale was found to be reliable, there were some issues involved about its validity across the two samples. In particular, although the dimension of acquisition value was found to be valid and generic, the validity of transaction value was very poor. Using principal components analysis, the scale items that were supposed to measure transaction value did not discriminate from those of acquisition value. Thus, the discriminant validity of the scale is doubtful, as it was not efficient in discriminating the two dimensions and posing them as clearly distinct components of the perceived value construct, assuming there are two dimensions.

One justification for the lack of discrimination between perceived acquisition value and perceived transaction value in the two studies might be the operational definition of transaction value. Defining transaction value as "the perception of psychological satisfaction or pleasure obtained from taking advantage of the financial terms of a price deal" makes the concept a bit confusing. This definition makes transaction value in a position to be confused with acquisition value. As a result, the statements quoted from Grewal et al.'s to measure transaction value do not look to be exclusive to transaction value. In other words, a customer who did not get any discount on price may still have the feeling that s/he got a good deal on price if s/he perceives the benefits acquired as being worthy, or more than worthy the money s/he paid. In this case the construct validity of the perceived transaction value scale is questionable, as it seems that the scale items' measurement of the construct does not match the conceptualization stated by the operational definition. This might have contributed a great deal to the overlap between transaction value and acquisition value.

Furthermore, having another look on the definition of transaction value – "the perception of psychological satisfaction or pleasure obtained from taking advantage of the financial terms of the price deal", it seems that the three items Grewal et al. used to measure transaction value emphasized only the first part of this definition. That is to say, the scale items were explicitly asking about "the pleasure" the respondents might have felt from taking advantage of a deal rather than asking them about their perception of the price deal and whether they see it as a "deal" or not!

Hence, an indirect, but probably more efficient, approach of measuring the actuality of transaction value is to assess the customers' perception of the service price as compared to their reference price. This will sound consistent with the conceptualization of transaction value as "a judgement of the value of the deal" or, in behavioral context, the consumer's reaction to a price, relative to the price s/he expects to pay for the service. Following these definitions, one of the acquisition value scale items seems to be more fitting in the transaction value scale. All this might have contributed to the mix-up of acquisition value and transaction value. Moreover, in marketing literature, price is defined as "the summation of all sacrifices made by a consumer in order to experience the benefits of a product." Based on this definition, offering a monetary discount to customers does not necessarily mean that customers will perceive it as a good "deal" if they see other sacrifices associated with experiencing the service as being much.

Furthermore, as "deal" refers to a temporary reduction in price, its influence is expected to be more apparent on price-sensitive segments of the market than it is on non-money-conscious people. Hence it is logic to expect that the pleasure from taking advantage of a deal (known as transaction value) will not be the same for subjects from both sides. Measuring price sensitivity along with a carefully designed instrument for measuring transaction value might be helpful in providing a better understanding of the latter, using between-groups analysis techniques. Another consideration that can not be overlooked is that the pleasure associated with transaction value might be a short-term mental status related to "finding" and taking advantage of a price deal. In turn, it might be more appropriate to measure it in the pre-purchase phase rather than the post-purchase one, or using experimental settings like what Grewal et al. did. Regarding the acquisition value scale, a further look on the definition on which Grewal et al. based their instrument raises some questions.

Initially, is the trade-off between benefits and cost in the acquisition value concept all about the internal benefits associated with the product or service and "the money given up to acquire the product"? This assumption ignores the fact that there are some other factors that may affect the customers readiness to pay more or less for the room/meal and, therefore, can not be neglected in any attempt to build a comprehensive value model. From all the above, two possible interpretations for these two studies' results need further investigation.

The first interpretation is that the instrument is appropriate in tracing the concept with relevant scale items, but actually the two concepts that lie beneath are the same thing. In other words, the model that hypothesizes that there are two dimensions of perceived value is not appropriate in the hospitality environment, and the instrument used was good enough to prove that. The second interpretation might be that the subjects were not able to discriminate between the two scales, that is, they saw the statements of both scales as the same. In other words, the model might be right but the instrument was not good enough to extract the empirical evidence that supports the model. This means that the instrument validity needs to be improved so that it can do the job more efficiently.

The strong theoretical base as well as previous efforts in this domain suggest that this supposition can not be ignored. Based on all the above, further research is needed to develop a better instrument for the measurement of service perceived value. This new instrument should be based on a solid theoretical background.

First, regarding the perceived acquisition value, the whole spectrum of possible benefits a customer may seek in a service should initially be defined, and so should the whole range of sacrifices that customer could possibly endure. A good starting point for this might be previous research efforts on benefits. Then, these benefits and sacrifices should be the foundation for new perceived acquisition value scale. These new scale items should be constituted by interchangeably interlacing the predefined benefits and sacrifices to reflect a trade-off between their various components.

On the other hand, for a better measurement of perceived transaction value, a new technique should be used. This new technique is to be based on tracing the customer perception of the price paid compared to his reference price. This way, transaction value will no longer be limited to, and can no longer be seen as indispensable to price discounts. Then the validity and reliability of the measurement tool is to be investigated.

This study empirically tested the dimensionality of perceived value in hospitality setting. The tool that was tested before with products did not maintain its validity when applied to hotels and restaurants. The content validity of both scales needs more investigation, as the items of the scales might be measuring the same constituent of the perceived value construct rather two dimensions. This is specifically relevant to the transaction value scale items that might have not been exclusive to transaction value and, in turn, failed to guide the respondents to the intended meaning. As for acquisition value, one factor that may positively contribute to the instrument content validity is to consider other types of benefits (for example, intangible benefits) and costs (for example, non-monetary costs) that were not considered by this instrument.

Developing an effective tool for measuring customer perceived value would be a substantial addition to the service evaluation literature. From a professional point of view, perceived value measurement will have major implications for marketers as it offers them a major source of competitive advantage, and a proficient tool to help them hone their strategies. A better understanding of the customer perceived value, and paying enough attention to its measurement will enable marketers improve their marketing practices.

Health and Safety

The learner is able to operate in a hygienic, safe and secure food preparation and service environment in a responsible manner and in accordance with relevant legislation. We know this when the learner is able to:

— Identify and apply specified hygiene and occupational safety practices as governed by relevant legislation in the preparation and service of food and beverages.

— Identify and apply correct food storage practices and procedures to meet specified hygiene principles.

— Demonstrate correct waste disposal practices and procedures to meet specified hygiene, recycling and environmentally friendly practices.

— Describe the implications of failing to comply with the relevant legislation and principles of hygiene, safety, security and environmental issues.

— State the types, effects and growth conditions of the main food poisoning and spoilage organisms.

— Describe and apply security practices and procedures as required in the hospitality industry, and suggest responses to a range of emergency situations.

— Understand and demonstrate a professional appearance, attitude, ethics and values in the preparation and service of food and beverages.

— Describe the origin and symptoms of infectious diseases, including HIV and AIDS, and their transmission possibilities in the food and beverage environment.

— Identify and apply basic treatment to common injuries that might occur in the preparation and service of food and beverages, with special attention to HIV/AIDS risks.

Food Production

The learner is able to understand and apply the principles of planning, organising, problem solving and evaluation as related to self and to practices and systems of food production.

— Identify and use a variety of large-scale and small-scale equipment.

— Explain and illustrate the design and layout of commercial kitchens.

— Interpret and follow a recipe with a basic understanding of preparation, cooking methods, culinary terminology, metrication and measurement of ingredients.

— Explain the principles of menu planning.

— Demonstrate a knowledge and understanding of the following food commodities - cereals, eggs, fruits, salads and salad dressings, scones and muffins, pasta, mince meat, sausages, dairy products, teas and coffees.

— Apply the concept of mise-en-place when producing and presenting a range of breakfast items and light meals using the commodities studied, to meet the principles of nutrition, menu planning and creativity or flair, giving preference to local commodities.

— Explain the kitchen brigade structure as it relates to kitchen operations and teamwork.

— Use the correct procedures for receiving, storing and issuing stock, and respond to quality and quantity problems.

— Cost a recipe.

— Plan menus for teas and light two-course or three-course meals in keeping with the principles of nutrition and menu planning.

— Demonstrate a knowledge and understanding of the following food commodities - poultry, fish, rice, soups, sauces, stocks, vegetables, yeast products, cakes and biscuits.

— Produce and present a range of teas and twocourse or three-course meals using the commodities studied, working effectively with other members of the kitchen and restaurant brigades, giving preference to local commodities.

— Discuss the use and benefit of computers in the administration of kitchen operations

— Maintain and keep records of food production, equipment and food items to ensure effective stock control.

— Cost and calculate the selling price of a meal and draw up a quotation for a function, including utility, infrastructure and labour costs.

— Plan menus for formal dinners and a cocktail function, taking into account nutrition and the specific dietary needs of consumers (including those with HIV/AIDS), national and international food trends and cultural uniqueness.

— Demonstrate a knowledge and understanding of the following food commodities - meat, vegetarian dishes, choux paste, pastry and desserts.

— Produce and present a range of dishes for formal dinners and a cocktail function using the commodities studied and taking cognisance of cultural interpretation of food trends and special dietary requirements, giving preference to local commodities.

Food and Beverage Service

The learner is able to understand and apply the principles of planning, organising, problem solving and evaluation as related to self and to practices and systems of food and beverage service and customer care.

- Identify, handle, clean and store the correct equipment for serving food and beverages in a restaurant.
- Apply the basic principles of customer relations with sensitivity for diversity (e.g. race, gender, age, disability and sexual orientation) while providing an excellent food and beverage service.
- Prepare and set up the venue and tables for a limited-menu buffet function (breakfast or light meal) taking into consideration the importance of aesthetic value.
- Describe and apply the concept of mise-en-place in food and beverage operations while following the correct service and clearing techniques of food and non-alcoholic beverages for buffetstyle breakfasts and light meals.
- Demonstrate a knowledge and understanding of the restaurant brigade and the necessity of contributing to effective working relationships and teamwork.
- Demonstrate an appropriate response to guest complaints about problems with kitchen production and service procedures.
- Prepare and set up the venue and tables for a range of teas and two-course or three-course meals using the commodities studied, working effectively with other members of the kitchen and restaurant brigades, giving preference to local commodities.
- Perform the correct service techniques and sequence of food and beverage services for table d'hôte menus.
- Maintain stock control by keeping a record of food and beverage equipment for the restaurant.
- Understand and demonstrate the basic principles of wine and malt service, paying particular attention to customer service and the applicable liquor laws.
- Prepare and set up the venue and tables for formal dinners and a cocktail function using the commodities studied and taking cognisance of the cultural interpretation of food

trends and special dietary requirements, giving preference to local commodities.

— Perform and maintain the correct service techniques and sequence of food and beverages for selective menus.

Quality of Life and Tourism Development Issues

Rural communities seeking to improve the quality of life for their residents often turn to tourism as a means to improve their economic position and create jobs to maintain the existence of their community. At the same time, rural residents who value their clean environment and social structure resist efforts that would result in a deterioration of their lifestyle. For development strategies to be sustainable, they must be socially equitable, provide economic security, and maintain the integrity of the environment. Faced with such a challenge, many community organizations have become proactive and are attempting to control and shape their own destiny through both collective organization and social action. Such involvement provides individuals with a direct link to the larger social and political structure and empowers individuals to effect changes.

Community Organizations

In estimating the scope of community organizations in the United States, two main issues tend to make the discussion somewhat obscure. First, the total number of community organizations or the memberships they reach are virtually impossible to estimate. However, some estimates by the Alliance for Volunteerism estimate more than 6 million voluntary associations, and a study by ACTION indicates greater than 40 million volunteers, or one fourth of all Americans older than age 13. Second, the range in the scope of grassroots community groups complicates such estimates considerably.

An understanding of the views of citizens who are involved in community organizations is critical to any development effort that seeks their cooperation and assistance. Community planners need to know how these residents view their quality of life and how they might react to proposed strategies. To date, little is known about community organization members' perceptions of tourism in a community. Hence, this sought to better understand community involvement through community organizations by comparing the similarities and differences among citizen groups based on various levels of their community involvement and perceptions of their community's tourism-related quality-of-life indicators. It expanded knowledge about how a specific subset of the population, that is, those who are members of community organizations, might respond to tourism development.

Community organization membership was operationalized in this study as self-reported membership in one or more of the following types of organizations: school related, religious, civic, service, hobby oriented, organized sports for children, organized sports for adults, and neighborhood. The specific research question this study sought to answer is whether highly involved residents differed from those who are not at all involved or less involved on three specific aspects. The research question was as follows: Are there differences in the way each group (a) viewed its quality of life in relation to its community, (b) evaluated the impacts of tourism, and (c) expressed support for different types of tourism infrastructure development?

The literature on community organizations has become a focal theme in urban research in recent years. Most of the research in this area has centered on defining the role of such organizations and their meaning to society. Some posited that they are place specific, volunteer driven, shaped by the direct involvement of members, and defined by problem solving as their principal reason for existence. They defined the role of community organization as a means by which residents acting collectively with little or no professional help take control of their neighborhoods. Their objectives are often to obtain better city services, to fight crime, to engage local youths in prosocial activities, to protest and clean up environmental problems, or merely to organize a block party. Other researchers have concluded that participants' economic resources or investments (e.g., home ownership) and the material benefit of protecting those investments were important reasons for their existence. From this perspective, it can be concluded that community involvement seeks to foster self-efficacy as residents work collectively to solve community problems. Others have researched their changing status during recent years. Some argues that concluded that neighborhood residents have learned that there are limited prospects for outside political or economic help in their struggle against large-scale agents of change-city hall, the "growth machine" (a powerful coalition of government officials and local businesses that are united in the pursuit of economic development), and big development interests.

Reasons for Involvement

Membership in community organizations at the individual level has been identified as an intrapersonal component of psychological empowerment that defines how people think about their capacity to influence social and political systems. It describes a self-perception that includes control, self-efficacy, motivation to exert control, and perceived competence. Citizen involvement in grassroots community organizations can be viewed as either an integral component of self-empowerment or as both a cause and effect of such empowerment. Thus, it is essential to understand why some individuals in communities are motivated to be more actively involved than others are. To date, there have been two major studies in the social psychology literature that have addressed community-focused predictors of citizen involvement in block associations.

They found that informal assistance facilitated block organizing. They also found that once a block is organized, association members engaged in more social interaction, which may lead to more neighborhood collaboration. From the same study, derived personcommunity predictors of involvement based on cognitive social learning variables (CSLVs). Their version of the CSLV expectancies includes self- and collective efficacy, which are similar to the concept of psychological empowerment. They found encoding strategies (residents' perceptions of satisfaction and dissatisfaction with community problems) to be a better predictor of involvement. One problem with this finding is that community satisfaction and perceptions may be related to involvement in different ways. Residents may be satisfied with their community as a place to live and, at the same time, be critical of community problems.

Thus, satisfaction alone may encourage involvement by enhancing other social cognitions and behaviors. Being satisfied with one's community may give residents a greater sense of community and collective efficacy and may result in more favorable interaction among neighbors, all of which are predicted to lead to greater collective involvement. A psychological sense of community is also important to community involvement. The results also suggest that involvement itself further enhances an individual's sense of community. A major study of block associations was conducted in New York City. It systematically examined both the physical and social context of crime, fear, and citizen involvement in community organizations at the block level. No significant relationship was found between involvement and reported crime, perceived crime problems, victimization, fear, and informal social controls, despite considerable block variability. The built environment (as opposed to the natural environment), territoriality, neighboring (e.g., loaning a tool or looking after each other's house), block satisfaction, and organizational efficacy, however, were significantly related to block association involvement, even after controlling for income, length of residency, and race. This latter finding suggests that perceived and actual problems or deficiencies in the physical environment may serve as catalysts for involvement and that community social cohesion may be an even more effective enabler of involvement.

Involvement and tourism

Several studies on resident attitudes toward tourism have determined that variability in support for tourism development differs by population segments. There is evidence to suggest that positive attitudes toward tourism may be related to how residents feel about life in their community. An expressed positive attitude toward tourism was positively correlated with a concern about the economic future of their community. Another relationship toward tourism might be a result of self-image and group-identity feelings rather than a belief that tourism will result in personal benefits. A few studies have focused on the relationship between attachment to a community and attitudes toward tourism. In some of these studies, the more the resident was attached to the community, the less support that resident expressed for tourism development. The findings of other studies were either inconclusive or contradictory.

There are three basic concepts were used to measure what was called attachment in the cited studies: (a) birthplace or length of residency, (b) sentiments about the community, and (c) involvement in the community. A more recent study demonstrated that the concept of attachment is composed of two elements, sentiment and involvement. The results of this study indicate that those who were willing to commit time and energy to improving their community were less optimistic about the impacts of tourism and somewhat less supportive of tourism development than those who evaluated their quality of life and emotional attachment to the community as being higher.

Respondents were asked to list all of the organizations to which they belonged. The total number of organizations to which each respondent belonged was calculated. Respondents were placed in one of four categories: no group membership, member of one organization, member of two or three organizations, member of four or more organizations. Frequencies and percentages were calculated. A one-way analysis of variance (ANOVA) was used to determine whether any of the observed differences in the level of involvement groups were significant with respect to their evaluation of their quality of life and the impacts of tourism and their support of various types of tourism infrastructure development. ANOVA allows for the comparison of mean scores from multiple samples to determine whether the differences in the means of the populations from which the samples were drawn are statistically significant. The null hypotheses assumed that the four levels of involvement means were equal for all variables. The analysis used an alpha level of 0.05. Tests for homogeneity of variance provided evidence of equality of variance.

In a telephone survey, there is always the potential of sample bias because all eligible respondents may not have telephones or may not be willing to participate. However, this threat is now considered to be minimal. The study is limited by the measurement of community involvement because it was based on the number of organizations to which individuals belong. No attempt was made to classify the types of organizations or to segment the population on the role respondents played in the organization or their level of commitment to the organization.

Approximately one half of the respondents were male (49.8%). The sample included a relatively balanced number of people in each age category. The vast majority of the respondents were White (90.5%), with a few other races being represented. A small number had been in the community less than 1 year (5.2%).

The respondents indicated that they evaluated their overall quality of life as generally good. Especially good were the quality of the environment, recreational, shopping, and employment opportunities. The quality of education was also rated fairly high. Only a few items were rated fair: driving flow and traffic flow, the quality of public transportation, and the cost of land and housing. The analysis found statistically significant differences in mean scores in several of the quality-of-life variables. Significant differences were found between the groups in their evaluation of the quality of the environment, recreation opportunities, cultural opportunities, and overall quality of life. In this case, the first null hypothesis was rejected because a Tukey b multiple comparison test verified that individuals who belonged to four or more organizations were more likely to evaluate the quality of the environment, recreation opportunities, cultural opportunities, and overall quality of life significantly higher than those of other groups. An observation of the means indicates that those who belonged to no community organizations evaluated the quality of most aspects of their lives lower than those that were the most involved.

The second null hypothesis was not rejected. No significant differences were found among the groups in reference to their evaluation of the impacts of tourism. However, those who belonged to no organizations appeared to be more optimistic than the average about the impact of tourism on employment opportunities, opportunities for shopping and recreation, the price of goods and services, the cost of land and housing, improvements in local services, relationships between residents and tourists, and the ability of tourism to preserve the local culture. This group appeared to be the most optimistic in more categories than other groups. Those who belonged to four or more organizations were also more optimistic than the average on three of the same items (recreation opportunities, the cost of land and housing, and preservation of the local culture). However, the latter group was more pessimistic about employment opportunities, opportunities for shopping, the price of goods and services, and the relationship between residents and tourists. Members of this group were, on the other hand, the most optimistic about the potential for improving traffic congestion and the crime rate.

Types of Tourism

Overall, there was considerable support for the development of tourism infrastructure. In fact, the groups differed little on the type of tourism infrastructure they would support or oppose. The highest level of support was found for preserving rural land and horse farms. Nearly equally strong support was indicated for improvements in transportation, the development of cultural and folk events, and cultural or historic-based attractions. Significant differences were found in cultural or historic-based attractions and cultural and folk events. Support for these types of cultural tourism increased as the level of involvement increased.

The relationship between group membership and concern about the built environment identified by Perkins et al. was confirmed. Residents who were members of a greater number of organizations evaluated their quality of life as higher than those who were not involved in community organizations did. They appeared to be slightly more supportive of specific types of tourism infrastructure development, especially those types of tourism infrastructure that will preserve the culture and history of their community. On the whole, the residents opposed large-scale infrastructure development such as a new convention center, theme parks, or a sporting events arena. It is interesting to note that there were no differences in the way the subsegments of the population viewed the impacts of tourism. It seemed as though residents, whether or not they were involved in community organization, were aware of how tourism would affect their lives. They realized that an increase in the number of visitors might provide increased revenues for government and better opportunities for employment, recreation, and shopping. It was clear that the respondents understood the economic benefits and costs. They appeared to be most concerned about traffic congestion and the crime rate. Residents in this community apparently evaluated the impacts of tourism similarly to those of other communities.

The lack of differences within population segments is important to tourism planners and developers because the viewpoints of the citizens that are most likely to influence public policy are not likely to be different from those of the general population. Similarly, the type of tourism supported or opposed by the various segments were alike. Even through significant differences were found in the intensity of support or opposition, in general all four groups supported cultural tourism infrastructure development and opposed tourism that required building on a large scale. Because the results indicate that there was little difference based on level of involvement in the support for specific types of tourism infrastructure, planners should develop relationships with community organizations for several reasons.

- The involved citizens appear to reflect the viewpoints of the general populace.
- The involved citizens are those who are proactive and want to affect the future of their community.
- The organizations provide planners with a direct link to those who are most likely to support or oppose their actions.

The findings of this research indicate that planners and developers could use their limited resources most efficiently by working with the most active members of the community. The involved citizens can be an especially valuable asset to the planner because their views are similar to those of the general population and impacts of tourism because they are somewhat more optimistic about their quality of life and less pessimistic about the impacts of tourism. In addition, actively involved citizens are likely to perceive that they can affect the outcome of a proposed development and may be more likely to volunteer their time and resources, especially for the development of cultural or historic events and attractions.

MUNCIPAL SOLID WASTE ORIGINATING FROM ROOMS AND RESTAURANTS

Since the Rio Earth Summit in 1992, the green movement has gained momentum in the hotel industry worldwide through the efforts of various associations and activities. Notably, when the Prince of Wales launched the International Hotels Environment Initiative (IHEI) in 1993, 11 international hotel chains agreed to work together and initiated the development of a manual to embrace a comprehensive campaign to advance environmental performance in the hotel industry. In the following year, another 16 hotel groups in the Asia Pacific Rim echoed this campaign and formed the first regional chapter—the Asia Pacific Hotels Environment Initiative. In the same year, the Hotel and Catering Institute Management Association participated in Green Globe, an environmental management awareness program initiated by the World Travel Tourism Council.

In Hong Kong, a survey conducted in 1992 found that about 30% of hotels had launched environmental programs, with varying degrees of success. The thrust of the green campaign in the local hospitality sector focused mainly on energy savings. Municipal waste management received very little attention until the mid-1990s. It is generally believed that the unenthusiastic response to reduce solid waste in hotels was due mainly to the anticipated high capital cost associated with the purchase of recycling equipment and the increased labor involvement. Furthermore, there was difficulty in converting the environmental impact of municipal solid waste (MSW) produced by hotels into a corresponding environmental cost. In the 1980s, the green issue in the hospitality literature in the United States centered on energy efficiency. Concerns about solid waste grew significantly in the early 1990s. In 1990 and 1991, trade journals raised the alarm about the "garbage crisis".

In 1993, some suggested future research directions in greening hotels were proposed, and a case study about solid waste minimization practices was subsequently undertaken in a megaresort. Research work, however, has largely focused on individual waste measurement and reduction practices. There has been little coverage on green accounting for pollutants such as MSW in lodging industry. In the nonhospitality field, accounting for the environment has received much more attention.

Contemporary environmental accounting research can be traced back to 1971. The hospitality industry's share of this green accounting initiation, however, is very small. The action plan for sustainable development, Agenda 21, adopted at the Rio Earth Summit 1992, has been a key factor in driving industry and business to recognize environmental management. Its chapter 30 has further encouraged business and industry to report annually on their environmental records as well as on their use of energy and natural resources. The first survey of green reports from 100 companies operating worldwide did not include a single hotel company. This suggests that the hotel industry in general has been slow to introduce green reporting.

In Australia, an opinion survey about the perception of the materiality of environmental information in company reports was conducted in 1997.

In 1998, the International Federation of Accountants released an International Auditing Practice Statement about the consideration of environmental matters in the audit of financial statements. It reported that accountants around the world expressed a great deal of interest in and a positive reaction to the topic. Further documents on this topic are being planned. In the light of these developments, this study investigates the MSW issue in the hotel sector. The objectives are (a) to estimate the minimum amount of MSW generated in guest rooms and restaurants in the hotel industry, (b) to estimate the amount of MSW produced in the period from 1986 to 2000, and (c) to cost the external effect exerted by MSW in the hotel industry. A new conceptual framework for predicting the minimum amount of MSW in the hotel industry and its environmental cost was developed. It is hoped that the information and benchmark built up in this study will be used to construct green indicators for future reports of hotel operations and statistics in the hotel industry. It is envisaged that the established norms will provide a foundation for further analysis on the environmental costs incurred by an individual hotel and by the hotel industry generally.

Because most hotels do not employ individuals trained in statistical analysis, the use of robust statistical techniques is inappropriate. Instead, all MSW ratios described in the study are based on the industry practice of analyzing performance on a per room and per check-in guest basis.

For the room department of hotels, there are four major identifiable categories of waste. The first type of waste is plastic toiletries, such as shampoo bottles, bath foam bottles, combs, shower caps, toothbrushes, and toothpaste tubes. The second category is unused portions of soap. The third type is slippers, and the fourth is newspapers. Midscale hotels account for 70% of the market share in Hong Kong. Therefore, samples of plastic toiletries, soap, slippers, and newspapers were collected from

20 midscale hotels in 1996. Electronic scales were used to measure the weight of these four types of solidwaste. For the solidwaste originating from hotels' restaurants, 14 samples from two midscale hotels were considered. The sampled solid waste included all items that were disposed of in plastic garbage containers, including paper napkins, paper place mats, straw, organic food remains, and so on. This solid waste was collected and weighed for 7 days in both hotels. All together, there were 14 samples. The number of meal covers was also recorded.

The theoretical framework of environmental accounting for the hotel industry's MSW considers the green costs of five independent variables, namely, in-room plastic waste, unused soaps, disposed slippers, discarded newspapers, and MSW originating from the hotel restaurants. The main equation for predicting the green cost originating from the minimum amount of MSW in the hotel industry can be expressed as follows:

$$EC_{msw} = (E_1)\kappa + (E_2)\kappa + (E_3)\kappa + (E_4)\kappa + (E_5)\kappa \qquad (1)$$

where EC_{msw} is the environmental cost of municipal waste created by the rooms and restaurants in the hotel industry, E_1 is the estimated amount of plastic waste produced in the room, E_2 is the estimated amount of unused soaps, E_3 is the estimated amount of discarded slippers, E_4 is the amount of newspapers, E_5 is the predicted amount of solidwaste originating from the hotel restaurants, and κ is a constant parameter associated with the cost environmental conversion.

To predict the minimum amount of each type of solid waste, that is, E_1, E_2, E_3, E_4, and E_5, a further five subequations were developed. The first four subequations are based on the assumption that the amount of weight of waste per check-in guest, multiplied by the actual number of check-in guests, is equal to the amount of waste produced by all check-in guests. The remaining subequation is related to solidwaste produced in hotel restaurants and is based on the product of the weight of waste per meal cover and the number of meal covers. Fifteen housekeepers and 10 restaurants managers were asked to determine the magnitude of the discount factors or adjustment ratios set in the subequations, as follows:

$$E_1(\text{plastic waste}) = (A_n D_n)(W_1 C \beta_1), \quad (2)$$

where A_n is the number of occupied rooms in year n, D_n is the double occupancy ratio in year n, W_1 is the average weight of total plastic waste per room in the sampling year, C is a constant (assumed to be 0.5), and β_1 is the discounting factor based on the actual consumption of plastic toiletries. Because not all rooms (A_n) were occupied by two guests, the estimated number of customers actually staying in hotel rooms could be obtained by multiplying the number of occupied rooms by the double occupancy ratio (D_n). The average weight (W_1) of plastic toiletries per room was obtained in the sampling measurement and was then divided by two (i.e.,$C = 0.5$) to reflect the weight of plastic waste per check-in guest. Discounting for the amount of disposed toiletries was considered because some bath kit items might have been used for more than 1 day. A discount factor of 20% was used for the period from 1986 to 1996.

Similarly,

$$E_2(\text{soaps' remains}) = (A_n D_n)\ (W_2 C \beta_2). \quad (3)$$

W_2 is the average weight of soaps collected per room basis in the sampling year, and β_2 is the discounting factor based on the actual consumption of soaps. The estimation of actual number of check-in guests followed the same principle used in equation E_1. Discounting was applied to the average weight of soap obtained in the sample analysis because the unused portions of soap were discarded. The discarded amount was estimated to be 50% of the original. Slippers are another major source of waste in many midscale hotels in Hong Kong. The equation to estimate the number of discarded slippers is as follows:

$$E_3(\text{discarded slippers}) = (A_n D_n)\ (W_3 C \beta_3), \quad (4)$$

where W_3 is the averaged weight of paired slippers on a per room basis in the sampling year, and β_3 is the discounting factor on the actual consumption of slippers. The number of users of slippers was assumed to be equal to the number of check-in customers. The average weight of the slippers was discounted because some slippers may be used for more than 1 day. After considering the reuse practice for guests staying for 2 days or more, a 20% discount factor was adopted. Newspapers are another category of waste produced in hotel rooms. The estimation of this sort of waste was also based on the multiplication of the number of occupied rooms and the adjusted average weight of newspapers, as follows:

$$E_4(\text{newspapers}) = (A_n)(W_4\beta_4), \tag{5}$$

where W_4 is the average weight of newspapers, and β_4 is the discount factor based on the weight of newspapers. The weight of the local newspapers increased in the past decade. First of all, the increase in the selling price of newspapers in the past provided the publisher a larger profit margin, allowing the press to enhance the content, ranging from overseas financial news to international sports news. Second, the economic boom in the past years also encouraged business and other entities to advertise more. To reflect the weight of the pre-1996 newspaper, the average weight of the sample newspaper was discounted by 10% for every 3-year period, working backward. The 10% discount was based on the average number of pages and can only be regarded as a rough estimate. To enhance the accuracy of this measurement, it would be useful if any environmental center could record the actual weight of each newspaper in future. Only one set of newspapers for each room was assumed in the calculation.

Solidwaste such as paper napkins, paper place mats, carton boxes, plastic film, and organic matter is generated in hotel restaurants. An equation that comprises the product of the number of meal covers in the industry and the average weight of waste per cover was applied to estimate the amount of waste produced. Thus,

$$E_5(\text{restaurants'waste}) = (N_n R_n \div S_n)(M_n)(W_5), \qquad (6)$$

where N_n is the average number of available rooms in a day in period n, R_n is the restaurant food revenue per available room in period n, S_n is the revenue per seat in period n, and M_n is the estimated number of meal covers served per seat (i.e., turnover ratio) in period n given in the annual survey. M_n is used to multiply the derived number of seats (i.e., $N_n R_n \div S_n$) available in the industry, and W_5 is the average weight of measured solidwaste per meal cover. Due to resource restrictions, only 14 samples collected in two hotels were used as an indicative reference for estimating the average waste per cover. Thus, it would be useful to do a larger scale study of the weight of different types of restaurant waste in future.

Environmental Cost Conversion

From the early 1970s to the late 1980s, HongKong did not have any long-term planning system for dealing with solidwaste. Since the publication of its statutory Waste Disposal Plan in 1989, the local government has been following this blueprint to establish an infrastructure to handle and dispose of a variety of waste. The infrastructure includes three large modern land fills and a network of nine refuse transfer stations (RTSs). Waste collected in the urban area is delivered to the RTSs, where it is compacted in purpose-built containers for onward transportation to the remote land fills. Waste collection from individual hotel premises is largely undertaken by cleaning companies contracted by the hotel management. The role of these cleaning companies is to take waste to designated refuse collection points at street level, where it becomes the responsibility of the municipal councils and private contractors to transport the refuse to the refuse transfer stations. The cost conversion exercise was based on four indicative environmental costs (κ): the cost of vehicular refuse collection, the operational costs (including depreciation) of RTSs, the cost of land fill site construction, and the subsequent operational costs (including discharging untapped methane gas, which may give rise to the greenhouse effect).

The environmental cost data established by Chung and Poon were based on 1994 market prices. To reflect the actual price levels in different years, the cost analysis was therefore adjusted according to the inflation rates in the respective years.

Quantity of MSW

The mean weight was based on the measurement made in 1996, and the discounting factors were estimated based on information from 15 experienced housekeeping staff. Because of hygiene and convenience, the reuse potential of plastic toiletries is low. This makes plastic toiletries the heaviest MSW at 0.594 kg per room. It is therefore suggested that more attention should be paid to the recycling of these plastic materials. For instance, the installation of lotion dispensers could be an alternative. Also, the selling of newspapers to waste collectors for recycling should be promoted, and the return of soap remains to special collectors should be considered. The amount of MSW generated from the hotel restaurants was estimated to be 0.751 kg per meal cover. This is slightly higher than the average of 0.665 kg reported in the United States. This could be due to the inclusion of Chinese restaurants in the present study.

Chinese restaurants tend to offer more menu items and more fresh items than their Western counterparts. This implies that more organic waste and more packaging materials are generated. Based on the estimated weight of the MSW, the number of guests, and the total number of guest rooms in HongKong, the amount of MSW generated by the local hotel industry was determined for the 15-year period. The sudden drop in 1997 was due mainly to the sharp downturn in the tourist industry (as a result of the Asian financial crisis) and the public's growing awareness of the issue of environmental protection.

Environmental Cost

Using 1994 as the basis for comparison, it was found that

vehicular refuse collection was the most significant among the four green costs studied. To reduce this pollution cost, hotel environmentalists should not only minimize MSW but should also put more pressure on the municipal council's vehicles and the light oil companies. The lowest amount, 18,859 tons, was recorded in 1986, and the highest was 24,191 tons recorded in 1993. These figures excluded the waste generated in room service. The total amount of MSW originating from hotels grew steadily from 34,811 tons in 1986 to 53,070 tons in 1996. The growth rate in this 11-year period was 52.4%. On average, the hotel industry's share of the total amount of the city's MSW was 1.5% in this period.

A set of environmental costs relating to solid waste in the hotel industry was produced, and some benchmarks for converting local hotels 'MSW into environmental costs were established. This study has developed a simple method that allows practitioners to estimate the environmental cost of solid waste and has shown that the inclusion of environmental costs is not difficult. Thus, it is expected that similar approaches and standard environmental costs can be developed for other pollutants and can be incorporated into management reports and statistical publications. In the long run, it is hoped that the established yardstick of green cost could serve as a useful tool in reducing the solid waste of hotel operations. In general, there are three accounting models. The first approach recognizes the actual and potential costs of waste management to a company and adjusts the policy accordingly. The second approach employs non financial data and sets up an information system that records the physical quantities of waste. The third approach, close to conventional accounting, charges all waste management costs back to the line management, who are more aware of the external impacts of its activities on the rest of the company. It is obvious that the first and the second approaches entail a large amount of research. The third approach is considered more feasible for the environmental accounting of MSW produced by the hotel industry. Based on these research methodologies and findings, we make the following suggestions. The executives

Table 1

The Weight of Municipal Solid Waste Generated in Rooms and Restaurants

	Per Room Basis					*Per Cover Basis*	
	Plastic Toiletries	*Laundry Bag*	*Paired Slippers*	*Original Soap*	*Newspapers*	*Room Waste*	*Restaurant Waste*
Mean	0.742	0.181	0.451	0.833	0.554	2.761	0.751
Standard deviation	0.078	0.011	0.065	0.055	0.081	0.119	0.100
Confidence intervals at 95%	0.705 to 0.778	0.176 to 0.185	0.420 to 0.481	0.575 to 1.091	0.174 to 0.934	2.204 to 3.315	0.693 to 0.808
Discount factor (in percentages)							
1986-1996	80	30	80	50	10a	NA	NA
1997-1998	70	20	70	40	10	NA	NA
1999-2000	65	20	70	40	10	NA	NA
Discounted mean							
1986-1996	0.594	0.054	0.361	0.417	0.554b	1.980c	NA
1997-1998	0.519	0.036	0.316	0.333	0.499	1.704	NA
1999-2000	0.482	0.036	0.316	0.333	0.499	1.666	NA

of individual hotels could consider inserting green indicators in their master profit and loss statements. The green indicators could appear in the notes section of the financial statements.

The suggested green indicator is an estimate of the amount of solidwaste consumed in terms of weight and environmental costs. To pass the green message down to operating departments, a more supportive practice would be to add such a green indicator, showing the green cost of MSW incurred, to individual departmental profit and loss statements. The same approach could also be considered to apply in environmental costing of MSW produced by the overall hotel industry. In fact, the majority of current tourism-related statistical reports emphasize financial and marketing information. Environmental performance indicators are rarely included in these reports. Therefore, we suggest that travel-related organizations such as industry associations, government bodies, and global hotel or tourism authorities could construct some green reminders or performance indicators in their statistical reports. For instance, certain annual publications, such as the Hong Kong Hotel Industry, the Statistical Review of Tourism in Hong Kong, and Trends in the Hotel Industry, would be good testing areas for such pilot schemes. In addition, the results and models of this study suggest possible further developments in the hospitality-related area of tourism satellite accounts (TSAs).

The traditional economic indicator of GNP, as codified in the United Nations System of National Accounts, masks the depletion of natural resources and hides the pollution costs of economic activities. There is therefore a growing body of published work on green accounts. In 1993, the United Nations published interim guidelines on an integrated System of Environmental and Economic Accounts (SEEA) and provided a common framework for green national accounting. In countries such as Canada and Sweden, the hotel industry's contribution to the GNP is reflected in the TSAs. The development of the TSAs has been on the economic side, and the revised TSAs were forwarded to the United Nations for comment in early 1998. It is envisaged that the next evolutionary phase in the development of the TSAs will involve this environmental element, in line with the United Nations' SEEA.

Environmental Uncertainty with the Hospitality Industry

The concept of environmental uncertainty is encountered frequently in the literature on organizations. When assessing the level of environmental uncertainty between industries, strategy and organizational theory research has considered two main dimensions: complexity and dynamism. The importance of contingency variables in macro-level research has been noted, and environmental uncertainty has generally shown a relationship with required levels of flexibility or rigidity in processes of the firm. Dynamism, in particular, has been shown to be an important moderator of the link between organizational decisions and performance. Although the contingency approach is generally accepted in strategy and organizational theory research, it seems to be underrepresented in macro-level hospitality research. It is suggested here that one reason for this is that generally accepted methods of measuring environmental uncertainty are too coarse grained to detect differences within a hospitality industry sector.

The alternate measures of dynamism and complexity that provide a more fine-grained assessment of these two constructs. The proposed method is exploratory in nature and is intended to encourage further discussion in this area. The proposed method has theoretical grounding in Schumpeterian economics, resource-based theory, and contingency theory. To test this method, aggregated macro-level data is analyzed for restaurant segments as defined by the National Restaurant Association (NRA). First, this discussion focuses on commonly used measures of complexity and dynamism. Second, the underlying theory of the uncertainty construct is evaluated. Next, exploratory methods are suggested and evaluated. And finally, future research for the development of valid and reliable measures of environmental uncertainty is discussed.

CURRENT MEASURES

Both environmental complexity and environmental dynamism are related to environmental uncertainty. Environmental uncertainty is viewed as a higher order latent construct that is caused by both complexity and dynamism. Environmental dynamism is defined as unexpected change that is hard to predict. Firms that operate in this type of environment face increased risk. Because change is hard to predict, members have a higher level of perceived uncertainty. Environmental complexity has been defined using two different dimensions:

— the variety and range of an organization's activities and
— the concentration dispersion level of firms within an industry or segment

A wider range of activities tends to increase information-processing requirements. The greater information-processing requirements are due to managers' perceived uncertainty when facing a more complex environment. The primary influence of the greater information-processing requirements is on organizational structure. This leads to divisionalization and decentralized decision-making authority. In addition, complex environments require high internal differentiation; resources must be used for extensive human resource training and to manage interdependencies. Environments low in complexity have more resources available to invest in assets and market promotion (i.e., external differentiation). The second dimension of a complex environment is concerned with the number, size, and distribution of firms within an industry or segment. Typically, members of a hospitality segment in a complex environment have low monopoly power and are "infused with entrepreneurial newcomers". Measures of complexity in the operations dimension include amount of diversification, breadth of product or service line, and geographical dispersion.

Measures of complexity in the concentration-dispersion dimension include movement to or from higher levels of concentration of firms within an industry segment, the number of firms within a segment, the diversity of firms within a segment, and their distribution. Although these traditional measures may be useful in assessing differences between industries, they appear too coarse grained to provide meaningful information in assessing differences between segments of a particular industry. For example, the currently accepted dynamism measures using secondary data rely on a number of implicit assumptions. The level of dynamism is measured by the volatility in industry performance, so this assumes that volatility is a proxy for unexpected change and (generally) that past levels of volatility will continue at the same relative levels for each industry in the study. Thus, if we are suggesting that a particular industry has a higher level of dynamism based on past levels of volatility, then by definition it is not unexpected change that is being measured but rather expected change (granted, we may not know where this change will happen). Because the level of dynamism can manifest itself in many ways other than financial measures of volatility, this analysis suggests that a richer measure of dynamism (and, hence, environmental uncertainty) can be achieved.

A second method of assessing the level of environmental uncertainty is to use subjective reporting or self-reporting by key informants of an organization. Although executive interpretations of the environment influence decisions and perceptions, it has been well documented that key informants' beliefs and expectations are biased toward confirmation. Because of these problems in measuring environmental uncertainty, it begs a number of questions for hospitality industry researchers. First, is the generally accepted approach to the measurement of environmental uncertainty fine grained enough to determine differences between hospitality industry segments? Second, besides using subjective data or traditional objective measures of environmental uncertainty, how else might this be assessed?

Variables

Variables included in this exploratory analysis included those that reflect theoretical measures of complexity and dynamism as well as being likely to be imperfectly mobile.

Age: Heterogeneity in firm age for this segment was chosen because it reflects the entrepreneurial entry dimension. If a significant difference exists between segments for this variable, additional interpretation of the results will need to be done to assess its impact (i.e., the proportion of young firms).

Affiliation type: This variable measures the proportion of firms in a segment that are single units, multiple units, chains, and so forth. It reflects the complexity dimension and entrepreneurial entry. As mentioned above, this variable was interpreted in a fashion opposite of the other variables, with a lower D value indicating greater heterogeneity (i.e., more single-unit firms).

Meal periods: This variable measured the variety of meal periods served in the restaurant segment. A greater variety of meal periods reflects a wider variety of activities and tacit knowledge within the segment. Tacit knowledge is defined as "the implicit and non-codifiable accumulation of skills that results from learning by doing . . . that is accumulated through experience and refined by practice".

Menu themes: The variety in menu themes was used as a measure of heterogeneity because it represents a level of idiosyncratic abilities between firms, specific know-how, and tacitness, which are not perfectly mobile.

Sales volume: This variable measures the proportion of firms within a segment that fall within a particular sales range category. A higher D value in the variable measures heterogeneity in volume for restaurant segments.

Location types: The variety in location type suggests a higher level of heterogeneity in firms and a wider variety of target markets within a segment. Types of locations include freestanding, hotels, clubs, shopping malls, and so forth.

Number of seats: The number of seats represents heterogeneity in size but also assesses differences in takeout capabilities and drive-through capacity and varies by meal period of the firm.

Size: Square feet: This variable is correlated to number of seats and sales volume but was included because it represents heterogeneity in amount of on-premise food preparation, service levels, partitioning of the facility, and so forth.

3

Monitoring Customer Satisfaction

Management is to be customer focused and really listen to customers. So, when a company decides to begin monitoring customers' satisfaction through a survey, the expectations are high. The company announces the process, develops a questionnaire, sends it out, and then awaits the results. The results trickle in, are tabulated, and a presentation is made to management. Many times the survey finds no surprises, offers few, if any insights into customer's attitudes, and after a couple of weeks the whole process is forgotten. The experience is disappointing. How can you use customer satisfaction monitoring as an opportunity to increase your customers' loyalty, and have a positive impact on your business?

Customer Satisfaction

Surveying customers seems simple on the surface, especially when there are few customers, but in reality customer satisfaction monitoring is complex. It is not easy to get solid, actionable answers from customers that can help you improve your company and increase customer loyalty, but it can be done.

They are not in any priority, but fall into three categories: designing the process, executing the survey, and analysing and acting on the results.

1. Decide the Purpose for Customer Satisfaction Monitoring

There are many reasons to survey customers. First, decide what you are trying to accomplish. Some people want to know how competitive their company is. Others want questions that relate to their mission statement and strategic plan. Still others will relate the questions to their continuous improvement program. All these reasons are valid, however, pick just one. When they are mixed together, the results are less than satisfactory.

2. Writing Questions

Managers may ask some questions like How's our quality?" "How's our selection?" "How's our on time delivery?", because they think 1) ultimately that is what they need to know, and 2) by directly asking the question they save the respondent time and reduce the risk of aggravating them. Nine times out of ten the customer will answer "great" because it takes less time than to answer the question meaningfully. These kinds of questions do not give you information that you can use to make changes in your company.

When companies get positive responses to questions such as the above, the managers usually have a brief celebration, don't gain any valuable information, and go back to business as usual. If the answers come back negative, there are discussions about what to do but usually the questions are so vague no one knows what to do, or has the budget to solve the problem, so the issues also soon disappear.

The solution is to ask most of the questions about actionable items. The quick way to find out if an item is actionable is to ask your managers, if this question comes back "dissatisfied" what can we do to change it to very satisfied? Examples of changing vague questions to actionable questions:

— (vague) How happy are you with our parts selection?

— (actionable) How many times have you called for a welding accessory and been told that we don't carry that part?

— (vague) How satisfied are you with our product quality?
— (actionable) How many times have you found scratches on the coatings of our parts?

The actionable questions tell a company several important things: 1) a quantifiable volume of lost sales — what this problem is costing the company in dollars; 2) the number of times a customer is aggravated; and 3) it gives a specific, finite set of parts or services to focus attention on. Management can take action on these questions.

The narrow focus of the actionable questions may steer some companies away from this type of question, however, with proper planning management should be able to provide input on which areas are the important ones for customers.

3. Understand What You Mean by Satisfaction

For many companies, satisfaction merely means you are allowed to continue bidding for jobs. Generally, customer satisfaction is composed of three areas:

— Importance—How relatively important is this issue to the customer?
— Expectation—What are the customer's expectations on this issue? How do excellent companies perform on this issue?
— Performance—How do we stack up on this issue? This is the last part of the satisfaction equation.

Michael Porter, a well known business author, has stated that companies that are in transition markets from growth to maturity, or have aging products, many times have inaccurate self-perceptions of their market position or capabilities. A statement such as 'we are the quality leader' may once have been true, but due to priority changes with buyers or competitors, it many times is no longer valid. An exceptional quality part may once have gotten you a big job but those standards move up. Previous quality levels may now be the expectation of the buyer.

4. Keep the Entire Process Concise and On Time

If the customer satisfaction project is dragged out management will forget about it, and forget the importance and original purpose. Keep the process moving forward with periodic updates for those with interest in the results. Customer satisfaction monitoring often takes a backseat to more urgent issues, and can have the plug pulled on it if something crucial occurs. Delivering the results in a timely fashion is as important as commitment to the process.

5. Keep the Analysis on a Level Managers Can Understand

Although you may understand the results of the conjoint analysis, if you spend most of your time explaining the technique to management before giving them the survey results, you may end up talking to an audience of blank stares. Results of customer satisfaction surveys are often used for employee performance reviews. If you are going to judge an employee's performance by your client's happiness, be very certain you understand what the results are saying and that the person being judged will understand them as well.

Most people without statistics coursework have an intuitive understanding of descriptive statistics (minimum, maximum, mean, mode, median, and standard deviation). Correlation and covariance are under- standable but give people much more than they need, and they will not believe what you are telling them, especially if the news is bad. If you are addressing results to other managers, give them suggestions on what to do about problems, or at least a sense of direction on how to address the issue. It is not enough to simply point out the problem. Remember, the best programs have addressed the question "What will we do if the answer is negative?" in the design phase of the survey.

6. Involve Others

You need full support of company management or you will

never get your customer satisfaction program off the ground. Either the results will be ignored or discounted, or even worse, sales and marketing personnel may claim you are pestering customers with unwanted interviews. Customer satisfaction monitoring must be a fully above board effort.

While it's important to involve employees and get them excited about the process, you do not have to involve them by inviting them to develop questions. If you do seek input from others in the survey development process, be certain that they clearly understand the purpose of the customer satisfaction monitoring activity.

A couple of questions in a lot of different directions may satisfy your employees, but will not give you a great survey tool. It's also important to share your company's commitment to customer satisfaction with customers so they realize the importance of their participation. This is best done with an introductory letter, signed by the president of the company. The letter shows the importance the process has for the company, and serves to introduce the interviewer to the respondent in a positive light.

7. Don't Be Afraid to Push Customers a Bit

Many companies are so afraid of aggravating customers that it inhibits them from communicating with them and developing insights about their satisfaction. They try to develop survey instruments that can be done in thirty seconds with yes or no answers. This provides meaningless answers in which the respondent does not take time to consider his feelings and many times circles all yes's. It makes the company administering the survey feel good for about a day, then the whole process is discarded.

Most experts seem to feel that a survey should not exceed two pages or you do risk aggravating customers, but within those two pages you can do a lot more to coax insights that can address problems or add value to your products or services. Ask customers about problem areas, but also consider what experiences they have had that were positive.

If you are trying to learn what customers think about a product, consider open ended survey questions in which you prompt them to tell the story of their experiences.

8. Prepare Your Customers and Involve Them

The best way to ensure you are touching on issues that matter to your customers is to ask them — What matters to you? It may sound foolish but it works. By asking them in the design phase of the survey, you can pinpoint their priorities and get directly to the issues that mean the most and produce the most loyalty. The best method for doing this is to work with a customer who is friendly enough to go out for a coffee or a beer. In a relaxed atmosphere, run a list of issues by the customer and ask them to rank ten issues by their importance to them. Once you know the important issues then ask additional questions to try and understand some of the subtleties that make that issue a sore spot for the customer. From that encounter you can begin building your questions for the survey. When the questionnaire is completed, run it by the same customer for feed back and to ensure that you have captured the issue that they described. Doing all the upfront work really pays off since you are dealing with issues that truly affect your customers.

9. For Your First Questionnaire, Keep Things Simple and In Control

For the first attempt, select customers that really matter to your company. Identify the best twenty-five and set a goal to interview all of them (a census, not a survey). As you gain experience and confidence, you might consider expanding the scope of your survey. For example, the first expansion should stay with customers. This way, the person conducting the survey does not have to deal with interview subjects who may have never heard of your company. Staying with customers, one might compare big buyers to so-so customers and find out why they differ.

Some managers think that since they are going through all the trouble of developing a questionnaire and conducting the survey, they might as well get the most they can from the process by including non-active customers, former customers, competitor's customers and potential customers in new markets. They see some advantages in comparing the attitudes of these groups and seeing how they differ. It's a good idea, however, it vastly complicates the process. In some cases, it may require more than one version of the survey. Without computer aided survey development software, it can become tricky keeping track of who gets what. It also may require developing random samples from potential markets. Without a background in statistics and some practical experience, this process is not usually successful.

10. Make Sure the Person Conducting the Survey Enjoys the Work.

Many customer satisfaction tracking plans fail because the person who does the work is dragged into the process unwillingly. In addition, the standard view is that this person will conduct the interviews, record the information, and report the results when he or she has free time. In the end, this process doesn't work because many people do not feel comfortable talking to customers. Consequently, the person never gets to the task, and the process drags on endlessly with many responses getting lost. Nothing aggravates a customer more than completing a survey, and then getting the same request, which does happen. Crucial to a good survey program is giving one person responsibility for the survey and develop a process to ensure that data is not lost or misplaced.

Enthusiasm sells the customer satisfaction monitoring process. If you are excited about the prospect of really learning what your customers think of you and how you can use that information as an opportunity to increase your customer's loyalty, then you will win over others both inside and outside the company.

BOOSTING ECONOMIC DEVELOPMENT

Over the past several decades, the tourism industry has become one of the fastest growing industries within the services sector. Its importance is set to grow even more as the economy transits into a post-industrial society. With the rapid economic expansion that the country has experienced, it is highly likely that the tourism industry will be the main driver to bring about both economic and social evolution. The level of contribution of the tourism industry to the country's economic growth has seen an increase over the years. It is expected, by the end of this year, the tourism industry will have contributed to roughly 4.7% of total GDP, and this contribution is set to grow to as much as 6.1% in the coming years.

Hence, it is important to ensure that there is sustainable tourism development to enable its economic benefits to be felt at all layers of the economy. Indirectly, this means that, in order to create a win-win situation for all parties, there must be a clear link with the other industries related to tourism development, no matter how obscure. Apart from contributing to economic growth, the call for greater attention to be placed on the tourism industry is related to its effect in encouraging economic diversification.

The tourism industry could serve as a cushion by reducing total reliance on the manufacturing sector. By tapping into new market sources for income, this not only promotes greater diversification and lessens the shock impacts from a particular industry, but it also contributes largely to the creation of new jobs in the services sector, in particular to sectors such as transportation, hotels and lodging, food and beverage, cultural and entertainment and even banking and financial services. Looking at this year alone, the tourism industry is expected to contribute 4.2% to total employment, which accounts for approximately 400,000 jobs.

Although it was only in the 1970's that the government realised the future potential of the tourism industry, the government has since placed greater emphasis upon it. Since then, the demand for Malaysia as a tourist destination has been growing at a healthy rate. With the exception of 1991 and 1996-98, the number of international tourist arrivals has been encouraging. In 2000, tourist arrivals stood at a whopping 10.2 million, surpassing the 9.5 million of Thailand, and much higher than the 7.69 million recorded by Singapore.

Notwithstanding, the growing recognition of the many contributions of the tourism industry to economic and social development, it is still worthwhile to note some operational issues that pose challenges to the tourism industry. Foremost, the tourism industry is still in great need for more funding and investments. Though the government has poured in approximately 2.1% of total government expenditure into developing the tourism industry, Malaysia still lags behind when compared to countries like Singapore, Indonesia or Thailand.

Singapore, for example, sitting at the top-end, has a high 9.1% of total government expenditure dedicated for tourism industry alone. This means that the Malaysian government would have to place perhaps a higher allocation in tourism expenditure and more investments in tourism-related projects, if it intends to compete on the same, if not higher, level as its regional competitors. The issue of safety and security also needs particular attention.

There is no doubt that the tourism industry is particularly sensitive to happenings in the country especially when these relate to tourist comfort, safety and security. Thus, for example, the haze hazard and outbreaks of localised viruses, which brought about health scare, caused a severe drop in in-bound tourist arrivals. Also, when the Asian financial crisis broke out, the tourism industry was again negatively impacted with in-bound traffic flow declining by almost 11% in 1998.

More recently, in the aftermath of the September 11 attacks on the US, there has been a substantial drop in air-travel, car rental and hotel bookings. From these incidents, it is obvious how important it is for tourism provisions and planning to ensure the safety of tourists and to avoid negative perceptions that are detrimental to the prospects for the tourism industry. Nonetheless, credit must be given to the government for being swift in taking action in responding to such crisis. During the Asian financial crisis, the government intervened to overcome the negative impact on the tourism industry.

The National Economic Recovery Plan, which was designed to draw up strategies from the public and private sectors to overcome the current financial crisis, earmarked the tourism industry as one of the leading tools to assist the country in its economic recovery. This helped the tourism industry to quickly rebound and helped the ailing nation to recover rapidly from the financial crisis. More recently, with the global economic slowdown rapidly setting in, the government has not only set aside RM110 million in the off-budget package, but in addition also thrown in a generous RM613.9 million for the Culture, Arts and Tourism Ministry under the 2002 Budget to boost the tourism industry.

Although it is expected that in-bound tourist traffic from the West would slow down to a trickle, the government is planning to compensate this by tapping and placing focus on new market sources, especially visitors from the Asian and Middle East region. In addition, the government has put forward plans to develop new tourist products and to expand existing ones such as eco-tourism, agro-tourism, cultural and heritage tourism among others, increase the market share and to create a competitive edge over other players.

The timing could not be more right since the United Nations has declared 2002 as the World Eco-Tourism Year, from which Malaysia is set to benefit much. Furthermore, since Malaysia has the advantage of being a country with diverse cultures and a rich heritage, the country will gain greatly by focusing on natural, cultural and heritage tourism. Although tourism resources serve as a crucial factor for development in the tourism industry, this alone will not suffice for a successful tourism industry. It is no secret that the success of the tourism industry also hinges inextricably on the quality of the training and education given to the people who are responsible in delivering these services. Therefore, there is a pressing need to place emphasis on human resource developent and to provide quality skill training to equip workers with relevant skills.

Since the tourism industry is a people-intensive industry, this is all the more reason to ensure that proper training, ranging from the operation and production level right up to the management level, is provided. Both the government and private sector have a shared responsibility to ensure that quality tourism-related services are provided, and to commit sufficient funds for education and training to develop the required human resources. This would mean that more effort could be expended to promote tourism-related careers, presenting stimulating interest in the industry as a source of employment.

The tourism sector will not develop to its full potential, if funds are mismanaged or misused for inappropriate programmes. Major programmes such as preservation and conservation of national historical sites and other tourism-related infrastructure must be properly planned and implemented. And, with sluggish performance and bearish sentiments expected in the near future, this calls for more intense and innovative marketing efforts to further promote the tourism industry.

However, this again must be well planned, with proper implementation in place so as to ensure that the marketing efforts have a full positive impact. If not, at the end of the day, poor advertising and promotional campaigns will not result in better tourism figures. It is vital that promotion and marketing campaigns are aggressive enough to overtake competitors like Thailand, Hong Kong and Singapore.

Excursion Tourism

This is a "virgin" market crucial to the successful launch of the "Discover Bulgaria" program. Presently, Bulgarian tour operators only offer "one day" excursions from beach resorts to nearby Bulgarian villages and monasteries without overnight stays. The economic benefit to communities away from beach resorts is minimal. This offer is targeted to beach-bound tourists as a diversion from "sun, sand and sea". Combination packages "one week mountain / one week beach" are not yet offered although such packages can provide a competitive advantage for Bulgarian tourism. Historical Societies, Alumni Clubs, Architectural Groups, Religious Groups are not yet target for Round Trip Tourism.

For the development of 8-14 days "Round Trip Tourism", new markets need to be targeted:

— The Experience/Relaxation seeking tourist
— The Culture / Communication seeking tourist.
— The Culture/ Nature Seeking Tourist

Creative Tour Packages and travel itineraries for a one - two week "Discover Bulgaria" program need to be developed with domestic and international travel partners who specialize in "Niche Markets" to really open up the cultural and natural riches of Bulgaria to the international tourist.

— Air- Bus- Lodging Packages
— Air- Rail-Lodging Packages
— Air- Rail Packages
— River Cruise-Bus-Lodging Packages
— River Cruise-Rail-Lodging Packages
– Mediterranean Cruise- Bus - Lodging Packages

Eco-Tourism

Although some tourist organizations such as the Pirin Tourism Forum have developed excellent collateral material to promote the history, culture, and nature of the region, the "tourist offering" have not yet been "packaged" and promoted to the international tourist seeking adventure and freedom to explore. International donor organizations including USAID, specifically the ARD Biodiversity Conservation and Economic Growth Project and the Bulgarian American Enterprise Fund, GTZ, the British Know-how Fund, the Swiss government agency, have provided substantial technical assistance and funding for developing the infrastructure for successful village tourism.

The Bulgarian-American Enterprise Fund (BAEF) promoting the development of enterprise and entrepreneurship in Bulgaria has a successful Hotel and Tourism Program. The program has invested in 100 hotels, disbursing 118 loans worth 16 million USD. The loans are typically used for privatization, reconstruction and furnishing of existing hotels varying in size from $20,000 to $2,000,000.

The clients include a wide range of businesses in the skiing resorts Bansko, Borovetz, Pamporovo, the cities of Shumen and Rousse, the Golden Sands beach resort and a number of smaller resorts on the southern coastline. BAEF maintains a web-site which promotes hotels in which they have invested. At present however, the site does not support on-line registration and the hotel rates published.

The site is currently being upgraded. The program is constantly growing and the existing portfolio shows good loan service ratios. BAEF however does not finance green field sites, or lodging operators in remote areas and tourist destinations. Private Bulgarian entrepreneurs have already developed unique lodging and recreation facilities in mountain villages such as Kovachevitsa, Leshten, Aprilizi and other locations. These entrepreneurs have found a way to market their offering on the domestic market but have not yet been linked to international niche tour operators. Financing for the development of "Bed and Breakfasts" remains a challenge, as banks are reluctant to take countryside real estate as collateral for loans because of lower liquidity.

The essence of village tourism is found in the statement: "One of the goals of the tourist is to penetrate the inside and back regions of the attractions in order to experience the authenticity of a place". The challenge is now to provide technical assistance to entrepreneurs in villages for further development of the infrastructure including lodging, arts and craft centers and tourist services. This village near or at national reserves and mountain areas need to be connected to the international market place through guidebooks. How transportation is provided and marketed to individual tourists is critical to the success of developing village tourism. Switzerland and Austria can provide the role model for developing the "Rail Pass"-Combination "Rail and Bus Pass".

The more affluent visitor will purchase "Fly -Drive Packages" offered by international niche tour operators and local car-rental partners. These packages can also include lodging at selected areas and entrance fees.

HEALTH AND SPA TOURISM

The competitive set for Bulgaria to compete "Health and Wellness Tourism" includes Germany, Austria, France, Italy, Spain, Hungary, Switzerland, Poland, Rumania, and the Czech Republic. According to the Ministry of Economy, there are a number of challenges Bulgaria is faced with when trying to qualify its "Balneological Centers" for inclusion in European national health care schemes:

— Need confirmation that Mineral Water is unique
— Need to upgrade qualification of medical personnel
— Need to upgrade the standards of medical equipment
— Need to modernize treatment facilities

This suggests that Bulgaria could develop a competitive advantage with developing a combined "wellness and health" and health market in key resort areas. According to a study by IUOTO (Health Tourism, IUOTO, Geneva Switzerland, there are approximately 1,100 health resorts- (bath in mineral water) in Europe. Many such health resorts provide wellness and beauty programs in addition to therapeutic and medical procedures. To succeed economically, many of these resorts offer combined skiing and health holidays, nature and health holidays, golf, and seaside and health holidays. Development of Health and Spa Tourism in Bulgaria is a capital intensive, long-term proposition which needs to start with the privatization of "Balneology Centers and Mineral Springs " in areas that have the potential to develop "Internationally competitive Wellness Resort Complexes".

The opportunity

The development of Health and Beauty Spas should focus on adding Spa facilities to the existing sea and mountain resort complexes and developing new complexes near major urban centers. The deliberate marketing focus should be on expanding seasons and increasing the competitive advantage. According to several studies conducted by Health Fitness Dynamics, Inc (HFD) a Florida based consulting organization, wellness and spa facilities with trendsensitive concepts as part of resort complexes can enhance the economic and marketing potential of the resort: Some of the key findings include:

- The 30-49 age group dominates the market
- Rest, Relaxation, feeling pampered and beauty services are most sought
- Resort with Spa's have a preferred booking status - marketing advantage
- Increased length of stay and higher perceived value for room rate
- Spa revenues come primarily from massage, facials, body treatment and nail care
- 59% prefer to purchase individual services rather then a package

CITY TOURISM

The potential of convention, incentive and "city break" tourism: SOFIA. Sofia has not been featured in City Programs since 1995. The presence of international hotel brands on the Sofia market enables the city to pursue this market to boost Hotel occupancies and the utilization of convention facilities. Without the expansion of the market, these operations remain below the economic target zones for sustained profitability.

The capacity of the international airport is underutilized. The number of visitors to the opera, theater, historic churches, monuments and museums can be increased to provide revenues for restoration and upkeep. Tour operators such as TUI have not yet included Sofia in their City Programs and the international airlines serving Sofia do not yet promote the city as a convention and "City Break" destination. The high cost of airfares is a major detriment to the development of convention and incentive tourism. International Airlines flying to Sofia enjoy consistently high load factors and in the absence of competition from Europe's Low -fair airlines, the airlines demonstrate an invert monopolistic behavior in the pursuit of aggressive pricing policies.

Sofia has developed the basic infrastructure and elements to develop and compete for the profitable business of major European conventions and as a "City Break" destination:

- International Airport in proximity of city destination
- Convention and Exhibit Facilities for 4,000 delegates
- Mid to Upscale Hotels (1,500 rooms) in proximity of Convention Center
- No Visa Restrictions
- Attractive Restaurants, Cafes, Pubs and entertainment facilities
- Guided tours to nearby cultural and historic attractions (Spouse Programs)
- Opera, Ballet and Theater Performances
- Post Convention Tours to Wine Country, Mountain (Ski) and Sea Resorts
- Business friendly atmosphere and global communication network

— Public Safety and Security
— Value for Money

An industry coalition made of airline representatives, hotels, the cultural center and other meeting facilities, restaurants, attractions, shops, meeting service providers, tour services operators is needed to represent Sofia at the International Incentive Market in Geneva.

Bulgaria needs a Master Plan: Tourism Development and Strategy

— The basic document outline should be as follows:
— Strategy
— Mass or Class Tourism, Environmental Impact, Benchmark
— Starting Position: 2002
— Profitable Tourism Products for Key Regions
— Basic Principles for the Development Strategy
— Government Qualitative and Quantitative Goals
— Environmental Impact for existing infrastructure and new developments
— European Travel Market Trends
— Tourism Potential of Bulgaria
— Assessment of Bulgaria as an Air, Sea, Rail, Bus, Private Car Destination Quality and Quantity of Hotels and Lodging Facilities
— Basic Infrastructure Development Strategy and Action Plan
— Sales and Marketing Plan

Bulgaria needs a post-privatization assessment of sustainable tourism development and overall economic impact

— Sustained Business Potential of Privatized Companies: Measure - Profitability Quality and Type of Business generated: Measure - Occupancy and Visitor Spending

- Foreign Exchange Earnings or Losses
- Ratio of foreign exchange earnings vs. foreign exchange outflows (imports)
- Increase in Tax Revenue
- Ratio between tourist tax revenue and total tax revenue
- Ratio between tourist tax revenue and public expenditures in favor of tourists
- Economic Impact of tourist projects between foreign ownership and local ownership
- Ratio of Market Access; Ratio of Staff Training and Development
- Level of new job creation and small business creation
- Control over development on the Regional Level
- Precise procedures applicable to all tourism development projects

Proposed actions:

- Provide Support for a "Discover Bulgaria" exhibit at the following international tourism fairs: ITB -Berlin; World Travel Market- London;
- Incentive Travel Market-Geneva; Tourism Fair-Moscow (all tourism enterprises, large and small, BATA affiliated or independent should have equal access to the booth)
- Support the development of an "Image Marketing" campaign for a "Discover
- Bulgaria" programs - video to be shown at airports, hotels, and tourist information centers
- Support for the Development of "City breaks" and Convention and Incentive Tourism. Enhance Bulgaria's competitive position: Grant
- Landing Rights for Low-cost Airlines

— Provide National and International Press Support for Tourism Activities News Releases, Travel Writer Program, Information centers at embassies abroad

— Support the development of "Village / Nature Tourism" Provide standards, credit and incentives for the development of "Bed and Breakfast / Private Rooms, and village based tour services Establish "Rail Pass System" for Tourists - Use Swiss Model Support the development of a National Directory for "Bed and Breakfast"

— Support the development of world-class Wellness and Spa Resorts Identify "green-field" sites and seek strategic developers, operators and investors Privatize and reposition sanatoriums as Beauty Spas and Wellness Centers

— Support the development of world class Golf and Conference Resorts Benchmark model: Moscow Country Club, Nakhabina

Tourism policy considerations and actions for all regions and summary recommendations

Environmental Considerations in view of changing consumer attitudes:

— Set up WTO and UNEP norms for measuring the impact of tourism development

— Fragility of ecosystem (species, flora, fauna) and biodiversity

— Waste management systems and waste-water treatment

— Drinking water safety; cost of consumption by tourist projects in communities

— Intensity of land use-tourist /density of land occupied by tourist structures

— Protection of atmosphere, noise, pollution and visual aspects (billboards)

— Tourism Construction Standards - Harmony with Environment

— Intensity of tourist transport by mode of transport

Tourism policy considerations and actions for all regions and summary recommendations

Social Measurements:

— Affect on traditional way of life

— Affect on cost of living

— Low or high economic impact of tourist activities (users of infrastructure vs. contributors to the local economy)

— Cost of public health and safety

— Intensity of tourist visitations

— Number of jobs by skill level created (seasonal/permanent)

— Affordability of restaurants, cafes, sport facilities by local population

Economic Impact

— Proportion of tourist activity to all economic activity in community

— Development policies linked to profitability of tourism enterprises

— Type and quality of business generated

— Proportion of local ownership

— Foreign Exchange earning and losses

— Ratio of tourist tax revenues and public expenditures favoring tourists

Tourism Concept Development and Planning in the National Interest

— Requires a clear strategic direction with the "New Europe"

— National, Regional and Community level co-ordination necessary for the development of a Master Plan

Privatization

— Changing Ownership models with legislative reassessments

— Focus on strategic investors and operators for larger projects

— Reconsider incentives to attract foreign investment capital
— Increase market potential by facilitating more hotel real estate transactions involving international hotel brands.
— Implement value based management performance metrics
— Separate property asset management from the hotel operation metrics
— Identify new financing mechanism for hotel and resort projects

Pricing

— Requires clearly differentiated approaches to avoid the business risk of excessive price competition and market / profit erosion -
— The Bulgarian tourism industry must consider the impact of transparency and price convergence with the introduction of the EURO and adopt different strategies to defend market and or · increase market share
— Consider challenges of transparent pricing when using the Internet

Tourism policy considerations and actions for all regions and summary recommendations

Lodging Facilities - Hotels and Motels

— Establish rating standards according to European norms
— Provide target market - oriented hotel product
— New licenses only for 3star plus facilities and amenities
— Focus on developing mid to up-market hotels and resorts

Lodging Facilities- Private Rooms and Bed and Breakfast

— Establish basic standards for comfort, sanitation and safety
— Achieve step-by step improvements in present offering
— New licenses only for 3star plus facilities

Lodging- Camping/ Mountain Chalets

— Upgrade facility, service and sanitary sanitary standards

— Minimize licenses for camping places

Expanding Marketing Potential

— Develop niche markets for cultural and back to nature tourism

— Seek co-operation from international niche-tourism operators

— Develop co-operative internet marketing with direct booking capabilities

— Consider the market potential of an aging European population when reconstructing hotel and resort facilities

— With increasing trade, focus on increasing business travel (trade shows, incentive travel and major international conventions - Consider the "European Package Travel Directive" when marketing destinations and individual resort locations.

— Partner with airlines for "City Promotion Packages"

Education

— Set up regional hospitality- vocational training centers - (service employees, cooks, reception, information centers, tour guides etc., - Provide for foreign vocational exchange programs

— Focus on Service as a behavioral capability and professional competency

— Consider E-learning capabilities when training hospitality workers

Technology

— Consider Room Allocations using the Internet as distribution channels for on-line bookings - need to consider a single image inventory - Consider the "position" /representation on the e-agent city site - Consider offering real time room availability and consistent pricing

Transport

— Seek expedient re-start of Danube Cruises originating / ending in Bulgaria (Consider affiliation with Casino Austria)
— Expand capacity for Black Sea/ Mediterranean Cruises originating in Bulgaria
— Upgrade the environment friendly rail transportation to tourism destination -Special Ski and Panorama Trains
— Improve attractiveness of Marinas and increase capacity
— Provide Solar powered boats for lakes and river excursions

CHANGES IN EUROPEAN TOURISM

The changing patterns in worldwide tourism, Europe, although losing market share, is still the main tourist destination. Within Europe there are, however, important regional differences in terms of international arrivals:

Table 1. International tourist arrivals in Europe 1990-1998 by sub region (million)

Year	Northern Europe	Western Europe	Central/ East Europe	Southern Europe	East Med. Europe	Total
1990	29.1	113.8	43.8	88.6	7.4	282.7
1995	37.6	116.7	78.9	93.7	11.4 3	38.4
1998	43.9	161.4	83.4	111.9	13.1	383.8
			Average annual growth rate			
1990-1995	5.3	0.5	12.5	1.1	9.0	3.7
1995-1998	5.2	4.0	1.9	6.1	4.8	4.3
1990-1998	5.3	1.8	8.4	3.0	7.4	3.9

As table 1 shows, there are wide variations in growth rates. Although in absolute terms Western Europe is still dominant, there are stronger growth increases in all other areas. Specifically it can be seen that the market share of Central and Eastern Europe, within European tourist arrivals as a whole, rises from 15.5 per cent in 1990 to 24.1 per cent in 1996, although, due mainly to the Kosovo crisis, this had dropped back in 1999 to 21.4%.

TOURISM IN EASTERN CENTRAL EUROPE

The momentous events of the late 1980s, which culminated in the collapse of communism in the former centrally planned economies of Eastern Central Europe, are common knowledge. One of the major consequences for the international hotel industry was the re-evaluation of tourism and the hotel industry within the economies of the nations in the region. Governments became more aware of the value of travel and tourism in generating hard currency earnings and creating employment and investment opportunities.

In the immediate aftermath of the transition from planned to market economies, international hotel operators eagerly anticipated the possibilities of entering a large, potentially very lucrative market that had been hidden by the iron curtain for more than half a century. It appeared that almost every major international hotel operator wanted to have a property in the region. This euphoria quickly evaporated, however, to be replaced by scepticism and cynicism on the part of international hotel companies, who had become impatient with the legal framework, administrative bureaucracy and inherent corruption in many of the countries concerned. It is clear that the massive challenges involved in changing from totally planned economies to free market economies could not be dealt with in the short- or medium-term, but rather within a timeframe of ten to fifteen years.

Specific problems that affected the hotel industry were the shortage of external funding, uncertainties on the part of international hotel operators over long-term political stability in the region, economic performance and property title. In addition, there was a lack of local capital to fund development projects, and per capita income was insufficient to generate domestic demand.

In general terms, there is an increasing body of knowledge describing and analysing key characteristics of tourism in Eastern Central Europe, including Kerpal, Medlik, Hall, McCleary and Whitney, Witt, Airey and Lennon.

Sociographic details

The size and scope of the region are indicated in the following table:

Table 2. Eastern Central Europe: size and population

Country	Population (mn, 1997)	Workforce (mn,1995)	Urban (%)	Landmass km^2	Population density habitant per km^2
Poland	38.6	19	65	312.68	123
Czech Republic	10.3	6	65	78.864	131
Hungary	10.2	5	65	93.036	109
Slovakia	5.3	3	59	49.036	109
Slovenia	2	1	64	20	100

As seen in table 2, Poland is by far the largest country in the region, both by population and area. The Czech Republic and Hungary are of comparable size in terms of population, although the Czech Republic is somewhat smaller in land area. Both Slovakia and Slovenia are much smaller countries, both physically and in relation to their populations. These factors obviously have a major effect on their respective tourism and hotel industries.

Peculiarities of tourism in former communist countries

The key difference between tourism in Western Europe and in Eastern Central Europe is the importance of the Marxist ideological legacy, which considered the service sector as "non productive". As a service industry, tourism was therefore of low significance among the priorities of national governments in the region. The main role of tourism was in rejuvenating the workforce and in providing collective holiday and recreation facilities. This peculiar state form of tourism provided domestic provision in the form of resorts for trade union members, and other sectors of society including, for example, mothers with infants, offering them holidays at reduced cost, or sometimes even free. This development of networks of tourist resorts has had a major impact on the distribution and nature of hotel and para-hotel stock in the region. The vacation centres, often in large numbers and of considerable size, tended to be of low quality.

In addition, the socialist model also took the form of cumbersome visa regulations, strict levels of security, regimented tours and restrictive currency regulations. Kerpal gives a clear account of the workings of the tourism "system" as practiced towards both local populations and foreign visitors.

As a result of such policies, in 1987, only 3% of international arrivals to Eastern Central Europe came from outside the continent and over 60% from within that region. There were also severe limitations on the local population within Eastern Central Europe wishing to travel outside the Comecon states, while Western visitors were often regarded with deep suspicion. With the exception of business trips or visiting friends and relatives (VFR), western visitors were "welcomed" only as part of an organised group. An additional factor was the effect of the policy on attitudes to service and client orientation, considered so important by marketing writers. Owing to the communist system, in which everybody had guaranteed employment, it was not considered necessary, or even useful, to take into account the needs of the clients. There was a form of "studied indifference" on the part of the service staff towards guests, which was prevalent throughout communist states.

It was not surprising, therefore, that this model of tourism organisation was not perceived as attractive to Western Europeans and tourists from outside Europe. As a result, the region missed the opportunity of mass holidays in the 1970s, which were subsequently exploited by Mediterranean destinations such as Spain and Greece.

Towards the late 1970s and early 1980s, there was a reassessment of the role of tourism, however, and governments began to realise its potential, especially in the creation of foreign exchange. The priorities of the XVth Communist Party Meeting in Czechoslovakia, had, for example set out the following aims for tourism in 1981:

1. development of mass sport and tourist activities, with the aim of regenerating the labour force;
2. promotion of friendship between nations;
3. generation of foreign exchange, particularly in the spa and transit tourism sectors;
4. improved utilisation of hotel, restaurant and spa facilities;
5. development of more sophisticated tourism services.

It is evident from the list, therefore, that tourism was beginning to be seen in a more positive light, and that the government had recognised the importance not only of the domestic market, but also of the different niches which had already proved popular with foreign tourists, but which needed to upgrade their quality.

Tourism's role in the restructuring of Eastern Central Europe

Despite the role that tourism has played in restructuring the economies of Eastern Central Europe, there are few explanatory models for tourism development in the region. Tourism was identified as an attractive sector for investment and development very quickly after the fall of the Berlin wall. "The region [Eastern

Central Europe] boasts a wide range of mass and specialist nice attractions, some of which far surpass anything Western Europe can offer".

These consist of natural attractions and features including mountain ranges, thermal spas, immense lakes, caverns and nature reserves (of which, for example, there are over 1,000 in the Czech Republic alone). There are also rich and varied cultural attractions including examples from the Greek, Byzantine and Ottoman empires, medieval castles, baroque churches, unspoilt villages and towns and the jewel cities of Prague, Budapest and Krakow. The region has a long tradition of folk art and music, opera houses and orchestra.

Many Western European and US tourism experts responded quickly to mandates from the European Union and other agencies to draw up tourism development plans and strategies at regional and national levels. The US consultancy company Arthur D. Little, for example, assessed the intrinsic value of Polish tourism and estimated that if Poland developed 170 tourist sites there was a potential for tripling tourism levels by 2004. The company believed that even through natural development tourism would grow by 70% between 1994 and 2004, increasing tourism revenues from US$1.6 billion to US$2.8 billion.

The journey to a market economy was evidently not going to be easy for tourism and hotel enterprises, however. On the one hand there were still frequent examples of extreme bureaucracy, backward technology, obsolete equipment and under-utilised maintenance and service departments, and on the other there was an urgent need to develop a more effective framework for market regulation. Quality control is still often outmoded, and there are major skills shortages, especially at the top management level in marketing, finance and change management.

However, there are significant advantages of doing business in Central and Eastern Europe for international hospitality enterprises, which include prospects of strong economic growth, a well-educated and relatively cheap labour force, proximity to the major tourist generating markets of western Europe (important also in terms of cultural affinity), combined with policies from national governments to attract foreign direct investment. Eastern Central Europe has vast areas of untouched natural countryside, and the region has experience of tourism, albeit within the communist framework mentioned above. Finally, tourism is an excellent mechanism for the development of small- and medium-sized enterprises, allowing easy access to many thousands of the working population as shown by Szivas and Riley, either working in the industry traditionally, or switching to it from other sectors.

As shown in figures 1 and 2, tourism has played an increasingly important role in the economies of the countries in Eastern Central Europe. As a major service industry, it has had an economic and social impact by exposing domestic enterprises to national and international market forces, encouraging FDI in tourist-related facilities, by stimulating comparative market advantage and niche specialization and finally by encouraging greater and closer interaction between formerly restricted host populations and the outside world.

Changes in Supply and Demand in the Tourism Industry in Eastern Central Europe

While enormous changes have taken place within the last decade in the tourism and hospitality industry, growth has not always been as exciting as anticipated. This has been due to such external factors as economic slowdown in some of the major source markets, e.g. Germany, and increasing consumer choice in tourism markets, especially in relation to cheaper airline travel, together with internal factors such as the pace of economic reform which proved to be slower than anticipated in a number of countries in the region.

Furthermore, the Kosovo crisis, which was virtually impossible to forecast, had a profoundly depressing impact that was widely felt, with negative repercussions for the image of the region as regards stability and security. Although the WTO and WTTC. forecast growth above the European average for Eastern Central Europe, the rate of growth has varied significantly from country to country.

There was great anticipation immediately post-1989, when tourism development and investment possibilities were perceived to have enormous potential. Tourism now does play an increasingly important role in the economies of the region. Six countries receive over $1 billion per annum from tourist revenues. In 1985 there were 36 million tourist arrivals, which doubled within a decade, and which are forecast to grow six-fold from the original figure by 2020. By 2020, it is estimated that one tourist in every three coming to Europe will choose a Central or Eastern European destination, and average annual growth in the region will be 4.4%, which is 1.3% above that of Europe as a whole.

The reasons for these optimistic forecasts include both internal developments, such as the easing of entry, exit and currency restrictions, and the growth of GDP in the region, together with increased disposable income and the mobility of many Eastern Europeans themselves, thereby stimulating domestic demand for tourism products. There was also increased recognition of the economic benefits of tourism by governments in the region. Externally, there was a change in the image of the region and more substantial Western media attention to it, as well as increasing Western involvement in aspects of tourism development, including improvements to infrastructure; financial support, especially from the European Union (EU), through both EU development funds and supportive trade policies and investments, as countries in the region apply for full membership of the EU.

Tourism balance of payments

The status regarding the balance of payments can be seen from figure 1. The tourism balance of payments was obtained by deducting tourism expenditure from the country of residence from that of tourism expenditure in other countries spent by outbound tourists.

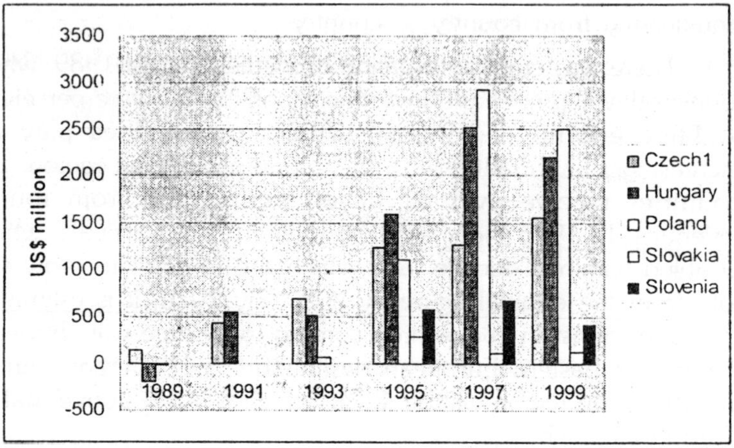

Figure 1. Balance of tourism payments, 1999, (S$ million)

As shown by figure 1 initially more money was spent abroad by outbound tourism than was generated from tourism within the respective countries. This was mainly because existing tariffs and prices were not immediately changed to market prices, so that state subsidies of tourism facilities were still required. This was compounded by the fall in the value and exchange rates of local currencies against the US dollar. The situation was reversed very quickly, however, so that the countries concerned generated more revenues from foreign tourists than their tourists spent abroad.

In the case of Hungary and Poland, within the two years this had increased dramatically. The Czech Republic, while increasing its revenues, has not, however, recorded the same level of growth as these two countries. Slovakia's balance of payments has consistently been of a much lower order of magnitude, and is significantly less even than Slovenia, a much smaller country in population and area.

International arrivals

Often industry analysts focus upon the level of tourist arrivals to a country as an indicator of tourism success. Figure 2 shows the evolution and projections of tourist arrivals in Eastern Central European countries from 1988.

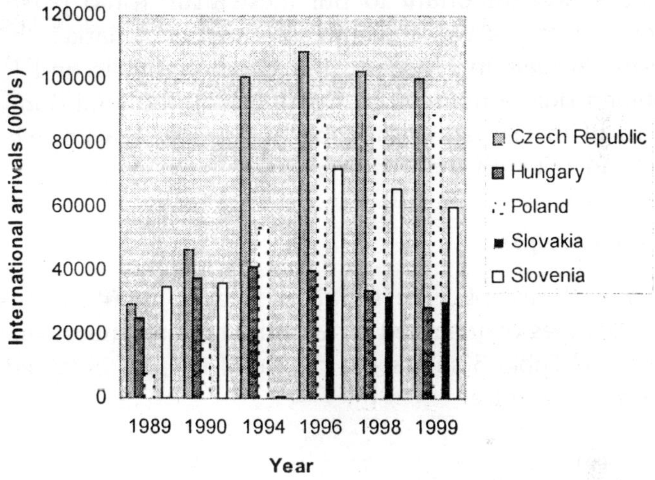

Figure 2. Tourist arrivals in Eastern Central Europe 1988-1998 (thousands)

As shown in figure 2, while there is strong growth in Poland, the Czech Republic and Hungary, international tourism in the region started from an extremely low base; additionally, the figures should be regarded with some caution, as arrivals contain a significant number of low-spending day trippers/excursionists, especially from other Eastern Central European countries, as well as cross-border traders and local cross-border customers for many services ranging from medicinal to prostitution, reflecting differences (and availability) of goods and services across borders.

Despite these caveats, however, the progress is impressive. By 1994, Hungary, Poland and the Czech Republic were in the top 10 rankings of the WTO, in 4th , 7th and 8th positions respectively. The change was the most dramatic for Poland, which had been ranked 16th in 1984. Unfortunately for the countries concerned, these huge increases were not sustainable over the longer-term, and by 1999 Poland had slipped to 10th place, with the Czech Republic and Hungary 13th and 14th respectively.

It is also important to put these figures into perspective by looking at the wider picture of European market share in tourism. Arrivals to Hungary, the Czech Republic and Poland combined only amounted to two thirds of the total number of arrivals of the largest destination in Europe, France, which in 1999 had over 73 million arrivals.

Tourist receipts

In terms of receipts, the situation is even more serious: the three countries only earned 50% of the total revenues generated by France. Table 3 shows the details of receipts obtained from tourism by country.

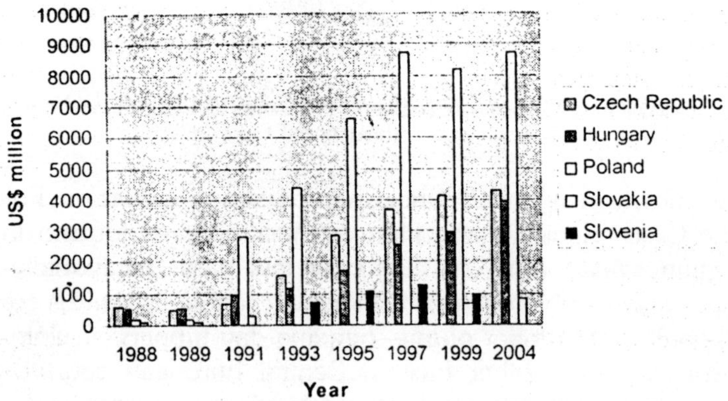

Figure 3. International tourism receipts in Eastern Central Europe 1980-2004 (excluding transport US$ million)

As seen in figure 3, the three major tourism markets of Hungary, the Czech Republic and Poland record the most impressive growth in tourism receipts during this period. The first two both increased their receipts during the period by a factor of seven, while in comparison with 1988 Poland does so by a factor of 42. Again at a much lower overall level, Slovakia and Slovenia have 9 times and 3.6 times more revenues respectively. Also of note is that despite relative stagnation in terms of tourist arrivals, within the last five years Slovakia and Slovenia have both managed to increase their receipts.

However, as with figure 2, figure 3 should be interpreted with some caution. Although it shows significant, even spectacular, growth in receipts, one should remember that the base was extremely low, when 61% of the international arrivals were from within Comecon countries, with extremely limited spending power. Central Eastern Europe still lags behind the rest of Europe in terms of per capita levels of tourism income generated. Although the region takes 25% of all European arrivals, it receives only one-eighth of the revenues .

These trends need to be taken into account by international hotel operators considering expansion into the area. Another equally important trend is the potential of the domestic market, as discussed in the next section.

The importance of domestic tourism in Eastern Central Europe

For many years it has been a criticism of Eastern Central Europe that there is no domestic demand. However, on closer examination of the data, it is clear that there are considerably inter-country differences, as shown in figure 4. Evident from figure 4 is the large share of Hungary's participation in domestic tourism, more than five times greater than that of the Czech Republic, which has a slightly larger population. Also clear from the chart is the major increase in Polish domestic tourism, with over 2.5 times the number of overnight stays in hotels in five years.

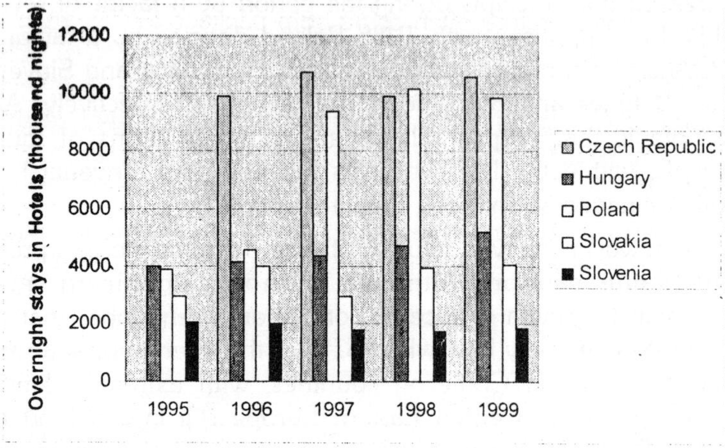

Figure 4. Trends in domestic tourism 1995-1999, by country

Given the potential size of the Polish market, this should be of interest to international hotel operators, especially those such as Accor who have "hard-budget" products like "Formule 1," targeted at the domestic market.

Current tourism markets

The diversity of physical and cultural environments within Eastern Central Europe offers significant possibilities for market segmentation. Tourism to the area has traditionally focused on particular attractions. Coastal tourism is well developed in the study countries, including the Polish Baltic littoral and Slovenia. It was recently reported at the annual International Hotel Investment Forum in Berlin that there is an increasing demand for such developments and for new projects involving golf resorts.

Winter upland tourism, for both the domestic and international markets, has long been a feature of the region in Poland, Slovakia, e.g. in the Tatra Mountains, and Slovenia, but the general quality of facilities and the winter sports product available is low in comparison with major western markets. The demand has therefore often come from package-tour companies, specialising in the less advanced, younger markets, and selling predominantly on low price. As in many Western European ski resorts, the lack of snow in recent years has also affected operators, which if prolonged may eventually have far-reaching results.

There is recent evidence, however, of new market niches being opened up, which may provide a higher value-added.

Potential Market Niches

Tourist supply in Eastern Central European countries has until recently been more accentuated on quantity rather than quality and has not been overly concerned with sustainability. This is now changing, as it has been recognised that one of the major trends in tourism development is towards sustainability, owing to the importance for the environment and providing for the future. In addition, it can be shown that, provided resources are properly managed, the economic return for the provider and so for the national economy can be higher than otherwise. Research is therefore focussing on targeting high-spending groups such as adherents of "eco-tourism", including nature and rural or farm tourism; the meetings, incentive conference and events markets (MICE); and cultural tourism, all of which attempt to extend the season.

"Green, "rural" and "eco-tourism"

There are many definitions of "eco" or "green" tourism. To be judged "truly eco," a tourism product should involve travel to a natural area, be supportive of the conservation of the biosphere, bring benefit to local communities and lead to a greater understanding of the natural or cultural environment visited . For our present purposes, the general concept of "green tourism" is more important than compliance with each and every possible criterion; green tourism is therefore taken to include nature and rural or farm tourism.

Paradoxically, when the image of Eastern Central Europe is often one of widespread pollution, and when large areas, such as the summer holiday camps around Lake Balaton Hungary, were transformed under unimaginative socialist schemes, the region as a whole was in reality under-urbanised by Western. European standards. There are indeed wide tracts of unspoilt countryside. In some countries, e.g. Poland, a large proportion of the population still live and work in rural areas, where farm tourism has been identified as a major possibility. Rural tourism is also an integral part of the tourism planning for Slovenia and has been identified as having potential in Slovakia and Hungary.

Other eco-tourism projects include the large, wooded, mountain region in Czech Bohemia, marketed as "Europe's green roof" and monitoring the effects of wolves in the Carpathian areas in Southeast Poland. In the winter, cross-country skiing also has potential, in contrast to its more destructive and energy- and capital-intensive Alpine cousin, classified as "hard tourism". The "softer" cross-country form is far less damaging, and makes good use of environmental assets. Such developments can complement and diversify rural enterprises, transforming them into tourism and leisure SMEs offering accommodation, food, local crafts, and other services, bringing improved incomes and standards of living, and the lessening of urban attractiveness and rural decline.

Eco-tourism is potentially a very lucrative market, when eco-tourists typically spend more per capita than the package tour "mass tourist". It is estimated that at present, however, the eco-tourist market represents only some 2-4 % of all travel expenditure.

Meetings, incentive, conference and events market (MICE)

The development of the meetings, incentive, conference and events markets (MICE) sector is directly linked to the development of business travel in both continehts and individual countries. Meetings and conferences are relatively underdeveloped in Eastern Europe, and the sector has been identified as having potential. The size of the market is estimated at 1-4% of business tourism, but the latter is difficult to estimate in certain countries, e.g. in a wide range between 6-35%.

For example, the WTO estimated 6.5% of travel to India was business travel, compared to 33.9% for Taiwan. The potential in Eastern Central Europe may be seen by reference to Poland, which, despite having 36% of arrivals as business travellers, has less than 2% of the meetings market. Table 3 shows the trends for numbers of meetings in Europe throughout the 1990's.

Table 3. Number of meetings in Europe, 1991-2000, selected countries

Country	1991/92	1993/94	1995/96	1997/98	1999/2000
UK	334	334	345	331	273
Spain	301	228	228	298	143
Germany	351	309	266	270	167
Switzerland	130	102	120	108	57
Hungary	95	88	117	79	86
Czech Republic	49	44	74	64	33
Poland	33	37	39	43	38
Slovenia	6	8	14	35	19

There are two main trends shown by table 3. Firstly there is a dramatic reduction in the overall number of meetings per country in the time period (which may be accounted for by the increase in the number of countries wishing to attract this kind of business). Secondly the share of the MICE market is relatively low in the Czech Republic and especially in Poland

Significant direct benefits may be generated from this type of business, including local government and private sector investment, increased employment and high average spending per delegate. Indirect benefits include improvements in local economies, the rejuvenation of depressed areas, revenues from taxation on delegates, and improved occupancy rates in hotels and restaurants, especially if events are held in the off-season. In contrast to the other forms of tourism, the business and MICE form is relatively price-inelastic, has a broad impact on the respective business sectors concerned, and does not follow the usual seasonal peaks and troughs.

Costs however should not be underestimated, with significant direct costs in the building and operating of the centres, and also heavy indirect costs in terms of upgrading the local infrastructure, and opportunity costs (such as building a theme park which could yield higher financial returns and generate more employment opportunities).

Cultural tourism

Although defining "culture" is even more problematic than defining "tourism", the conceptual definition used by Richards is adequate for this relatively brief section. Cultural tourism is "The movement of persons to cultural attractions away from their normal place of residence, with the intention to gather new information and experiences to satisfy their cultural needs" It is the learning factor that is the most important constituent of cultural tourism.

A typology of cultural tourism resources could include the following:

Table 4. Typology of cultural tourism resources

1.Attractions	Monuments
	Religious buildings
	Public buildings
	Historic houses
	Castles & palaces
	Parks & gardens
	Defences
	Archaeological sites
	Industrial-archaeological buildings

	Museums
	Folklore museums
	Art museums
	Routes
	Cultural-historic routes
	Art routes
	Theme parks
	Cultural-historic parks
	Archaeological parks
	Architecture parks
2. Events	Cultural-historic events
	Religious festival
	Secular festivals
	Folk festivals
	Art events
	Art exhibitions
	Art festivals

Within Europe the importance of culture and the possibilities for cultural tourism have been compared economically to that of the major motor vehicle producers of the USA, and recognised as deserving priority by political decision makers such as the European Union.

In Eastern Central Europe there are examples that fit into every category of the typolology, which will add to the already abundant European richessse. Examples of cultural tourism already evident in the region include examples of cultural tourism centred around monuments (which is also sometimes referred to as Heritage tourism), include the cities of Prague, Budapest and Krakow, which have been well publicised. Additionally there are, especially in the Czech Republic, many smaller historic towns that are richly endowed in cultural monuments.

Art events are also widely held with "high culture" being represented by Poland's "Warsaw Autumn" contemporary music festival, the Czech Republic's "Prague Spring" music festival and the Hungarian Budapest summer opera and ballet festival. There is also a range of national, regional and local dance groups, choirs and folklore music events. In addition there are a wide range of theatres, art galleries and open-air village museums. The latter were constructed to give a sense of national pride and identification, rather than for foreign tourists. One such example of a village museum is to be found near Luhochiviche in the Czech Republic, and there are over 30 in Poland.

On the accommodation side, there are a number of guide books and listings offering stays in historic palaces and country houses "Indeed Poland" describes over 20 historic properties throughout Poland including the 13the Century Cistercian monastery at Podklasztorze. Other segments being developed include wine tourism in Slovakia (centred around Pizinok, Modra and Valtice) Hungary and Slovenia. Much of the tourism development is in the development of wine routes that are included in tourist maps and in specialist viticultural maps of the countries. For example in Hungary there is detailed information on the 22 wine producing regions (Hungary is the eleventh largest wine producer in the world), published by the Hungarian Agricultural Marketing Centre.

Due to the region's diverse religious background, there are numerous churches, monasteries, synagogues and shrines that lend themselves to religious tourism. Jewish heritage tourism, for example, has enabled clients to trace their family roots and visit museums, Jewish neighbourhoods and ghettos, and include visits to memorials of the holocaust and concentration camps in Poland and the Czech Republic.

Re-emphasis on spa and health tourism

Owing to the presence of mineralised water in many of the countries in Eastern Central Europe, there is a tradition of spa and medicinal tourism going back several centuries. Under the ancien régime, some of the resorts became fashionable through patronage from the aristocracy. Unfortunately, however, many of the establishments over time were managed along institutional lines for a largely domestic population, and so suffered from a lack of investment. The Danubius chain in Hungary has specialised in this niche, and are now also internationalising into neighbouring countries. Spa tourism is excellently placed both to tap into the senior or "grey market" that is increasingly health-conscious and to diversify into sports or activity tourism. In contrast to regular tourism in the region, spa tourism has longer stays (often 1-2 weeks) and can be high value-added.

EMERGING INTERNATIONAL HOTEL INDUSTRY STRUCTURE IN EASTERN CENTRAL EUROPE

Many of these factors relating to supply and demand in Eastern Central Europe have had a major impact upon the structure of its hotel industry. As mentioned in the supply of hotel accommodation before 1989 was met almost exclusively through national hotel chains, despite the fact that some international chains, such as Accor, Bass (Holiday Inn) and Hilton had been present since the 1970's and 1980's. The major national chains can be seen in Table 4

Table 4. Major national chains in Eastern Central Europe

Country of Origin	Company Name
Czech and Slovak republics	Tourinvest
	Interhotel Cedok
	Interhotel Bratislava
Hungary	Hungar Hotels
	Danubius Hotels
	Pannonia
	Eravis hotels
Poland	Ortbis hotels
	Polo hotels
Slovenia	Kompass hotels
	Hotels Bernadin
	HIT
	VAS hotels
	HTP

In terms of numbers of rooms, some of these chains (Orbis, Hungarhotels and Pannonia) were among the largest in the world in the early 1970's, and on that score were cited in 45th, 48th and 83rd positions among the 100 leading hotel companies.

Changes in capacity by country

While statistics available for the region can be misleading and are not always comparable, certain conclusions can nonetheless be drawn. There have clearly been major changes in the supply of hotel rooms since the fall of communism. Figure 5 shows the dynamics of hotel room supply.

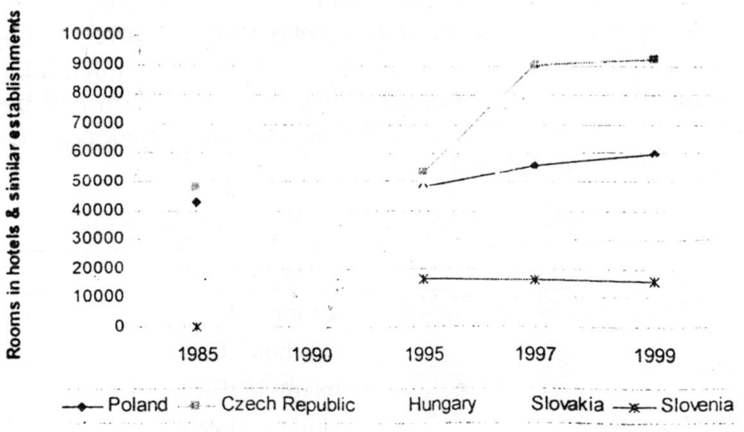

Figure 5. Room supply by country, 1985-1999.

As seen in figure 5, the most dramatic change has been in the Czech republic, especially from 1995-1997, when room supply almost doubled, although it has since stabilised. This may be due to the fact that tourism in the Czech Republic was heavily centred on Prague, and initially there was a chronic shortage of rooms in the capital. Growth, albeit at a reduced rate, is also apparent in Hungary and Poland. The two smaller hotel markets in the study, Slovakia and Slovenia, have experienced fluctuations in their hotel room supply over the period. This is likely to be the result of the closure of certain state hotels, as subsidies became harder to find.

Structure of hotel supply

After the fall of communism the lack of appropriate hotel accommodation was identified as a major problem in the region. The European Bank for Reconstruction and Development (EBRD) stated, "the lack of modern hotels and commercial facilities is constraining the development of the private sector".

Before this, tourism academics and hotel analysts had also been highlighting the need for mid-market and budget accommodation in the region. Figure 6 shows the distribution of room supply in the different market segments by country

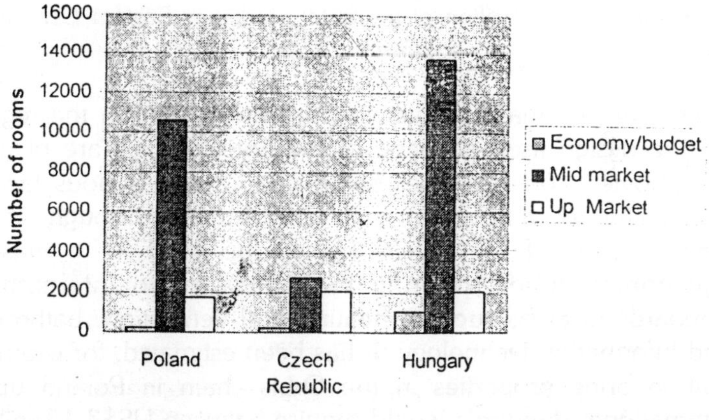

Figure 6. Room supply by sector and country, June 1999.

Figure 6 appears to belie the experts at first glance, as the vast majority of rooms are in the mid-market sector. The problem, however is not the supply, but the quality of the hotel stock: the head of development strategy for Kosice City Council (Slovakia), Mrs Rozila Mundra, was reported to say "our problem is not lack of capacity, but the quality of what we have,". Figure

7 gives more detail with the composition of the market in terms of hotel classification.

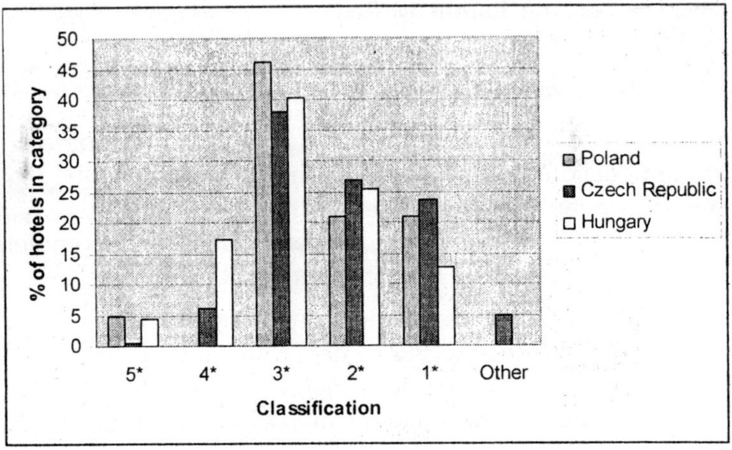

Figure 7 Composition of the hotel market in Eastern Central Europe, 1998

There are two main problems with hotel supply in the region: (1) the design itself of many of the hotels, which are of post-war, Soviet, concrete-block style; and (2) the serious lack of investment for renovation and refurbishment throughout the working lives of the hotels. Hence the need for a massive injection of funds to bring the hotels up to international standards in areas such as heating and ventilation, bathrooms and information technology. It has been estimated, for example, that to bring properties in the Orbis chain in Poland up to international standards would require between US$3-15 million per property.

Other important characteristics of the hotel market concern the market share of the major companies in the respective countries, and concentration in the industry.

Hotel industry concentration

As mentioned above, before 1989 hotels - as components of travel and tourism enterprises - were owned entirely by the

State. In contrast to the rest of the European hotel industry, which in this period displayed signs of classic service fragmentation and SME dominance, the hotel markets in Eastern Central Europe were heavily concentrated.

Different governments pursued varying methods of dealing with this concentration, either adopting "short sharp shock therapy" or adopting a more evolutionary approach. Some governments (e.g. in Hungary and Poland) wished to privatise the hotel stock by finding buyers who would purchase the chains' entire portfolio of hotels. Other governments (e.g. in the Czech republic and Slovakia) sold individual properties, so that by 1999 over 90% of the hotel stock in these two countries was privately owned and run. This had an obvious effect on concentration in the industry, as shown by table 5.

Table 5 Hotel operator concentration ratios, 1999 (market share % of turnover)

	Leading Company	Leading 2 Companies	Leading 3 Companies
Poland	37	65	90
Hungary	28.6	46.5	49.1
Czech Republic	3.2	6.2	8.2
Slovakia	4.6	8.1	9.4

There is a wide variation in levels of concentration, especially between Poland and the Czech Republic. The high level of concentration in the former is due mainly to the influence of the semi-privatised national company Orbis on the national market. In Hungary, the indigenous chain Danubius acquiring individual properties and a smaller chain, which largely determined the level of concentration in the national market. This came in parallel to the Accor joint venture with the other indigenous chain, Pannonia, which accounts for almost 18% of the market. The German-based hotel company Kempinski controls 2.6% of the value. The situation in the Czech and Slovak republics is therefore the reverse of that in Hungary and Poland, with no real leaders controlling the markets.

International hotel operators' locations and choice of entry mode

International hotel chains appear to be pursuing a classic "hub and spoke" development strategy, searching for gateway city locations and adopting a very cautious approach. Despite academic and industry experts stating for almost ten years that the need in the region is for mid-market and budget accommodation, the properties developed have almost exclusively (with the exception of Accor) been at the upper and luxury end of the market.

There are several chains with over half a dozen properties in the region (Marriott, InterContinental, Accor, and Vienna International). The latter is one of the large numbers of Austrian companies serving the business community in the region. Choice of location is again of note, with Holiday Inn and InterContinental having a spread of properties in four of the five countries, while Vienna International heavily focuses on the Czech (and principally Prague), market.

Accor has adopted the most ambitious strategy, with its joint venture with the Pannonia chain in Hungary: with its major presence, the company has begun begin the distribution of its main Ibis, Mercure and Novotel brands.

Holiday Inn has also been adventurous, signing a franchise agreement with Global Hotels Development Group (GHDG) to develop 20 hotels within Poland over 20 years. The agreement gives Holiday Inn approximately 4% of revenues in return for its expertise and brand name. Total investment is approximately US$116 million, with construction of four Crowne Plaza Hotels (five star), 4 Holiday Inns (mid range), and ten Holiday Inn Express (budget). GHDG also intends to modernise existing properties and include them in the chain.

Best Western has also developed its marketing consortium in the area, with independent hoteliers subscribing in Prague, Brno and Ljubljana

It is useful at this stage to have an overall view of hotel chain activity in the region, and per country. Table 6 gives an overview of the major hotel chains presence.

Table 6 Profile of hotel chain operations in Eastern Central Europe, September 2001

	Poland	Czech Republic	Hungary	Slovakia	Slovenia
Total rooms	59'704.00	92'138.00	57'674.00	27'983.00	15'753.00
Hotel group rooms	17'048. 00	8'543.00	17'548.00	346.00	306.00
No. Hotel operators	11.00	14.00	16.00	1.00	1.00
No. Hotel brands	15.00	18.00	23.00	2.00	2.00
No Hotels operated by publicly quoted operators	75.00	14.00	64.00	2.00	2.00
No. Hotels operated by domestic groups.	79.00	24.00	100.00	n.k	0.00

As may be seen in table 6, the Czech and, in particular, Hungarian hotel markets have the highest chain penetration. At first glance the Polish and Hungarian markets appear to be very similar. The major difference, however, is in potential, for Poland has 15-20 secondary cities which would support mid-market and budget hotels; Hungary, less than a third of the size of Poland in population and area, is much more limited.

Previously, there were two major brakes on tourism development - a lack of capital and no domestic demand. There are now signs, however, that local and regional entrepreneurs are appearing who have the capital and the inclination to invest in hospitality enterprises. In Poland, for instance, Electrum SA, a holding of several Polish companies, has created Elector, with the intention of developing a chain of approximately 100 hotels across the country. The company are seeking to franchise the Elektor brand name, with partners taking a 49% share in individual properties.

An additional issue considered crucial for development by international hotel operators is that of potential sales in the region. Table 7 provides data on projected sales by country.

Table 7 Hotel sales by country, 1999-2004

	1999 US$ MN	% Growth 1995-1999	2004 US$ MN	% Growth 1999-2004
Czech Republic	1585	101.3	1637	3.2
Hungary	264	63.8	387	46.5
Poland	2379	88.1	2172	-8.7
Slovakia	79	71.5	93	17.7

As this shows, the growth in hotel sales after 1999 has been extremely varied, with reduced but substantial growth still continuing in the Hungarian, and to a lesser degree the Slovak, markets. Growth in the Czech market is much reduced, however, and in the Polish is in decline. This figure should be treated with caution, however, based as it is on the assumption that domestic tourism will decline. International tourists are forecast to increase slightly in this period, however, and while it is evident that tourism infrastructure will have to be improved considerably, an actual decline, seems unlikely, rather than a very modest growth. Clearly, however, there is an urgent need for improvements in Poland's tourism infrastructure, which is currently acting as a major barrier to development.

4

Better Motivation to Customers

A comfortable room, good food, and a helpful staff can make being away from home an enjoyable experience for both vacationing families and business travelers. While most lodging managers work in traditional hotels and motels, some work in other lodging establishments, such as camps, inns, boardinghouses, dude ranches, and recreational resorts. In full-service hotels, lodging managers help their guests have a pleasant stay by providing many of the comforts of home, including cable television, fitness equipment, and voice mail, as well as specialized services such as health spas.

For business travelers, lodging managers often schedule available meeting rooms and electronic equipment, including slide projectors and fax machines. Lodging managers are responsible for keeping their establishments efficient and profitable. In a small establishment with a limited staff, the manager may oversee all aspects of operations. However, large hotels may employ hundreds of workers, and the general manager usually is aided by a number of assistant managers assigned to the various departments of the operation. In hotels of every size, managerial duties vary significantly by job title.

General managers, for example, have overall responsibility for the operation of the hotel. Within guidelines established by the owners of the hotel or executives of the hotel chain, the general manager sets room rates, allocates funds to departments, approves expenditures, and establishes expected standards for guest service, decor, housekeeping, food quality, and banquet operations. Managers who work for chains also may organize and staff a newly built hotel, refurbish an older hotel, or reorganize a hotel or motel that is not operating successfully. In order to fill entry-level service and clerical jobs in hotels, some managers attend career fairs.

Resident managers live in hotels and are on call 24 hours a day to resolve problems or emergencies. In general, though, they typically work an 8- to 10 hour day and oversee the day-to-day operations of the hotel. In many hotels, the general manager also is the resident manager. Executive housekeepers ensure that guest rooms, meeting and banquet rooms, and public areas are clean, orderly, and well maintained. They also train, schedule, and supervise the work of house-keepers, inspect rooms, and order cleaning supplies.

Front office managers coordinate reservations and room assignments, as well as train and direct the hotel's front desk staff. They ensure that guests are treated courteously, complaints and problems are resolved, and requests for special services are carried out. Front office managers may adjust charges posted on a customer's bill. Convention services managers coordinate the activities of various departments in larger hotels to accommodate meetings, conventions, and special events. They meet with representatives of groups or organizations to plan the number of rooms to reserve, the desired configuration of the meeting space, and the banquet services. During the meeting or event, they resolve unexpected problems and monitor activities to ensure that hotel operations conform to the expectations of the group.

Assistant managers help run the day-to-day operations of the hotel. In large hotels, they may be responsible for activities such as personnel, accounting, office administration, marketing and sales, purchasing, security, maintenance, and pool, spa, or recreational facilities. In smaller hotels, these duties may be combined into one position. Assistant managers may adjust charges on a hotel guest's bill when a manager is unavailable.

Computers are used extensively by lodging managers and their assistants to keep track of guests' bills, reservations, room assignments, meetings, and special events. In addition, computers are used to order food, beverages, and supplies, as well as to prepare reports for hotel owners and top-level managers. Managers work with computer specialists to ensure that the hotel's computer system functions properly. Should the hotel's computer system fail, managers must continue to meet the needs of hotel guests and staff.

Working Conditions

Because hotels are open around the clock, night and weekend work is common. Many lodging managers work more than 40 hours per week. Managers who live in the hotel usually have regular work schedules, but they may be called to work at any time. Some employees of resort hotels are managers during the busy season and have other duties during the rest of the year. Lodging managers sometimes experience the pressures of coordinating a wide range of functions. Conventions and large groups of tourists may present unusual problems. Moreover, dealing with irate guests can be stressful. The job can be particularly hectic for front office managers during check-in and check-out time. Computer failures can further complicate an already busy time.

Employment

Lodging managers held about 69,000 jobs in 2002. Self-employed managers-primarily owners of small hotels and motels-held about 50 percent of these jobs. Companies that manage hotels and motels under contract employed some managers.

Training, Other Qualifications, and Advancement

Hotels increasingly emphasize specialized training. Postsecondary training in hotel or restaurant management is preferred for most hotel management positions, although a college liberal arts degree may be sufficient when coupled with related hotel experience. Internships or part-time or summer work are an asset to students seeking a career in hotel management. The experience gained and the contacts made with employers can greatly benefit students after graduation. Most bachelor's degree programs include work-study opportunities.

Community colleges, junior colleges, and some universities offer associate's, bachelor's, and graduate degree programs in hotel or restaurant management. Combined with technical institutes, vocational and trade schools, and other academic institutions, over 800 educational facilities have programs leading to formal recognition in hotel or restaurant management. Hotel management programs include instruction in hotel administration, accounting, economics, marketing, housekeeping, food service management and catering, and hotel maintenance engineering.

Computer training also is an integral part of hotel management training, due to the widespread use of computers in reservations, billing, and housekeeping management. Additionally, over 450 high schools in 45 States offer the Lodging Management Program created by the Educational Institute of the American Hotel and Lodging Association. This is a two-year program offered to high school juniors and seniors, which teaches management principles and leads to a professional certification called the "Certified Rooms Division Specialist". Many colleges and universities grant participants credit towards a post-secondary degree in hotel management.

Lodging managers must be able to get along with many different people, even in stressful situations. They must be able to solve problems and concentrate on details. Initiative, selfdiscipline, effective communication skills, and the ability to organize and direct the work of others also are essential for managers at all levels. In the past, many managers were promoted from the ranks of front desk clerks, housekeepers, waiters, chefs, and hotel sales workers.

Although some employees still advance to hotel management positions without education beyond high school, postsecondary education is preferred. Restaurant management training or experience also is a good background for entering hotel management, because the success of a hotel's food service and beverage operations often is important to the profitability of the entire establishment. Graduates of hotel or restaurant management programs usually start as trainee assistant managers.

Some large hotels sponsor specialized on-the-job management training programs that allow trainees to rotate among various departments and gain a thorough knowledge of the hotel's operation. Other hotels may help finance formal training in hotel management for outstanding employees. Newly built hotels, particularly those without established on-the-job training programs, often prefer to hire applicants who have hotel management experience.

Large hotel and motel chains may offer better opportunities for advancement than small, independently owned establishments, but relocation every several years often is necessary for advancement. The large chains have more extensive career ladder programs and offer managers the opportunity to transfer to another hotel or motel in the chain or to the central office. Career advancement can be accelerated by the completion of certification programs offered by various associations. These programs usually require a combination of course work, examinations, and experience. For example, outstanding lodging managers may advance to higher level manager positions.

Employment of lodging managers is expected to grow more slowly than the average for all occupations through 2012. Additional job openings are expected to occur as experienced managers transfer to other occupations or leave the labor force, in part because of the long hours and stressful working conditions. Job opportunities are expected to be best for persons with college degrees in hotel or restaurant management.

Increasing business travel and domestic and foreign tourism will drive employment growth of lodging managers. Managerial jobs are not expected to grow as rapidly as the hotel industry overall, however. As the industry consolidates, many chains and franchises will acquire independently owned establishments and increase the numbers of economy-class rooms to accommodate bargain-con-scious guests. Economy hotels offer clean, comfortable rooms and front desk services without costly extras such as restaurants and room service. Because there are not as many departments in these hotels, fewer managers will be needed.

Similarly, the increasing number of extended-stay hotels will temper demand for managers because, in these establishments, management is not required to be available 24 hours a day. In addition, front desk clerks increasingly are assuming some responsibilities previously reserved for managers, further limiting the employment growth of managers and their assistants.

Additional demand for managers is expected in suite hotels, because some guests-especially business customers-are willing to pay higher prices for rooms with kitchens and suites that provide the space needed to conduct meetings. In addition, large full-service hotels-offering restaurants, fitness centers, large meeting rooms, and play areas for children, among other amenities-will continue to provide many trainee and managerial opportunities.

Earnings

Median annual earnings of lodging managers were $33,970 in 2002. The middle 50 percent earned between $26,110 and $44,670. The lowest 10 percent earned less than $20,400, while the highest 10 percent earned more than $59,420. Salaries of lodging managers vary greatly according to their responsibilities and the segment of the hotel industry in which they are employed, as well as the location and region where the hotel is located. Managers may earn bonuses of up to 25 percent of their basic salary in some hotels and also may be furnished with lodging, meals, parking, laundry, and other services. In addition to providing typical benefits, some hotels offer profit-sharing plans and educational assistance to their employees.

CREATING COMFORTABLE GUEST ROOMS

Majestic Canopy

Give a plain twin bed majesty and drama by topping it with this simple sheer canopy. To fashion the canopy, you'll need approximately 7 yards of fabric. (For a different size bed, estimate the yardage needed by measuring the width of the bed and tripling the measurement. The fabric should be long enough to gracefully drape across the bed and to the floor on either side.) Hem the raw edges with a needle and thread, or use fabric tape or glue for a no-sew option. Attach two 2-foot-long wood dowels to the wall with L-brackets. Then hide the brackets with large tassels slung over the dowels. Drape the fabric over the dowels, letting it fall in front of the dowel ends to hide them. Or, finish off the dowels with round wood finials screwed into the ends.

Details Say Welcome

There are many things you can do to make guests feel welcome in their sleeping quarters, even if you have just a sliver of space to offer. Appoint a guest room as you would your own room, with attention to design and detail. And think of what needs they may have. You want to avoid a guest having to ask you for something.

— Think about who is most likely to use the room and determine the beds you'll need. A queen is good for couples, but if you don't have the room, consider twins, a daybed, or a trundle bed.

— Supply proper bedding for the season: lightweight blankets and sheets in the summer, and jersey or flannel sheets in the winter, plus extra blankets and a throw.

— Stock the closet with a variety of bed pillows—soft, hard, flat, fluffy, down, synthetic—so guests can choose the one that's most comfortable for them.

— Top the bed with an array of throw pillows for a comfortable, luxurious resting spot.

— Treat a guest room as you would your own bedroom. Incorporate color, pretty fabrics, and accessories to give it a finished look.

— Always include an alarm clock and reading lamp, and make room for a bedside table or nightstand to rest them on.

— Make sure guests have place to store clothes and empty luggage.

— In warm months, add a tabletop fan to the room.

— Pay attention to window treatments and how light enters the room at different times of the day. If light is a problem, adjust the shades or curtains accordingly.

Versatile Guest Rooms Content

Hosting overnight guests, and making them feel welcome, can be simple when you have a well-appointed guest room. It's often difficult to dedicate an entire room for guests when it might be used sporadically. To maximize the day-to-day function of your home, create a combination guest room and home office suite. And, if you have an empty corner, tuck in your favorite piece of exercise equipment. That way you'll use the room every day, year-round. Here are some keys to a good guest room:

— *Include a good bed*: A pullout sleeper sofa or a futon can't compete with a full-size mattress. Whatever type of bed you choose, make sure the mattress is firm and that it's comfortable—sleep on it yourself for a night or two.

— *Allow space for unpacking*: Some guests prefer to live out of a suitcase. Some like to unpack. Prepare for both with an empty chest of drawers and a luggage rack. Leave enough room on bedside tables for personal items such as jewelry or books.

— *Consider small appliances*: An alarm clock for the nightstand prevents guests from having to rely on the host. It's also nice to include a portable fan, telephone, and TV, if you have extras.

— *Stock up on samples*: Think like an innkeeper and purchase inexpensive travel size toiletries such as shampoo, conditioner, hand lotion, disposable razor, and hair spray. Tuck them in a basket by the sink.

— *Give them privacy*: A common mistake for many hosts is to think you need to spend every moment of the visit with your guest. Be the first to suggest some private time by saying you're going to take a nap or read for a bit; then arrange a time to meet.

Remodel with Guests in Mind

Accommodating extended-stay guests, such as parents visiting for the summer (or winter) or a young relative "crashing" between semesters, requires thoughtful planning to make the visit a success. Part of the plan is to allow your guest some privacy. If you're building or remodeling, you have an excellent opportunity to create a separate, welcoming space. Here are some suggestions:

— Close some doors. Strategically placed doors can help create temporary private space for guests. A main-level bathroom might have one door connecting to a guest bedroom, for example, and another to a hallway. When visitors arrive, the hallway door can be locked.

— Show guests where to park. A separate driveway can prevent confusion about where guests should park. And a private entrance can keep you from being disturbed by comings and goings.

— Clone your master suite. Duplicate your upper-level master suite on the ground level, and your guests will enjoy the same luxury and privacy you do. Also, later in life, you can switch the spaces if illness or injury prevents you from climbing the stairs.

— Give visitors their own kitchen. A small kitchenette with coffeemaker, refrigerator, and other items prevents guests from feeling uneasy about asking for a drink or sandwich. Don't forget staples such as paper plates, paper napkins, cups, silverware, and condiments. If your guest space has room for a dishwasher, add one.

— Install a small laundry. Laundry facilities are a nice addition for guests. If your space is tight, consider a stacking unit. Then tuck a hamper, laundry soap, and dryer sheets nearby.

Desigining the Guest Room

Welcome guests with a room that's just as cozy as it is good looking. For many of people, the guestroom is merely a collecting place for mismatched furniture and extraneous linens. Rather than shortchanging your visitors, take a cue from these homeowners, who took a patchwork spare room and transformed it into a functional and inviting place. Lowe's is happy to provide this information as a service to you.

Flooring

Wool carpet (US Floors, London Collection, Mayfair Design, Cream, Model 300121, special order)

Paint

— Wall paint (American Tradition, Aged Blue #94-23A, satin)

— Trim paint (American Tradition, Chalk #91-42B, semigloss)

— Headboard and nightstand paint (American Tradition Signature Colors, Laura Ashley, Stone 2 #608, semigloss)

Lighting

— 2 swing-arm lamps (Design Trends, Classic Bronze)
— 2 lampshades (14" pleated, Design Trends, Silver)
— Night-light with rotating shade (American Tack & Hardware Nite Lite)

Miscellaneous

— 2 (3-drawer) nightstands
— 6 cabinet knobs (1 1/4", Belwith, Traditional Oil-Rubbed Bronze)
— Oval mirror (28 1/2" x 34", Gardner, Wrought Iron)
— Compact refrigerator (1.6-cubic-foot, Whirlpool)
— Over-the-door hook (Classico by Interdesign, Chrome)
— Mesh wastebasket
— Skill level: Beginner
— Rough cost estimate: $2,000
— Rough time estimate: 4 days
— Lowe's Installation Available

Flooring can be professionally installed by Lowe's. Carpet is a key decorating element that you can incorporate in every room. It absorbs noise, insulates and reduces heating costs, and provides a cushion for comfort. Even better, it's easy to maintain. In this space, a 100% wool carpet with a textured loop pattern replaced the existing carpet. The classic style and neutral color will last for years to come with proper care.

Carpet is certainly a vital style decision, but how it fits your room's purpose is paramount in making the right choice. In this guest bedroom, the soft, yet short-napped wool Berber holds up to traffic and is also a safe choice for most anyone who will be a guest in the room, whether their steps are steady or they require assistance. Think about who might set foot on the carpet before you make your final purchase. And consider the following general information as you narrow down your search. Several factors determine a carpet's quality: how it is constructed, the pile, and the material from which it is made.

Carpet Types

Woven carpets tend to be more costly because of their weave, while tufted and bonded varieties are the least expensive. Most household carpet is the tufted kind, which means that the yarn is stitched on a pre-woven backing.

The pile of the four main types of tufted carpets—twist pile, shag pile, loop pile, and velvet pile—is cut to different heights and forms unique designs.

Carpet Grades

Carpet is graded according to durability. Some types are intended for high-traffic areas, and others are suited for light wear. Quality carpet typically has a jute backing and requires a separate underlay. It should be professionally installed, which, as a service to you, Lowe's can do. Less expensive carpets have a foam backing and don't require an underlay.

An over-the-door rack helps guests keep their belongings organized and close at hand. A fresh coat of paint on the walls and trim gives this tired room a much-needed face-lift. A soothing blue color was selected for the walls, and a neutral was used on the trim. Build a headboard that suits your décor and won't break the bank. Here, square dowels and moulding corners from the millworks department were painted a complementary hue and attached to the wall.

Start with the bed. Ideally, you should provide your guests with a full- or queen-size bed to ensure maximum comfort. But whatever its size, dress the bed with luxurious linens that boast a high thread count. A collection of comfy pillows and extra blankets adds a homey touch.

In addition to storage, this chest provides a convenient surface on which to place personal items.

Light up the room

A nightstand and ample reading light are must-haves in a guestroom. In this room, unfinished three-drawer nightstands were painted and placed on both sides of the bed. Oil-rubbed bronze knobs were added to complement the classic bronze swing-arm lamps. Guests now have plenty of light for reading, and a spot to place personal belongings, such as eyeglasses, a box of tissues, or a stack of magazines, is within arm's reach. Items such as mirrors and bedside lighting can make guests feel more at home.

Add extra touches

Equip your guests with everything they need, so that they don't feel as if they have to impose on you for every need.

1. Add an alarm clock. Visitors who prefer to rise at a specific time may hesitate to bother you if they need an early wake-up call.
2. A wastebasket is a necessity.
3. For anyone not accustomed to the layout of your house, a night-light is essential.
4. A mirror in the bedroom will allow guests to prepare for the day in the privacy of their room.
5. Offer an over-the-door rack, as well as space in the guestroom closet for hanging clothes.
6. A compact refrigerator is a perfect addition to the guestroom. Stock it with bottled water, juices, and an assortment of snacks.

CHANGING LODGING SECURITY

The lodging security is changing daily. A hotel's reputation is, without doubt, its single most important asset. No matter how professional the hotel's services may be or how good a value may be offered, no one respectable will stay at a hotel if a bad type of activity is allowed to take place openly. It is probably safe to say that prostitution has been around as long as the concept of inns for travellers. Some of the comments frequently heard about prostitution is that it is a victimless crime and that society should not care what consenting adults do in privacy. However, prostitution is a problem that, if not controlled, can ruin a hotel's reputation. The word controlled was used intentionally, for prostitution cannot and will not ever be eliminated.

The security objective should be to reduce such activity to an absolute minimum. There are a number of simple control methods a hotel can employ. First, guest registration procedures must be established and followed closely. All guests must be required to show valid photo identification such as a driver's licence and preferably a credit card when checking in, even if they are paying cash in advance for their stay. The reason for the tight registration process is that most streetwalkers will not carry identification.

The more sophisticated "call girl" or "escort" type of prostitute will have identification, but she or he also represents less of a threat to the innkeeper. The second method of control can be utilised in properties that have computerised front desk procedures and can print out a complete list of all guests by room as well as list the number of occupants registered in that particular room. Once given that list, particularly at night when guests are returning to their rooms with visitors they may have just met in the local bar, the security officer can screen all incoming guests at the front door. This method has two benefits. First, the innkeeper is entitled as a matter of law to additional revenue if a second person is staying in the room. Second, if in fact the "visitor" is a streetwalker, not only will he or she not have identification as noted above, but the guest may not want to risk having a second person listed on the registration folio. The final two methods of prevention include employee cooperation.

The housekeeping department will know if a certain guest-room has heavy traffic going to and from it and can alert security. Secondly, hotel managers must maintain a no-tolerance attitude toward prostitution while supporting security in its efforts to deal with the problem. Common meeting places for prostitutes are lobby pay telephones, bars, and easily recognised hotel fixtures such as chairs, plants, and the like. There are two general types of problems associated with bars, restaurants, stores, and the front desk in a hotel. They are check and credit card fraud, and theft of merchandise including food and beverage items. Incidents involving "walk-outs" are common when non-paying customers enjoy a meal and/or drinks in a hotel and then proceed to leave without offering to pay for the items consumed.

Unfortunately, this type of crime is only a misdemeanour in most states and innkeepers are very limited in what they can do after the event. Frequently, if the patron is caught leaving, they can be confronted and—if they refuse to pay—be held long enough for security or the public police to arrive. The thief then can be identified for future reference or prosecution. The amount of the loss usually is not worth the time required to prosecute, so it is recommended that the name and description of the individual be recorded and distributed to all outlets in the hotel. Credit cards very often are used as a means of payment by patrons because of their convenience and the generation of tax records for business purposes. This convenience, however, has caused some problems for the hotel operator, particularly in food and beverage outlets and stores.

The security department must face problems ranging from guests using stolen cards and cards over their allowable limit to dishonest employees inflating gratuities or even writing in gratuities. The best means of avoiding these and other scams is to develop detailed policies and procedures for authorisation of use, and to train employees to follow the procedures. Charging store merchandise to a guest-room, for example, must somehow be verified first.

Management must then follow up to ensure compliance with the rules, and violators should be dealt with appropriately. If security is called to investigate alleged wrongdoing by employees and the allegations are proven, swift and severe disciplinary action should be taken after all levels of disciplinary action are considered. Disciplinary action can range from counselling to termination. The sale and use of illegal drugs are major issues in any industry, but appear more complicated in the lodging industry. The innkeeper must be concerned not only with employees, but also with guests and patrons who become involved with using and selling drugs.

The use of drugs by employees on or off the job presents some serious consequences for both performance and safety. With the cost of workers' compensation insurance rising so high and representing one of the largest line expenses for liability, employers must address the increased use of drugs by employees. Only recently have employers begun to consider the possibility that some employee accidents are directly related to drug use on or off the job. Morale problems are likely to arise among employees who want to do their job well, but see others not performing because of drug use.

Furthermore, a work environment that allows employees to sell drugs to co-workers will create the impression that management does not care or is incompetent. Although still controversial at this stage, employers may wish to consider the possibility of drug testing on employees who either have declining performance levels or who have exhibited unusual behaviour or evidence of drug use. A number of legislative reforms on intoxication on the job have been enacted recently, including denying benefits in cases in which accidents are alcohol- or drug-related. Talk to legal counsel about your state's legislation.

Effective ways to deal with substance abuse problems are complicated. The long-term solution is education and awareness, not policing employees. The hotel should have an Employee Assistance Programme (EAP), which may reduce the incidents and cost of alcoholism and other abuse at work. Yet we must be realistic and acknowledge that both alcoholism and drugs do exist in the lodging industry. Most hoteliers wait until drug dealing is rampant before they act on tips about drug usage. This does more harm than rapid action because, by the time management reacts to the problem, more employees are involved and affected, which may result in having to remove more staff from the hotel.

Security managers also can consider using undercover investigators posing as employees to determine who the dealer and buyers are, as evidence for termination. Drug use or sale by guests is not an unusual problem, but is one that hotel operators should be prepared to resolve. It is very unlikely that a hotel manager will be able to prevent a guest from using drugs in the privacy of his or her room. If however, the manager becomes aware of such use, action should be taken. Limited use (e.g., smoking a marijuana cigarette) may best be handled by warning the guest that repeated activity will result in removal from the hotel. However, evidence of more serious use (such as large parties with cocaine left out in the open) may require assistance from the local police. It is common for drug dealers to use large urban hotels to conduct their drug deals, for the size of the hotel usually will ensure their anonymity. Certainly, no hotel operator wants to see her or his hotel aired on the evening news as a result of a major drug bust. Liaison with local, state, and federal law enforcement agencies is vitally important.

Most law enforcement arrests involving drugs occur off property; however, the legal case may be developed around the actual activity that took place while on hotel property. Training all hotel staff about drug activity awareness will assist security in preventing illegal sales, manufacture, or use of drugs on hotel premises. Depending on the size and location of a hotel, certain types of public figures are likely to stay as guests on occasion. In larger, convention-class hotels, political figures are often in attendance for social events. Public figures, whether they are politicians or people such as rock stars or sports teams, often will draw crowds. These crowds may be admirers, or they may be demonstrators protesting the appearance of the individual.

In either instance, security is faced with the difficult task of controlling the crowd while protecting the public figure. One should not assume that the local police will always take care of or even be aware of these problems. Instead, the security manager should be prepared to work with the authorities in planning for the person's arrival, stay, and departure. Occasionally, hotel security will not receive any advance notice of the person's arrival. However, if your hotel security procedures include how to handle this type of scenario, coordinating this process should not take very long. Generally, though, there will be varying amounts of lead time available before the event. If this time is adequate, detailed planning will avert risk with minimal difficulty.

The hotel may make reasonable regulations governing the conduct of its guests; provided such regulations are applied to all persons, without discrimination. These regulations can be designed to prevent immorality, drunkenness, or any form of wilful misconduct, e.g., loud obnoxious behaviour, drug activity, etc., that may offend other guests, may bring the hotel into disrepute, or may be inconsistent with the generally recognised properties of life.

The hotel has the right to evict any guest who wilfully violates these rules. Obviously, the eviction must be done in a reasonable manner. If guests refuse to leave the hotel after their attention has been called to the violation and they have been requested to leave and given a reasonable opportunity to do so, the hotel may forcibly evict them. The hotel may use only such force as is reasonably necessary to accomplish this goal. Management personnel and security officers should be carefully instructed on this point and the hotel should obtain the assistance of the local police.

When a hotel guest becomes ill with a contagious disease, the hotel management, after notifying the guest that she or he must leave, has the right to remove the guest in a careful manner and at an appropriate time to a hospital or other place of safety, provided this does not imperil the guest's life. As a practical matter, however, it is preferable to consult with an attorney and report these matters to the proper local authorities. Usually the local authorities will take charge and remove the sick guest. The illness of an indigent guest should be reported to the local department of welfare, communicable diseases should be reported to the local health authorities, and psychiatric cases should be reported to the police.

Security managers must ensure that they are knowledgeable about many types of crime, with special attention to those that may occur at a hotel—even if one would normally think they are unlikely to occur. For example, a hotel shuttle bus left a hotel an route to the airport with a group of tourists and was hijacked. The hijackers, posing as guests, had boarded the bus and waited. As it pulled out of the airport, one of the men pulled a gun and ordered the driver to head in another direction while his accomplice robbed the tourists of jewellery and money at gunpoint.

Floods, fires, hurricanes, blizzards, tornadoes, hazardous chemical spills, and power outages are some of the disasters that pose a threat to hotels. However, because it is nearly impossible to know for certain when these disasters will strike, hotels must have an emergency plan to protect themselves from these devastating events. Needless to say, this requires advance planning, and it can be challenging to imagine most risks. Once the risk analysis is completed, however, the security manager must determine priorities. Putting the risks in order of priority will also assist in creating a successful emergency plan. Within this plan, three separate groups of people need to be established.

Operations is made up of managerial representatives who oversee administrative issues and ensure that the emergency is being handled according to the plan. The emergency response team (ERT)—sometimes called the HEAT, "Hotel Emergency Action Team"—actually seeks out the root cause of the emergency (i.e., fire, bomb, etc.). The logistics group supports the rest of the hotel such as banquets personnel who assist function people in evacuating ballrooms, engineers who keep generators and other equipment operating, and others who do important parts in an emergency yet go unrecognised during the event. It is very important that the emergency plan identify and explain the duties of each position by department for each type of emergency. The plan also should include notification sheets to make personnel aware of situations. Another vital section of the plan should be how to deal with the post-emergency situation: getting affected areas cleaned up, reinstating guests into the hotel comfortably, and getting employees back to work.

The security manager should try to coordinate efforts from the "command centre" to cordon off and preserve damaged areas. The task of photographing, inspecting architectural designs for defects, and adding up actual damaged property claims and estimates needs to be accomplished as quickly as possible. Only after everything has been photographed and documented should the clean-up phase begin. Once a plan has been developed, it should be reviewed and critiqued by other management staff for accuracy. In addition, the plan should be tested at least annually.

Finally, all emergency situations should be followed up with an after-action analysis describing in a positive manner the procedures followed and those done incorrectly. This analysis is a learning tool for the staff that should be used with constructive criticism. The Hotel and Motel Fire Safety Act is designed to produce the safest lodging properties in the world. Most hotels have emergency plans and fire prevention equipment in place. However, more often than not, human error or failure is the root cause of life and property tragedies: Someone fails to report a hazard, or an employee disregards an emergency procedure even after he or she was trained properly. It should be noted here that any defence against fire must be viewed in two parts, fire prevention and fire protection.

Fire prevention, which usually is the hotel's major preoccupation, entails the control of heat sources and the elimination or isolation of the more obviously dangerous fuels. This commendable effort to prevent fire must not however, be undertaken at the expense of an equal effort for fire protection. Fire protection includes not only the equipment to control or extinguish fire, but also devices to protect the building, its contents, and particularly its occupants, in the event of fire. Fire doors, fire walls, smokeproof towers, fire safes, nonflammable rugs and furnishings, fire detector systems—all these are fire protection matters, and are essential to any fire safety programme.

A hotel should also have an outline within the procedures about how to handle the media. The community and others will want to know what exactly is going on. Designated media locations are important so that interference by the press is totally eliminated. Ad hoc interviewing of employees and victims of the crisis should be prevented. The media must not be allowed to manipulate a crisis scene into a three-ring circus. In most states, hotels are not required to provide medical services for their guests. In busy hotels, however, a large percentage of the calls for security services will be medically related. These calls will range from simple abrasions and burns to serious trauma.

Even if your hotel is in the middle of a large city with several hospitals and ambulance services, significant delays can be expected before expert assistance will arrive. Yet although many of the calls security receives in a given day will require some medical assistance, it generally will not be enough to justify the cost of a full-time physician who would need to be available twenty-four hours a day, seven days a week. Security personnel, or any hotel employee who is likely to respond to calls for such services, must be properly trained.

The key is to train for the level of services you are prepared to provide, and no more. Once medical assistance has commenced, you are expected to carry it out properly. The legal liabilities that arise against persons in such situations generally relate to how they performed the aid for which they were duly qualified. A security officer must not attempt to perform CPR on a victim if the officer has not been certified to perform CPR. The level of training recommended for most hotels is basic first aid and CPR, both of which generally are available through the local chapter of the American Red Cross and are of nominal expense.

In a very large property, some security employees can be trained as Emergency Medical Technicians (EMTs). The risk of such advanced training is that guests may come to expect it all the time, yet manpower or budget constraints may prohibit having an EMT on each shift 24 hours a day. Most hotels will have some level of emergency evacuation plans on hand. Whether the plans are simple or sophisticated depends on the security manager's exposure to disasters and knowledge of the subject. The risk analysis that the security manager conducts also will include evacuation vulnerabilities. Ensuring that a hotel can handle certain crowds is easy enough; however, ensuring that you can get the crowd out safely in the event of an emergency can be challenging. Evacuation from high-rise buildings is even more of a challenge. Usually there are only two avenues of travel up and down for high-rise buildings—elevators and stairs.

The security manager must be aware that, in order to exit when an emergency occurs, human beings will naturally go toward the door through which they entered the hotel or function room. Therefore, if a hotel uses ballroom exits only in case of emergency situations, someone has to be designated to inform the patrons and guests which way to exit. These guests and patrons also do not check for a hotel's fire exits when attending events such as weddings or dances. Another contributing factor to confusion in an emergency situation is when the room or corridor the crowd is in does not have windows, as this leads to a psychological effect which disorients people as to where they are and how to exit the hotel.

Hotel security departments must learn to overcome these types of problems until the time comes when elevators are made safe to use in case of an emergency. Evacuation plans for employees need to be established and detailed information must be provided so that step-by-step plans can be offered. New employees should get a basic overview of evacuation plans during their orientation programme within the first few days of employment. Additional training should be given once in a work environment or department. It is important for employees to be very comfortable within their environment, knowing the nearest exits and stairwells.

Casinos are being developed in historic or refurbished structures, and river boats are being used to operate as floating casinos or moored casinos. There are also casinos in purpose-built facilities, which may have limited non-gaming amenities. With gambling, there has been a trend toward allowing people to have greater control over their choice of activities and to be more responsible for the consequences of their own actions. But this principle has not been applied uniformly over the so-called "vices" such as alcohol, tobacco, illicit drug use, prostitution, and pornography. These vices have economic and social impacts on the hotel and/or casino similar to the impacts of gambling. The likelihood of these vices being introduced into the casino is very high.

Security managers should study their local gambling and lottery ordinances to find out what is and is not allowed. In addition, they should check with their local public prosecutor to find out what cases he or she is willing to act on and how the courts interpret gambling statutes. It is a known fact that the gamblers as well as persons who attempt to conduct scams are all well-versed in gambling laws. Don't be surprised to find people who attempt to challenge casino games, testing the parameters in order to commit acts which may be on the legal borderline. Likewise, don't be afraid to ask for help from a gaming investigator in identifying marginal cases. Emerging casino security practices, using CCTV equipment, call for gaming machines and tables to be individually identified with a location mark and casino logo.

The identification, coupled with video recordings, allows taped incidents to be admitted as evidence in gaming commission hearings as well as in court. The casino security strategy is people-watching, which is nothing new. Employee theft is not new, either, especially when millions of dollars pass through the hands of employees each day. As visitors and employees come up with new ways to cheat, many eyes should be watching. The most effective deterrent is people watching people, with most watchers out of sight. Hundreds of cameras can be hidden inside domes or behind ceiling panels. Pan/tilt capabilities, colour monitors, and strategic placement all contribute to cover every square foot of a casino floor. It is important for security staff to study what they see on those cameras to determine if angles should be changed, people should be followed, or if a zoom shot should be taken of a pile of chips.

Most states allow tapes from casino crimes to be admissible as court evidence. Crowding is a problem, due to the fact that river boat designers cram as many gaming positions onto each boat as possible, to take advantage of the enormous revenues generated from each position. One advantage to river boat owners is the fact that the boat is cruising—therefore, passengers do not have the option of leaving and frequently gamble more than they normally would. To alleviate the risks associated with congested spaces, security needs to be involved in the floor planning stage of construction to ensure that foot traffic patterns and passenger movement have been considered. Another concern is that air circulation is poor in crowded spaces, and smoke-filled air can become an irritant, leading to a less-than-optimal gaming experience for many guests.

Surveillance is very important in casino security environments, where criminals range from casino dealers and employees to "railbirds" who steal chips from the sides of tables while patrons are not paying attention. Surveillance specialists look for targets of theft where the stakes are high. Crimes take place in areas of intense action, where more chips are being played or the value of the game is high. Surveillance specialists also look out for known troublemakers and have a central supervisor or pit boss for every ten tables. Usually, the staff working in surveillance security have worked in hotel security and are knowledgeable enough about guests' traits and mannerisms to assist them in identifying problem people.

Another issue for casino security is that the budget needs are far greater than most security departments' needs, due to the vast amount of technology necessary to conduct professional surveillance operations. Storage of video equipment, for example, is an important factor because tapes must be retained in case they are needed for prosecution of criminals or other legal matters. Most surveillance specialists are concerned about having updated and timely identification of known criminals, along with their method of operation. Knowing about these techniques is crucial to casino security professionals and will keep them keen on typical tricks of the trade. One way in which the surveillance specialist can be made aware of these criminals and their methods is through networking systems set up in cities with casinos to share information about incidents that occur at various sites.

This networking system can communicate by fax, telephone, or other methods. The relationship and coordination between the specialist operating the surveillance equipment and the security officer on the casino floor is also crucial. Casino security and hotel security, as professions, need to be recognised as excellent career paths that offer upward movement. These positions develop special talents that should be rewarded accordingly. Both education and experience must be continuous and security professionals must be allowed to grow with the industry.

Hotel chains that have surveillance experts need to allow them to assist the industry as it grows by sharing information, training, knowledge, because it is not a competitive area. Every security department—regardless of the lodging facility size, number of employees, or even number of security staff, for that matter—must have some form of training. Training programmes for security employees fall into two separate categories: a programme for newly hired staff, and regularly scheduled training or ongoing training for staff. From a potential liability perspective, it is essential to train all security employees before they handle calls on their own and, further, to ensure that the training programme reflects the actual job. For effective development and implementation, the lodging security personnel training plan needs three characteristics:

— the programme must be well rounded;
— training must be continuous, and
— proper documentation of all training must be maintained.

In most facilities, training will be tailored around management concerns. Well thought-out programmes will reduce the risk of inadequate training and can be an important aspect of strategic security planning. Inadequate training has been a major downfall of lodging security for years. This is also an area that receives the most criticism whenever legal issues arise about an incident. Inadequate training claims are based upon either spending an insufficient amount of time on a topic and/or not addressing issues that will be encountered on the job. For example, if a security officer routinely receives calls for medical assistance, it would be unreasonable not to provide some training in basic first aid. The need for improved training is higher now than ever because the pressure from the public (guests and patrons) has been compounded with the recent recognition of crime rates. Most people today in any profession are measured by the amount of education and training they have received, which qualifies them to perform their job.

For lodging security professionals, both proficiency and success are based on experience and training. Keeping abreast of the current lodging security issues is another important factor. All lodging security personnel should receive the same initial orientation and policy handbook as every other employee. Then, when the security staff members arrive in their departments, the training programme is outlined in respect to their positions.

In the traditional role of hotel security, concerns for or involvement with a liability problem usually was a result of coincidence. Management often was reluctant to involve security because it had questionable confidence in the staff. Instead, it handled liability issues in a public relations fashion. With the phenomenal growth of litigation throughout society, and particularly in the lodging industry, security has taken on major responsibility to investigate, report, and develop prevention programmes for many of these problems.

Hence, it makes considerable sense, for example, for the contemporary hotel security manager to be responsible for overseeing and managing most general liability problems, including the loss of guest property, claims of guest injury, damage to or loss of guest vehicles, and employee accidents. The most common claim guests make against a hotel is that some of their property has been stolen from their guest room.

Security personnel must be cautioned not to assume that all reports of lost property necessarily mean that the property has been stolen. It may simply be misplaced or missing. It is common for victims of loss to blame someone else. Therefore, adequate information must be gathered to determine whether the item was in fact stolen or simply misplaced by the guest. The reason is obvious—lost property requires one type of investigative approach, while stolen property involves another.

In a lodging setting, however, the guest, unless he is informed, cannot be expected to understand and appreciate the threats that exist which are peculiar to that city, that neighbourhood or to that property. Although he has a certain obligation to assist in his own protection, he cannot be expected to provide his own "protection package". The threats which a guest faces in his guest-room are seemingly unlimited. Certainly any threat common to the lodging industry and shown in the Protection Management Matrix may exist in the guest-room.

The nature of each threat, the significance of it and the protection considerations against it will vary from property to property. There are, however, some protection considerations which are virtually universal and which should be incorporated into any guest-room protection countermeasures. Confidentiality of the guest-room location is vital. No audible announcement of the guest's room number should be made at the front desk or at any location. When providing the key to the guest, he should be informed of the room number by the use of a card or key holder or some other nonverbal means.

Obviously, when the bell staff is used, the room number again should never be verbalised but rather the bellperson should be informed of the room location in the same confidential manner by which the guest was notified. When receiving inquiries regarding a guest, whether by phone or in person, the confidentiality must again be maintained. A guest's right to privacy is a vital and long-standing tenant of lodging and should never be violated.

When a request is made for a room key by a person claiming to be an occupant of that room, positive identification must be made of that person prior to issuing a key. Standard identification methods should be established and used as appropriate. The locking system utilised at the guest-room door is a major consideration in this countermeasure.

Basically systems available to the hotelier fall into one of four general categories. They are key in knob, standard mortise locks, mortise locks with programmable cylinders and/or removable cores, and electronic lock systems. Key-in-knob is a system in which the key channel is actually within and a part of the doorknob itself. It is activated by inserting the key directly into the knob and the channel.

This is probably the least effective of all systems, is considered generally insecure and in fact is prohibited in some states as a hotel/motel guest-room locking system. The word "mortise" means, literally, "a hole, groove or slot into or through which some other part of an arrangement of parts fits or passes". This system usually consists of a face plate, with the doorknob and an unconnected separate key channel on the exterior side of the door and a deadbolt arrangement on the interior side of the door.

Mortise locks with programmable cylinders and/or removable cores allow for quick key combination changes. Electronic lock systems allow for a unique selection of keying combinations whenever a new guest is assigned to that room, whenever a compromise or key loss is suspected and whenever management determines that such action is warranted. New and more sophisticated systems are reaching the market on a continuing basis and the choice for the hotelier is a difficult one. If there is a single rule-of-thumb to follow, it is that whatever system is chosen, it offers higher protection if the locking combination can be changed on a random or programmed basis whenever required.

Door and frame construction as well as attendant locking hardware should be of such quality and workmanship as to minimise the ease by which an intruder can bypass them by force. Obviously, the hinges should be located to preclude the pins being pulled from the exterior. Glass, either in the door or in a panel near the door, should be of such strength and of such configurations as to minimise the possibility of an intruder breaking it and reaching into the room and accessing the locking system.

The lock bolt should be configured to minimise forceful entry and of such strength as to minimise being cut. Self-closing automatic locking devices should be standard. Connecting room doors are those doors which are placed between guest-rooms to allow for access from one guest-room to another or to enlarge the rented space from one-room to two-or-more-room capacity. Historically, these doors often have been of lesser construction than the main guest-room door.

In fact, the threat which is posed to the guest by inappropriate connecting room door design, maintenance or construction warrants special attention. Single connection door arrangements are strongly discouraged. Instead, there should be two separate doors, each void of all hardware on the inside. In effect, then, there are two doors facing one another, neither with locking hardware and with space between them. On the guest-room side of each door, however, there should be provision for the guest himself to provide added self-protection. Only guests occupying both rooms simultaneously and in concert with one another or hotel/motel staff should have the ability to access both rooms. View ports should be installed in the guest-room door. The exception to this guideline would be in the case of those door/room configurations in which adjacent glass panelling allows observation of anyone immediately outside the guest-room door.

A minimum 200-degree viewing angle is considered acceptable. A second view port for disabled persons is recommended and is in fact required in rooms complying with the Americans with Disabilities standards. Secondary and additional protective equipment is appropriate on the main guest-room door, depending on the locking system utilised. Many door locking systems have a double locking dead bolt and single action panic release features installed within the system. Many states require the hotelier laws of that state to be posted prominently within the guest-room. The limits of liability in so far as the loss of personal belongings are normally shown and are posted so that the guest understands those limits.

Also, normally noted on these postings are the considerations of safe deposit and property safekeeping facilities available at the property. All too often, however it is the hotelier himself who has not kept his knowledge current. Announcements concerning what actions the guest ought to take in order to secure that door to the fullest extent possible should be posted on or near the back of the guest-room door. Use of the safety chain, if applicable, should be explained as should the use, if appropriate, of the dead bolt. All double locking procedures should likewise be explained. Use of the view port and methods of securing any connecting or sliding/patio doors should also be addressed. Personal injuries due to accidents occur more often in the bathroom than any other portion of the guest-room.

Postings, therefore, regarding tub safety, use of any grab bars, slip-and-fall deterrent bathmats, etc. should be considered. If particular use of electrical equipment in the bathroom is desired, warnings regarding their use should be posted. The guest-room telephone is more than a convenience. It can be, literally, a life-saving guest protection device. Consider posting prominently and distinctly on the phone faceplate a notation of the number to be called to summon help. Of even greater concern, obviously, is the system devised to both answer immediately and prioritise any emergency calls. Several methods are possible to accomplish this immediate handling of any emergency call. The emergency number can be channelled, like all operator calls, into a central switchboard. If this is the system chosen, care should be taken that when the emergency number is dialled, it has an extremely distinct ring—much louder perhaps or with a distinct tone.

Some hotel chains/properties have adopted a procedure whereby the guest is advised to dial an outside number such as 911 to request emergency assistance. Great care and planning are essential before such a procedure is established. Whatever method of immediate response is adopted, the recipient of the call, whether a front desk clerk, a switchboard operator or a security officer, must be trained and scripted in quick and accurate response. Many municipalities using the nearly universal 911 system have developed scripting which is quick and concise and makes misinterpretation or extraneous conversation of a minimal concern. The use of a warning light which is activated along with the distinct ring adds greater assurance that the operator will note the call immediately and cease all other duties to respond to it.

The emergency line might also be channelled into a continually manned security office, dispatch point or control centre. Again, the ringing apparatus and arrangement must be such that the ringing tone is clear, distinct and unique and is inevitably responded to immediately. Consideration should be given to installing a system so that the room number is displayed when a call is received. Automatic taping of the ensuing conversation is a plus.The lodging industry is long past the time when it was felt that education of guests about threats and dangers and protection methods were contrary to the "host image".

On the contrary, such announcements and notifications are now considered absolutely essential by most professional hoteliers. The bell staff should be scripted and instructed in all protection aspects of the guest-room. They should direct the guests to the TV announcement, if there is one, even turning the TV on and to the particular announcing channel so that the guest gets an early opportunity to view and hear it. The bellperson should also call to the guest's attention the guest-room service directory and highlight the fact that there is a section regarding protection. Finally, the bellperson should mention the entire range of protection devices, techniques and announcements present in the room. He should discuss all subjects ranging from the use of the door devices, safe deposit system to advice about safety and fire protection.

Training for Securities

Manufacturing firms are virtually assured of failure without trained employees. Retail establishments have failed because they did not have trained employees. Public utilities, financial institutions, health care organisational, without exception, are highly likely to fail unless the personnel responsible for the product or the service which is intended to be delivered to the public are trained.

In all service industries a significant number of employees apply and are employed with little or no previous formal education or training. Even those who arrive with some degree of basic skills are not knowledgeable or informed of the particulars and peculiarities of their new property environment. The training process begins at the time the employee begins his employment and continues until lie leaves that employment is crucial to the success of the property, In literally every department, every manager must accept that fact.

Property success will not evolve unless and until every employee in every department is afforded the process of training in guest protection. Such training is vital because the lodging industry has a high turnover rate. Such training is vital because the lodging industry employs such a high rate of previously untrained persons.

Such training is vital because the lodging industry is experiencing, not unlike many other industries, rapid technological changes. The three objectives designed to accomplish the training process are:

— Teach employees to perform new and unfamiliar tasks.

— Assist employees in improving current skills.

— Assure that the guest will be protected.

The highest level of management on a property has overall training responsibility. In most individual properties, this means the general manager. Often he assigns the responsibility to the human resource department, a unit usually well situated to oversee the plan. However, the actual conduct of training is often a vastly different concern and thus requires a vastly different approach. Determining needs are the initial consideration of guest protection training—the preparing of a statement of training objectives. Such a statement allows for a common beginning point for all levels of employment from the prospective of management as well as the work force.

Guest Management

A typical day might find these workers tracking down tickets to a hot concert in town, making reservations at a hip new restaurant, picking up dry cleaning, carrying luggage, welcoming guests, opening doors, or booking reservations. But whatever their exact duties or job titles, guest services representatives have the basic task of making hotel guests feel like they are, well, at home.

As front desk people, concierges, telephone operators, doormen, bellmen, and reservation agents at hotels, resorts, motels, and inns, guest services representatives are the "public face" of a hospitality enterprise. Guests instantly get a good or bad feeling about where they are staying, often based solely on the helpfulness and friendliness of these workers. When a concierge goes out of the way to get information for a guest, or when a reservation agent is especially courteous and helpful, it can ensure that a first-time guest becomes a regular.

While hotel and resort guests love excellent service, providing it is not always easy. Guest representatives must remain courteous, tactful, calm, and helpful, even when hotel guests are rude and demanding. If a concierge or desk clerk blows his cool, the hotel's reputation--and the concierge's or desk clerk's job--may suffer. Even after a horrendously long day, guest representatives must be as friendly and helpful to the last guest at the end of their shift as the first one in the beginning. "How may I assist you?" is a phrase practically stamped on these workers foreheads. And even if a hotel is teeming with guests on the busiest weekend of the year while five staff members are out sick with the flu, guest representatives must remain unflustered and serene, as peaceful as zen monks. Needless to say, these jobs require a certain type of personality for success.

Guest services representatives work in hotel front office departments, which may be very large, with hundreds of employees, or very small. They may have specialized assignments or broad ones, depending on the size of the department and the hotel.

Specific tasks vary by specialization, but all guest services representatives do the following:

— Greeting guests, offering assistance, and recommending hotel and area services
— Keeping an eye out for problems, from unsatisfied customers to untidy restrooms, and making sure they are reported to those who can fix them
— Reporting and documenting safety hazards, conditions, or unsafe practices
— Read about concierges in Boston
— Read a personal profile of a hotel porter

Areas of Specialisation

In very large hotels, the front office is usually subdivided into sections such as reservations, registration or the front desk, bell service, telephone, concierge, and guest transportation. Many people may be employed in each area, with managers and assistant managers to supervise them.

In small hotels one or two guest services representatives may handle all of these responsibilities. In this case they are usually called front desk agents. In very small hotels, inns, and bed and breakfasts, one person may handle these and many other tasks, from housekeeping to food service to maintenance.

Reservations agents keep up with hotel booking. They handle group room contracts negotiated by the sales department and correspond with groups and travel agents to answer special requests for rooms and rates. They enter information into the computer and retrieve it when needed. They see that the front desk, housekeeping, and other departments, such as food service, receive daily information on expected arrivals and departures.

Front desk agents work behind the main desk where guests register when they arrive and check out when they leave. They make sure that guests have the rooms they booked, take payments, ask about any other needs the guests have, and generally try to sell and promote hotel services.

Bellmen assist guests with luggage

Doormen open the hotel door for guests entering or leaving. They also assist guests with luggage, call taxis, and direct traffic moving in front of the hotel. Concierges perform many services for guests including arranging hotel services, recommending local amenities, and booking transportation, restaurants, and tickets. In resort hotels concierges tend to focus on leisure services.

At business and conference hotels they also have to know a considerable amount about business services like where to find legal secretaries, translators, or computer repair. Guest transportation agents drive guests in hotel vehicles. They usually drive to and from the airport or between hotel outbuildings, but some hotels provide more extensive transportation services. Telephone operators take incoming calls and direct them to the proper room or department. They also take messages for guests and answer simple questions.

Education, Certification, and Licensing

Most large hotels provide extensive training to their employees and do not require higher degrees for their entry-level staff. Many people begin working in guest services jobs with just a high school diploma, especially if they have completed a program in hospitality services. However, people who want to become managers, and in some cases even assistant managers, need a degree, preferably in hotel management. Associate's and bachelor's degrees are available from many colleges.

Both are useful, but a bachelor's degree is usually necessary for upper level management, and an MBA for the executive level. Some hotels, especially the top ones, prefer to hire college graduates for their front desk positions and see this as an entry level management position.

Are you in high school? Ask about the Career & Technical Education programs in Hospitality Management and Hospitality Services. These programs can lead to hospitality skills certification from the American Hotel & Lodging Association and the National Occupational Competency Testing Institute (NOCTI). Find programs in hospitality at high schools, technical centers, and community colleges

Guest services representatives advance by moving from entry-level positions within their department to supervisory positions. In most hotel chains it is difficult to move into management without a degree. Service representatives can also advance by moving from smaller, less prestigious hotels to larger ones. Wages in luxury hotels are significantly higher than those in budget hotels.

Where they work

Guest services representatives work in the lobby and front office of hotels and resorts, many of which are located in cities and in resort communities such as beaches and ski areas. The recent tough economy has hurt the hotel industry, which has always been cyclical. The industry responds quickly to the overall economy, slowing in recession years and rising in expansion.

In recent years the 2001 terrorism attacks and increased concerns about security have dealt a particularly hard blow to the hospitality industry.

However, regardless of the state of the economy, there are usually a lot of job opportunities in guest services because there is a high turnover among hotel workers. In addition, to high turnover, it is likely that more jobs will be created in this industry as people continue to travel and new hotels continue to be built. New technology has changed the job of guest services representatives over the last decade.

Computerized record keeping has cut down the amount of paperwork that front desk workers do. Guests can now check out automatically, view their bills on television screens in their room, and get messages on in-room answering machines. However, guests still want, and will probably always want, direct and personal service from hotel staff. In Virginia, opportunities in this field may increase as more hotels and convention centers are constructed across the state. Major new hotels and convention centers are planned in Richmond, Virginia Beach, Hampton and Roanoke, VA.

Salaries in the Guest Service

Salaries in this career are generally low, as they are throughout the hospitality industry. Guest service representatives usually earn $17-30,000 per year, depending on the hotel's size, prestige, and location. Those representatives who have an opportunity to earn tips from guests—such as doormen and bellhops—can earn more than workers who are generally not tipped, like front desk clerks.

ROLE OF INFORMATION TECHNOLOGIES

Wireless applications enable guest services

High-speed Internet access is being installed throughout many midscale and above hotel brands as a standard for guests

["HSIA surges into midscale hotel segment," April 5, page 30]. In most cases, hotels require wireless HSIA in public space and might also suggest it for the guestrooms for the convenience it offers.

As wireless networks become more widely installed and used, hoteliers will look for ways to take advantage of them to improve their operations and guest services. Many wireless products are available as vendors try to get ahead of the wireless curve. "We find, adapt and invest in technology that's already in use in other industries and wait patiently for it to pay off," said Jay Troutman, president of Aptech Computer Systems, a business intelligence software vendor based in Pittsburgh. "In some cases, the technology has been proven and paid off in other industries eight or nine years before it takes hold in hospitality."

Business intelligence

Aptech's Execuvue is a business-intelligence product designed for management companies and ownership groups with multiple properties. It's used by operators in management companies to report and compare data and to find best practices and by asset managers among ownership groups. More than 1,000 hotels use it to report information, including about 400 Starwood Hotels & Resorts Worldwide properties, Troutman said.

The wireless version of the product has been available for three years, but has not caught on with hoteliers, Troutman said. Wireless technology at the hotel restaurant point of sale is in its infancy, according to Keith McNally, c.e.o. and founder of Ameranth Wireless, a systems integrator based in San Diego. The company conducts 80 percent of its business in the hospitality industry, which includes hotels, restaurants, casinos, theme parks, stadiums and cruise ships. With wireless point of sale, wait staff use handheld electronic devices to send orders to the kitchen.

The E-menu is an Internet-connected electronic menu that offers diners a wealth of information. A hotel restaurant with about 100 seats would need about 12 E-menu tablets because guests don't need them during the entire dining experience.

Service delivery

When a guest reports a request or maintenance issue, hotel employees can log it into GuestWare or a two-way paging device, such as a pager or cell phone that includes two-way messaging. The calls are dispatched automatically to the appropriate runner, who responds and closes out the call via pager, which communicates back to the guest-service agent. The software is designed to streamline work flow and provide information to improve processes.

"Some hotels use walkie-talkie radios instead of wireless pagers," Benjamin said. "The problem with them is that they are noisy and the user has to remember what was communicated to them. Wireless devices are easier because users don't get bogged down with verbal or written information. They don't have to remember anything."

The GuestWare communication server communicates with two-way messaging devices, such as pagers. GuestWare is a brand standard at Marriott Hotels & Resorts and is used at Kimpton Hotels for guest recognition. Other uses

— Members of Fairmont Hotels & Resorts' guest recognition program can uses a wireless-enabled HP iPAQ pocket personal computer during their stays for instant messaging or access to corporate e-mail. Guests using the iPAQ can access information ranging from local attractions to weather updates while in the hotels' public areas and conference rooms.

— Hilton Hotels Corp. installed IBM self-serve kiosks at two of its hotels in New York and Chicago to allow guests to check in and check out by scanning their credit cards.

Hotel interior design stimulates and satisfies guest expectations of service, quality, and comfort; as such, it represents the realization of hospitality design. Respecting the enormous investment that goes into creating these environments, successful hotel design also factors in timelessness and durability to increase overall longevity.

The manifestation of hospitality design balances pragmatic concerns—such as function, safety and economics—with tangible environmental elements—such as FF&E (furniture, fixtures & equipment), flowers & plants, music, art & objects—that create the desired ambiance. Harmonizing these approaches sets the stage for hospitality design based on solid, long-term operational and functional foundations.

With design proposals based on thorough knowledge of hotel operations, and accurate cost data, we can establish concrete budget proposals at the planning stage of the project. ILYA's comprehensive perspective, concept control, and detailed design direction strengthen the relationship between pragmatic and environmental factors to create balanced, integrated environments.

In addition to meeting the functional requirements specific to hotels, a sophisticated and comfortable atmosphere is created through comprehensive and detailed coordination of interior finishes, and FF&E. Here, the choice of materials in guest rooms and public spaces—furniture, accessories, lighting fixtures, window treatments—require particularly close attention. Interior finishes, materials, textures, colors, and lighting are critical factors both in effecting a dramatic presentation of the space and manifesting hospitality design.

ILYA's furniture & decorating services include international furniture procurement and custom furniture. Sophisticated environments that meet both client and user needs do not emerge from cosmetic design. Experience shows that they only develop by striving to optimize function, quality, and safety while respecting budgetary, timing, and implementation parameters. Designers work together with architects and engineers making use of cost and technical data and construction supervision know-how compiled from ILYA's achievements to date. With support from staff based in New York, and a network of collaborating specialized consultants, we are fully prepared to meet the wide ranging needs—including MEP (mechanical/electrical/plumbing) planning—of designing complex facilities.

SUCCESSFUL INTERIOR DESIGN

More Americans eat out each week than participate in an other single form of entertainment. As Americans depend more on meals away from home, dining has become what they do to relax and unwind. If you have ever traveled in Europe, you notice that the dinner meal is eaten much later than in the United States and these meals have a celebratory air about them - people are heavily involved in conversation and the dinner is viewed as an event.

As living has gotten more hectic, Americans have begun to view dining as a one-stop form of nourishment and entertainment. A 1993 Roper Starch survey found that 34 percent of adult Americans had eaten out in a one-week period, whereas only 14 percent had seen a movie and 9 percent participated in some other event. The National Restaurant Association says that trend has increased in the last three years. With so much interest and money riding on food, it is extremely important for restaurateurs to develop trends that positively impact customers - including an interior design that appeals to potential customers. This is particularly important since the average American eats 198 meals out a year and spends $855 million on an average day on meals away from home.

So how do restaurants program profitability and success into their interior design? Based on current trends in the industry and working with restauranteurs to design appealing, and profitable, restaurant operations, the following elements are critical for successful restaurant design.

Know your Market

Determine what your customers want. This may sound like a daunting task but all it really takes is a little research. Who do you talk to? Talk to your customers if you are an existing restaurant. If you are designing a new restaurant, talk to your competition. You would be surprised how talkative your competition is, especially if they are successful. Getting feedback from your existing customers is extremely important. Chances are these people dine out at other restaurants and can tell you what they like and don't like about the design of these restaurants.

Talk to your competition - they will tell you what went right with their design and what went wrong. You will also get the added advantage of seeing their design in action. Do market research - look at the demographics of your location, analyze your competition and determine if there is a niche for your idea. Also, you will be giving your customers what they want.

Know the Trends

This is related to the aforementioned element but goes a step further. In the information-based society, people can find out more information at a faster rate - and things keep getting faster and faster. The TV Food Network has been started and is available on most cable television services. People can get information about restaurants quickly and easily. With more information, potential customers can be more discriminating in their restaurant selection.

Interior design influences a restaurant's atmosphere which impacts the customer's decision-making process. Some of the recent trends in restaurant design based on the work at RAS and discussions with experts in the restaurant industry incorporate the following elements:

1. An upscale, but casual, theme - Tony Clark's, a recently-opened restaurant in Philadelphia conforms to this design theme - and has been overwhelmingly successful in its fledgling stage. The Striped Bass also falls into this category. The upscale, but casual design trend appears as though it will carry us into the new millennium.
2. Entertainment-themed restaurants - Planet Hollywood and Hard Rock Cafe are excellent examples of this trend. Also,

a prototype restaurant for Philadelphia Park, a thoroughbred racetrack and The Turf Clubs, off-track wagering facilities.

3. An exhibition cooking area where your chef is visible. The American public likes to see who is preparing their meals. This design also brings chefs out of the kitchen. If your chef is well-known, it will be a great marketing tool for you.
4. Neighborhood feel - People do business with people they know and like. It is the same with restaurants. Restaurants are creating interior designs that make people feel like they belong. It helps to remember the customer's name, too - Remember the television show Cheers?

Use an Experienced Restaurant Interior Designer

Although you might not think so, all interior designers are not alike. A restaurant interior designer is different from a residential interior design who is different from a health care interior designer and so on... An interior designer you use should have experience in designing restaurants. They usually have a portfolio of their work to show you. It is an excellent way to look at the designer's creativity and design ability. Pictures are always worth many words, right? Also, an interior designer should understand the operations of a restaurant - the flow of the food from the kitchen to the customer's table, the flow and circulation of restaurant design from a customer's and employee's viewpoint and knowledge of finish specifications for restaurant furnishings, including durability and feel of furnishings.

Don't Forget Profitability

Remember you have a budget you need to stick to. Also, keep the employees in mind when you design the restaurant. Create a design that facilitates their movements in and out of the kitchen. This will create seamless service that will make customers happy. It will also contribute to high employee morale. Internally market your design to your employees. They may have some ideas to share with you based on their practical experience.

Most importantly, emphasize to your interior designer the need to adhere to your budget and that your restaurant should run smoothly and look good. Tell your interior designer to create an interior that is programmed for profitability - this is where the designer's value is really reflected based on their experience. Your restaurant's interior design - as well as great food and great service - has to appeal to restaurant patrons so they keep coming back.

5

Managing Environment for Better Customer Satisfaction

Corporate environmental strategy and accountability has risen to prominence in government and business policy particularly over the past decade. This has increasingly been reflected in the management and accounting research agendas and literatures internationally. Community environmental concerns have come to affect a widening range of industries. However most research into corporate environmental strategy, control and reporting has focused on the mining, manufacturing and chemical industries, especially those heavy industries where the potential for direct pollution and degradation of the environment is most obvious and appears to be the most significant.

Increasingly however, community environmental concerns have begun to extend to businesses in the service industry. Thus, firms in the service sector are beginning to face up to the challenge of implementing appropriate environmental management practices. Among these stands the international hotel industry which has begun to exhibit signs of taking up environmental strategies as part of some hotels' core missions and profiles.

A number of factors contribute to the importance of environmental strategy and management in this industry. First, it represents a foremost part of the hospitality and tourism industry, one of the largest global industries. Second, with the growth of national and international tourism, the hospitality sector and the hotel industry in particular, are assuming a higher public profile and may increasingly attract the attention and scrutiny of community groups, environmentalists and regulators. Third, more affluent consumers may increasingly demand "green" accommodation, and regulation may intensify for better waste disposal, and improved water and energy conservation etc. With the heightened interest in environmental strategies, comes the challenge of not only developing corporate environmental objectives and strategies but also achieving effective implementation.

One key to effective implementation lies in the linkages between environmental strategies, corporate accounting and management control functions. For example, there is a need to develop a better understanding of environment-related costs and benefits as inputs to conventional management accounting. Bartolomeo et al. reports on the results of a trans-European project to investigate links between environmental management and management accounting functions of a business. The results suggest that opportunities exist for companies to become more active in environmental management accounting and control and that the pressures on them to do so will increase. Arguably this requires a strategic approach to environmental management, accounting and performance evaluation. Before this can happen however, research is needed in these areas, both in relation to the specific needs of the hospitality industry and possible contributions from the broader accounting and management control disciplines.

A Structuration Theory Foundation

Giddens' structuration theory has now been employed over many years by some researchers as a lens for both constructing and critiquing organisational strategy, accountability, information systems and the like. Structuration theory recognises a close and reciprocal relationship between social structure and human agency. It combines the notions that people act with purpose and in so doing, create their own environment and the social structures of that environment, while at the same time, those emerging social structures also determine people's behaviour and actions. As they both create and are shaped by emergent social structures, people develop meaning in their actions and exercise power through those structures that are continually transformed and reproduced through people's actions.

Thus for Giddens, action and structure are both media of interactions between people as well as being outcomes of those interactions. This suggests that for organisations, systems such as management control systems, management information systems and corporate planning systems, have structures that are produced and reproduced through organisational members' interactions. They in turn facilitate structures and shape the form and patterns of those interactions. Thus structures do not simply constrain human activity, but also enable those activities. This is what Giddens terms, the duality of structure.

Management control systems, management information systems and corporate planning systems can essentially be conceived as part of social systems having three major properties:

1. structures - systems of rules and resources
2. modality - means by which structure produces action
3. interaction - actions taken by organisational members working within these systems

There are three types of structure conceived by Giddens: signification, legitimation and domination. Signification refers to organisational members' making sense of actions and deriving meaning from them by drawing on meanings they derive from control, information and planning systems. The modality through which this is produced is largely the development of people's interpretive schemes, namely the ways in which they conceive and interpret the world around them. Legitimation refers to the moral sanction and thereby legitimacy derived by organisational members from these systems.

The modality through which this is produced is largely that of the creation and maintenance of accepted social norms -

of belief and behaviour. Domination refers to the power derived by organisational members from the authorisation of actions and allocation of resources facilitated by these systems. The modality through which this is produced largely relies upon the facilitating role played by organisational planning and control systems that authorise actions and allocate resources. Thus for each of these three types of structure, there is a corresponding modality and interaction. Thus the interaction of people with the structure results in actions and interactions that in turn produce communications, rewards and sanctions, and the power to achieve desired objectives and outcomes.

Structuration theory offers a perspective on organisational strategy and accountability that is distinct from a purely functionalist or systems based view. It offers a focus on the interaction between structural and human factors that influence how both operate. Its view of power is not unilateral, but rather recognises the exercise of power in social relations and for the purpose of altering the course of events, at all levels of the organisations, and by subordinates as well as superiors.

Environmental Policies and Strategies

Environmental management might best be summarised as the suite of strategies, actions and controls that are aimed at reducing an organisation's dysfunctional environmental impact and includes both technical (hardware) and organisational (software) activities. It broadly covers issues such as environmental impact, sustainability, resource management and pollution control. In the specific case of hotels, environmental management consists of operations that cover aspects of consumption of energy, water and other resources; food waste production, waste management and pollution emissions.

Empirical evidence shows that hotels have begun to respond to the need of environmental management. The first step in the process, as suggested by Elkington and Burke, is the formation of an environmental policy. Brown reports that in their sample of UK hotels more than 40% of the respondents stated that they have an environmental policy, while 60 did not have one. Kirk's sample of general managers in Edinburgh shows an even smaller number, with only 19% having a written environmental policy at the time of the study. A subsequent study showed comparable numbers of 22% having an environmental policy. Given the evidence that only a small number of hotels have a written environmental policy, another way to ascertain commitment to environmental management may be in terms of the implementation of environmental initiatives.

Brown found some evidence that environmental initiatives are being operated in her sample of UK hotels. Examples include recycling of cans, paper and food, less frequent change of bed linen, and "green" purchasing policies. However, more than 60% of the respondents were still failing to adopt these types of green initiatives. Gil et al. examined hotels' environmental management in terms of the practices they adopted to reduce their negative impact on the natural environment. These practices included quantification of environmental costs and savings, environmental training programmes, green purchasing policies, energy and water-saving actions and recycling. They found the extent of implementation of environmental practices to vary with various contingency factors such as age of facilities, size and chain affiliation.

Environmental Strategy Drivers

In a survey of 262 3*, 4* and 5* Spanish hotels, Gil et al found that various factors had an effect on the degree of implementation of environmental practices. These were hotel size, age of facilities, chain affiliation and pressures from operations management and internal and external stakeholders. It is noteworthy that except for stakeholder pressures, the other factors are all internal organisational factors.

In a study of a total of 85 hotel managers in Edinburgh, Kirk looked for a relationship between the presence of a written environmental policy and characteristics of the hotel such as size, ownership and classification/grading. While he found no significant association, this result could be due to the small number of respondents declaring a written environmental policy. Brown reported that the most cited reason for implementation of a number of typical environmental measures has been cost. This emerged as a significantly more cited reason than care for the environment, customer pressure, regulatory requirement and competitor action. Indeed managers ranked care for the environment as a less important concern for hotel management than factors such as quality and customer care. Somewhat surprisingly, they also viewed competitors' actions as the least important criterion.

Based on a survey of General Managers (GMs) of hotels in Edinburgh, Kirk reported that the most significant benefits of environmental management they perceived were the positive effects on the local community and public relations. This perception was enhanced by the presence of a written environmental policy. GMs of hotels with a written environmental policy perceived greater potential benefits in terms of increased profitability and marketing advantage compared to GMs in hotels without a written policy. Hotel size and classification also had an effect on general managers' perception. Managers of large hotels, and hotels with classification of 3* to 5* perceived greater positive public relations benefits from environmental management.

Research into hotel patrons as drivers of environmental policy and management reveals somewhat mixed evidence. A survey of frequent travelers revealed that: (1) they want to stay in hotels that show concern for the environment, but (2) they are not willing to pay extra for it. About 70% of those sampled say they are likely or extremely likely to stay in a hotel with a proactive environment policy, while 26% say that it does not matter to them. About 50% do not think that hotel room rates should change in environmentally active hotels.

One other potential driver that cannot be ignored is the effect of environmental strategy on firms' financial performance. Yet again, the empirical evidence regarding this is rather mixed. Some studies have reported a positive relationship between environmental strategy and financial performance while others have reported a negative relationship. Research into environmental policy and strategy in the international hotel industry therefore reveals a spectrum of factors driving the environmental agenda. Large hotels, those with more recently constructed facilities, and those belonging to large chains appear more likely to be environmentally active. From the point of view of hotel management, two major motivators emerge in the form of cost reduction and enhancement of public relations.

Nevertheless the evidence for a relationship between environmental strategies and better financial performance is mixed. Furthermore, while stakeholder pressure is cited as a significant driver, evidence from hotel patrons suggests that they are favourably disposed towards environmentally conscious hotels but vary in their preparedness to pay a premium for this.

The Environmental Control Gap

One potential reason for the hotel industry's muted support for environmental management strategies may be due to how hotel managers are controlled and evaluated. Managers surveyed by Brown reported that they are controlled both by budget and achievement of profits. Environmental reporting and achievement of environmental targets were generally viewed as being unimportant control criteria. Thus, the managers were judged primarily by financial performance. When asked if environmental improvements should be recognized as part of the reward system, 71% responded that they should not.

In a subsequent survey of 106 managers from UK hotels, Brown found that their perception of importance placed on control criteria was consistent with the earlier study. The three most important forms of reporting cited were achievement of budget, maintenance or improvement of profit and reporting of customer complaints. The same criteria were reported for hotels with and without an environmental policy. However, those hotels having an environmental policy (over 40% of respondents) did perceive a number of other reporting requirements as significantly more important, including environmental reporting and environmental target achievement. Brown concluded that hotels with environmental policies have not incorporated environmental reporting in their control system to any great extent.

As in other industries, the hotel industry reveals a mixture of contradictory tendencies and trajectories in environmental management and strategy. While a proportion are developing environmental missions, policies and strategies, the frequency and level of hotel commitment to these is highly variable, the motives for commitment to these are mixed, and managers remain primarily focused on traditional short term budgetary and financial performance targets. This traditional focus is reinforced by the control systems to which they are subjected. Yet it is in control systems design and implementation where arguably the greatest potential for the effective integrated pursuit of operational, financial and environmental strategies lies.

Hotel Performance Measurement

The problems faced by organisations in designing optimal performance measurement and evaluation systems are not peculiar to the hospitality industry. In recent years, new performance measurement frameworks have been developed to meet the changing competitive demands faced by organisations. Criticisms have been directed at traditional systems due to their focus on measuring short-term financial outcomes, which are lag indicators. These fail to measure factors of strategic importance to the organisation and facilitate early intervention. To refocus manager attention upon the longer term strategic issues, frameworks such as the balanced scorecard and EVA have been increasingly adopted by organisations. Based on the rather limited research available in the hotel industry, it would appear that the hotel industry has adopted such frameworks only to a limited extent.

Surveys of hotels in Europe indicate that most hotels are still emphasising financial measures, despite their well-documented limitations. Harris and Mongiello surveyed GMs of chain-based European hotels, and followed-up with interviews with a selection of GMs in UK and Italy. The questionnaire asked respondents to indicate which key indicators they would choose if information was available and the actions taken in relation to the results of each indicator. The key indicators given were based on a balanced scorecard with financial, customer, operational and human resource perspectives. The results show greater use of financial and customer-related indicators as a basis for actual actions taken by the GMs.

Similarly, a study of UK hotels reported that the highest rated measures monitored were financial dimensions of performance - profitability had the highest rating, followed by turnover and cost control respectively. Overall, the hotels appear to pay significantly less attention to non-financial dimensions. While the non-financial performance measure rated most highly was quality of performance, other measures such as innovation received scant attention. These findings are not limited to Europe - GMs in Australia also put significantly more emphasis on financial indicators in evaluating subordinates' performance.

Overall, the empirical evidence regarding the performance measurement and evaluation process in hotels suggests a predominantly simplistic, short term, financial, limited scope operation. In particular, Brown and McDonnell voice concerns in three areas. First, hotel information systems lag behind the range of techniques available (e.g. monitoring multiple dimensions of performance). Second, despite the high level of interest shown in human resource and marketing issues, current performance measurement and evaluation systems are weak in these areas. Finally, they argue that hotel companies must develop performance measures unique to their circumstances and needs. Collier and Gregory's field study of investment appraisal in the UK hotel industry also found that investment analysis techniques employed to evaluate capital investment and expenditure proposals were much simpler than they had anticipated, the approach being largely dictated by the dominant leadership of one individual or by the board's degree of specialist knowledge of the hotel industry.

Guilding's field study of the impact of owner-operator structures on hotel capital budgeting found that when either hotel owner or management adopted a short term planning horizon (eg. intending to sell the hotel or not to renew a management contract), this significantly reduced attention to longer term strategies by both parties. Such industry practices clearly carry the potential to seriously limit strategic management of both operations and environment.

In order to better address the needs of hotel companies, Brown and McDonnell suggested the use of the balanced scorecard approach. They illustrated this by developing a balanced scorecard for a 5-star hotel in England. Since then, several other cases of balanced scorecard adoption have been documented in the literature. Hilton Hotel developed the balanced scorecard as a way to quantitatively track financial and non-financial data that have an impact on the company's strategic plan and to ensure consistency among all Hilton properties. Hilton's balanced scorecard included performance measures focussing on revenue maximisation, operational effectiveness, customer value, and brand management standards.

White Lodge Services (WLS) Corporation started developing its balanced scorecard system in January 1997 to monitor performance at both the property and corporate levels. WLS manages a hotel portfolio consisting mainly of Marriot limited-services franchises, namely, Courtyard, Fairfield Inn and Residence Inn. Their balanced scorecard elements included employee and management turnover, internal operational and human resource practices, guest satisfaction, and financial success. Performance improvements were reported in several areas during the first two years of the balanced scorecard's implementation. These included improvements in quantitative measures of revenue, profitability, as well as greater alignment of objectives between owners and property managers. Neither reported balanced scorecard had environmental performance as a significant focus.

Whilst it is encouraging to find examples of hotels that have experimented with the balanced scorecard, very little else has been documented in the literature with regards to the adoption of other new performance measurement frameworks. In a sample of 18 hotels, Atkinson and Brown identified only one company that had developed and implemented a balanced scorecard. There was very little evidence of the adoption of other new performance measurement frameworks. For example, the concept of activity-based costing and its application to customer profitability analysis, while potentially beneficial to hotels, has received little exposure in the hospitality literature. In a research report looking at management accounting in hotel groups, the authors found that there was a consistent failure to implement activity-based costing in the cases studied.

A Strategic Management Approach

Phillips notes that although the balanced scorecard is gaining in popularity, it is not without its shortcomings. For example, some companies fail to define the measure of success that needs to be emphasised, but instead have used indicators that are easy to determine. Moreover, he argues that existing performance systems have been fixated on individual techniques such as the balanced scorecard but have neglected the process of overall organisational performance measurement. To address this shortcoming, Phillips proposed a hotel performance measurement system that goes beyond technique to focus on process and structure and links the three areas of strategic planning: formulation, implementation and evaluation.

The model is a contingency model consisting of the following key elements: (1) Inputs and processes - based on the resource based view of the firm, (2) environmental characteristics - including market turbulence, competitive turbulence and technology turbulence, (3) strategic orientation - using Miles and Snow typology, and (4) Outputs, markets and outcomes - using performance measurement systems, such as balanced scorecard to monitor outcomes of processes. The proposed model was illustrated using a four-star hotel located in England. A similar model was proposed by Webster drawing on systems theory where the organisation with its activities and processes fits its environment and has both inputs from it and provides outputs to it.

The major elements of the model are the environment, the inputs, the organisation and the outputs. The model can be used to perform a strategic analysis of a company and was illustrated using a case study of Swallow Hotels in the UK. In general however, there is little research done on strategic planning and management control processes utilised by hotels. Phillips provided some empirical evidence of a positive relationship between strategic planning and performance. However, the significance of the relationship depends on the exact measure of "performance" (different measures of efficiency, effectiveness and adaptability were used in the survey).

Other studies tend to focus on specific elements of the strategic management process, for example, environmental scanning. Olsen and Roper provide a review of research in strategic management in the hospitality industry and found that it is still grounded in the classical view of strategy as a highly rational process. They conclude that there is much scope for significant research in strategy as applied to the hospitality industry and in particular argue for additional research to be conducted to develop the relationships among the key elements in order to provide synthesized views of how they interact to produce successful strategies.

Unveiling Budgetary Practices

The currently available empirical evidence regarding existing budgeting practices in hotels is based on surveys and limited case studies of UK, US and Scandinavian hotels. Budgets are commonly used in hotels and most are prepared for the purposes of control and performance evaluation. Schmidgall et al. made comparisons between the operations budgeting practices of US and Scandinavian hotels using a survey methodology. The approach to budgeting used by hotel chains was found to be bottom-up in both samples (US: 79.5%; Scandinavia: 64%). This compares with only 54.6% of UK hotels surveyed by Jones. However, for budgeting at the hotel-level (rather than the chain-level), while the majority of US respondents (65%) still use a bottom-up approach, the Scandinavian respondents exhibited a greater variety of approaches (38% being top-down, 35% being bottom up, and the rest a combination of the two). Prior to developing the budget, a majority of respondents set tentative financial targets. The most commonly used target is net income (51.5%) followed by return on owner's equity (15.5%).

In a subsequent study of US hotels, Schmidgall and Defranco report similar results, with a majority setting either sales (33%) or net income (31%) financial targets prior to developing the budget. After the budget is developed, further revisions are still commonly made, since budgets are usually prepared months in advance of the operating year.

Flexible budgeting does not appear to be widely used. This could be explained by the relatively high fixed costs of hotels which diminish the advantages of "flexing" the budget. While most hotels prepare annual operating budgets, fewer appear to prepare a long-range planning budget. Yet Schmidgall and Defranco have found a positive relationship between the sales level of a hotel and the likelihood that the hotel would prepare a long-range budget.

Overall it would appear that the hotel industry focuses on traditional short term budgeting, treating budgets as their primary tools for control and performance evaluation. The emphasis is on financial targets of net income or sales. However few organisations prepare long-range budgets. Thus the focus is on short-term financial measures that require frequent updating given the environmental uncertainties surrounding the organisation. These are the very criticisms that have been directed at traditional budgeting — its inefficiencies and ineffectiveness in meeting the needs of the information age.

Given the concerns with traditional budgeting, some have advocated that companies adopt "better budgeting" processes. One example is zero-based budgeting (ZBB) which has been adopted in varying degrees in different countries. For example it is used much more by US hotels (42%) than Scandinavian hotels (7%). The rate reported for UK hotels is even higher than the US at 52%. However, it must be noted that this rate is based on a survey conducted a few years later than those reported by Schmidgall et al.. Despite a proportion of hotels adopting "better budgeting practices", some researchers have argued that this does not address the problem that the fundamentals of budgeting create barriers to competitiveness.

Instead, they advocate a new approach encompassing a more comprehensive range of steering mechanisms. These include techniques such as rolling budgets, balanced scorecards and activity-based management, incorporated into a framework that also emphasizes behavioural dimensions by developing an appropriate organisation al culture. Some of these improvements in budgeting have been adopted by hotels, and one example of Lakefront Hotel is provided by Brown and Atkinson. Lakefront Hotel is a 1200 room property located in Chicago and is widely considered as a "flagship" operation within the well-established international company which is managing the property. Its annual plan is supplemented by frequent revised forecasts and updates that are developed through team work and are widely communicated. Its approach to performance management and control is also more balanced, and performance indicators include both external and internal quantitative data as well as "softer" performance indicators.

These strategic indicators include long-term leading indicators of future performance and short-term measures of outcomes already attained. So the picture of the hotel industry budgetary practice is largely one of short term incremental budgeting focussed on net income or monetary sales. While a degree of innovation in budgetary systems is evident in a significant proportion of some national locations, there remains considerable scope for innovation and experimentation with more comprehensive, broader based strategic and financial steering mechanisms.

Strategising Environmental Change

In order to develop hotel environmental strategy, successfully implement it, and then evaluate its impact (both financial and non-financial) on various stakeholders, those strategies must be created and managed holistically and linked to the overall management control system of the organisation. The environmental strategy must first and foremost be a synergistic part of the hotel's overall corporate strategy if it is to create value both organisationally and environmentally. Given the evidence from the studies of hotel environmental management and planning and control systems discussed above, the further development of environmentally responsible strategies in the hotel industry beyond minimum legislative compliance or in the absence of government regulation, will require a balancing of hotel owner and management incentive with positive environmental outcomes.

Strategising hotel environmental change on this basis invites the development of a comprehensive strategic management framework. Such a framework reflects a structuration theory approach to the development and implementation of environmental values, objectives and actions. Opportunities exist for embedding environmental strategy into the hotel organisation through signification, legitimation and domination structures. All three are capable of impacting on and being themselves reinforced by the actions of hotel owners, managers and employees.

The following framework is presented as a potential foundation for the further investigation and development of hotel environmental management processes and outcomes. Environmental strategies require a foundation which establishes the basis for overall strategic direction. These consist of a set of governing corporate environmental policies that reflect consideration of:

— The organisation's strengths, weaknesses, opportunities and threats

— Mandatory environmental legislation and regulations in countries in which it operates

— International industry quality standards (eg. ISO14001) and guidelines
— Environmental policies and strategies employed by hotel industry leaders
— Community and patrons' concerns and preferences

These policies will reflect and be driven by emerging environmental values which themselves can drive longer term action through their roles of articulating the organisation members' meanings and sense-making their customer, operational and environmental roles and responsibilities (signification) and through their roles of embodying and legitimising emerging norms of environmental responsibility (legitimisation).

These two structures have the capacity to generate major environmental strategy actions and outcomes in addition to the more formalised management planning and control systems that an organisation may develop. The resulting broadly specified environmental policies require translation into environmental objectives in both operational and financial terms. These form an integrated part of the organisation's overall objectives, being framed in a common medium to longer time horizon, supported by related strategies and subject to measurable key performance indicators (KPIs) where feasible.

Given the evidence concerning hoteliers' strong cost control orientation and hotel patrons' environment-cost trade-off preferences, the effective implementation of environmental strategies may, at least in the early stages of environmental strategy development and change, be facilitated by the adoption of "Environmentally Efficient Resourcing" (EER). EER offers a focus upon the linkage between environmental objectives and strategies, and integrated environmental and financial outcomes for both hotels and patrons. Thus under EER, hotel environmental strategy and management is oriented towards the integration of environmental and operational enhancement in the pursuit of positive outcomes for longer term environmental, operating and cost efficiency. This involves environmental strategy in contributing to and being held accountable for:

— A net reduction in the organisation's dysfunctional environmental impact.

— Associated cost savings, cost containment or agreed upon cost increments.

— Operational efficiency improvements or maintenance of longer term operational efficiency targets.

— Development of a positive environmental reputation amongst communities and patrons.

— A consequential positive impact on patron demand and payment for accommodation and services.

This essentially reflects a balanced scorecard philosophy, but incorporates environment as a key feature, and drives strategy development rather than being used purely ex post to evaluate outcomes. Once more, this philosophy reflects the mutual interaction of hotel organisation members' actions and structure whereby their emerging sense-making of the relationship and balance between operational, financial and environmental values and objectives becomes more clearly agreed upon, articulated and pursued. As employee understanding of and support for this philosophy develops, it also has the prospect of gaining moral legitimacy as a valued and agreed upon set of behavioural norms.

The effective operationalisation of EER hinges on its implementation, evaluation and control. This can be applied at three levels:

— *Level 1.* At the deepest level of owner and management values and philosophy. This involves a morphogenetic change of deep seated organisational culture and its core values towards a deliberate and major commitment to fundamental principles of environmental protection and remediation - in both core beliefs and extensive action that commits significant financial, human and operational resources. This implies a focus on signification as a crucial structure whereby people make sense of their environmental versus operational and financial responsibilities.

— *Level 2.* At the related operational business and functional strategy level. This involves the translation of the core values into feasible objectives and the implementation of practical environmental strategies for the instigation or improvement of environmental management. This can be pursued particularly through the legitimation structure whereby the crafting of specific environmental objectives and strategies begin the process of creating norms of belief and behaviour which influence management and employees' perceptions and behaviour alike and in turn reinforce the legitimacy of the pursuit of environmental responsibility values and objectives.

— *Level 3.* At the environmental control level. This requires the design, measurement and monitoring of environmental, operational and financial KPIs covering periods from short to long term. These are oriented towards the control of both environmental resources and impacts and related financial resources and impacts. This control level embraces domination structures involving the authorising of environmentally proactive behaviour and the allocating of resources to facilitate such actions. It is this structure that can be brought into action by strategic management, management control and management information systems modalities.

Given the empirical evidence for a strong predisposition in the hotel towards short term profit and cash flow targeting, the operation of EER at Level 1. most probably represents a longer term state for hotels that have attained the more advanced stage of corporate environmental strategic positioning. These will have a well developed and deeply held core set of environmental philosophies, a longer term strategic orientation, and an integrated suite of operational, environmental and financial KPIs. They are more likely to have combined signification, legitimation and domination structures in their overall pursuit of proactive environmental strategies for longer term hotel implementation.

In the shorter term, hotels without prior commitment to environmental strategies are more likely to engage in morphostatic change, whereby some elementary environmental principles are adopted, leading to incremental short to medium term environmental strategies only partially integrated into the overall strategic management and control system. This represents the beginnings of environmental change while still retaining previously held priority core commitments to other operational and financial objectives. This represents a partial approach which may work through attention to legitimation and domination structures whereby some norms of environmental responsibility are developed and some action is authorised and resources are allocated to selected environmental strategies.

Some might argue this to be a form of rebuttal or apparent accommodation without the organisation taking on any real change in its fundamental philosophy or beliefs. Nevertheless it is arguable that some positive environmental outcomes and impacts may be generated by this incremental approach. Even if environmental change is addressed at Level 1 via a morphogenetic approach, Level 2 operationalisation of EER will be required if any positive impact on hotel environment is to be achieved.

Environmental objectives must be articulated simultaneously with operational, and financial objectives, if related strategies are to be developed and responsive actions triggered. Without Level 2 operationalisation, values and philosophies remain just that. Implementation of actual and effective environmental change management cannot follow without specific plans and related commitment of resources, responsibility, and accountability for outcomes - major arenas of legitimation and domination structure.

Level 3 represents an essential performance control and input to further cycles of environmental strategising. It prompts design of information systems to answer the question "How will we know when (or if) we've got there?". The development of environmental KPIs and their integration into the hotel's existing system of KPIs is essential for the ongoing actioning of

EER at Level 2. At this level, it is most likely that a suite of strategic steering mechanisms such as rolling 3 to 5 year budgets and balanced scorecards, may be developed and applied.

The challenge is for them to focus strategic implementation upon the balancing of short and long term objectives, to maintain a dual orientation towards both operational and financial targets, and to pursue environmental improvements in a market sensitive manner. This fundamental Level 3, embodies a profoundly domination based structure. Systems of decision-making authorisation and resource allocation are developed to facilitate specific implementation and control actions essential for securing outputs and meeting objectives - operational, financial and environmental.

What becomes increasingly clear, is that for EER to produce longer term tangible environmental outcomes, it must ultimately operate at all three levels specified above. Any lesser number of levels being addressed is likely to result in environmental outcomes that are not sustainable over the long term, produce negligible short to medium term results, are readily jettisoned in favour of short term financial KPIs, or at best produce some policies or procedures that amount to little more than tokenism.

What EER does offer hoteliers is the opportunity to pursue environmental change strategies in the context of their industry and their own organisation's particular profile and constraints. Furthermore it draws together environmental, operational and financial issues for joint evaluation and action, offering the opportunity to develop environmental strategies incrementally and as part of the overall hotel management planning and control system and processes. Being pursued via all three levels and across all three structures of signification, legitimation and domination, EER offers the prospect of incrementally building and reinforcing environmental values, actions and outcomes that match operational and financial counterparts in organisational significance and duration. In addition it keeps open the hotelier's choice as to whether they pursue a position of environmental leader or follower within the hotel industry or within a segment or region of that industry. Finally, it recognises the importance of industry and organisation context, organisational values, adequacy of policy foundations and effectiveness of steering mechanisms for implementation and control.

6

Technologies and Facilities to Customers

Five years ago, e-mail had not yet achieved the almost universal presence it now enjoys as a means of professional and personal communication. Mobile telephones were still relative curiosities, owned essentially by early adopters. Most small businesses were still using dial-up connections to the Internet and flip charts were still as likely to be used for presentations as PowerPoint. Tens of thousands of business travellers flew daily over the twin towers of the World Trade Centre, having undergone only the most cursory security checks before boarding.

The astonishing pace of technological progress, and the apparently unstoppable urge to travel faster and further, mean that predicting the trends that will characterise the conference, incentive and business travel markets over the next five years is not an easy task. For those of us operating in these sectors of business tourism though, it is absolutely vital that we achieve a degree of understanding of the ways in which we shall be using technology and transport by 2009: in the products we promote, organise, sell and purchase.

There is no doubt that technology will continue to evolve at a remarkable pace over the next five years. Corbin Ball, predicts that over the next few years:

Computers will get smaller and cheaper; processors will get faster; batteries will hold a charge longer; displays will have better resolution and be more flexible; data projectors will get smaller, cheaper and brighter; and broadband internet will get faster and ubiquitous. There will be a doubling of performance tied to price every 18 months into the next decade. The phrase 'faster, better and cheaper' will continue to apply to most of the technology products we buy". Over the next five years, mobile phone technology will evolve particularly rapidly, and we shall see a gradual convergence of the PDA and the mobile phone.

Corbin Ball has forecast that mobile phones, with access to wireless broadband, will be able to be used as mini-PDA phones with access to high-speed Internet connections through multiple channels including Wi-Fi, Bluetooth and even faster wireless formats. He notes that a number of products are being developed on these mobile platforms for the meetings industry itself, including mobile registration, networking, surveys, audience response, interactive programs, electronic attendee lists, product directories and lead retrieval systems.

USE OF THE INTERNET

We live in the age of 'digital Darwinism'. The permanent Internet revolution is constantly changing the way we live, survive and, we hope, thrive. This revolution is most evident in the way business is conducted in the meetings, incentives and business travel market. This is a market dependant on storing, using and processing vast amounts of data; something that information and communications technology does extremely well.

Using the Internet for Distribution

Web-based booking tools have been slower to penetrate the corporate market than the leisure travel market. It is generally accepted that by the end of this decade, due to pressure from corporate buyers and suppliers' desire for cost-savings and distribution efficiencies, the use of the Internet for making reservations will be well established as the preferred distribution channel for all forms of business travel.

A recent IBM Business Consulting Services report predicted that, overall, on-line travel bookings will approximately double in volume between 2004 and 2007. More hotel rooms being booked electronically. One aspect of this trend is that the use of electronic distribution channels for the booking of hotel rooms will continue to grow. This will be particularly evident in Europe.

However, the total of European hotel room nights is increasing faster than the world average of 3.3%. Between 2002 and 2003 there was an increase of 4.7% in the number of hotel rooms in Europe booked electronically through the Global Distribution Systems (GDS) and key Internet travel sites. The region's 2003 ADR improved 10% over 2002, also outperforming the worldwide average increase of 0.9%.

By increasing competition and obliging GDS's to diversify their revenue streams, deregulation will provide improved technology and new products from which individual business travellers and their employers will directly benefit. Lower fares and better service are also widely predicted, adding to the 'push' factors that will stimulate additional travel for work-related purposes.

Deregulation will enable the GDS companies to offer more competitive pricing and packaging alternatives to attract more travel suppliers, especially low cost carriers, which may result in more content for end users. By 2009, the GDS's should be in a position to provide those seeking to purchase business travel with one single place to obtain a complete array of the lowest fares and rates, thus eliminating the need to search multiple sources.

Internet for Site Selection

The virtual world will continue to advance, via the Internet, in the site selection process. Virtual hotel and conference venue tours are already an established feature of site selection and site promotion, but the next five years will see a steady increase in their use, as destinations, venues and hotels become much more sophisticated in using panoramic photography, 3-D modelling, multimedia, and even on-line chat and web conferencing to make the selection process easier for event organisers.

The applications of the Internet will only be limited by the imagination of the users. Meanwhile, new ideas are not in short supply. For example, in February 2004, Meeting News magazine reported that the Atlanta Convention and Visitors Bureau was using 'video e-mail' to help incoming groups promote their events and the city itself to potential attendees. The service is provided free to the CVB's largest convention clients, and involves custom video messages being made that include invitations promoting the features of the upcoming meeting and direct encouragements to the viewer to register on-line. According to the CVB's Director of Marketing, the technology places images directly in front of the customer in an accessible and timely manner: *"It's a cost-effective direct outreach when advertising dollars are stretched and conventions are looking to CVB's for new offerings"*.

The streaming-video messages appear in a browser window, playable by Windows Media Player. While the service is free for large convention groups, a sliding-scale fee applies to other groups based on their size, to cover production costs for custom clips. As the use of the Internet for site-selection purposes becomes ever more ingenious and creative, the use of that medium to research venues will also continue to expand over the next five years. More and more event planners will be logging on to the Internet, rather than opening the filing cabinet full of brochures and venue guides. This will lead to considerable timesavings.

Access to destination and venue information via nearly instantaneous technology has already reduced response time dramatically, as elements of the site-selection process that used to take days or even weeks can now be measured in minutes or hours. Sending RFP's (Request for Proposal's) by post to several properties and waiting for responses to be mailed back will be nothing but a dim and distant memory by the end of the first decade of the 21st century. Event planners will be assisted in their site-selection task by the plethora of websites that will continue to be developed, offering searchable meeting facility databases with everything to be found in a traditional sales kit: photographs, menus, floor plans with room dimensions, automated RFP forms that can be sent to multiple facilities with a click, 'hot dates', and, most recently, on-line auctions. Writing in the June 2003 edition of Convene magazine (US), Sara Torrence predicted that over the next few years, venue sites would add new, desirable features:

- Interactive floor plans
- An attachment capability
- Sections that are currently missing from most RFP's, such as goals and objectives and audience profiles
- Not just 'hot dates' but also generally available dates and rates
- Information about hotel security and enabling technologies in properties

She also forecast that advance website bookings of larger meetings are likely to increase. As website selection continues to expand internationally, there would also be a standard format to handle the demand. The MPI 2004 Futurewatch Survey is among those sources predicting this trend. The survey highlighted that growing Internet use was set to continue into 2004. Meeting planners responding to the survey indicated that they expected a 20% increase in use of the Internet to research venues, in addition to an increase of 23% in 2003.

The way to Sustainable Tourism

The annual search for sunshine and seclusion away from the crowds is becoming more difficult. And with the number of international tourist arrivals predicted to more than double from 668 million in 2000 to an astounding 1,561 million by 2020

(WTO) it's going to get a lot tougher. Alongside this constant quest for more interesting and exotic vacations, sits the very real issue of sustainability because – unless current business practices and social attitudes adapt – the environmental and social consequences of continued growth in tourism may be too high a price to pay.

Sustainable development is a complex issue for the tourism and leisure industry, touching much more than environmental issues and conflicts, such as the impact on ecosystems and biodiversity and the generation of large volumes of waste, in themselves challenging enough. It also embraces the moral and human context such as economic and social justice, access to information and democracy in decision making. Though these challenges seem to be ones of intellect and ethics for a small percentage of the world's population, for a much larger and growing number of people, the effects are real and have lasting impacts.

Establishing a united front on sustainable development is not easy. This has not been helped in the past by a lack of business drivers for significant change and a lack of will or vision in some parts of the world. However, key changes are gradually putting sustainability issues higher up company agendas. These include: growing pressures for companies to be accountable for the environmental and social impacts of their activities from stakeholders; as well as the need for governments to establish frameworks that drive sustainable tourism growth to ensure long term sustainability in tourist destinations.

Tourists are also demanding higher quality and more 'experience based' products. Undoubtedly, tourism, leisure and travel bring many benefits. The industry creates jobs, encourages the injection of foreign exchange, provides much-needed rest and recuperation to holiday-makers looking for new experiences and adventures, and helps companies maintain and develop international business relationships.

Counting the Cost

— An average golf course in a tropical country can use as much water as 60,000 rural villagers. It needs 1500 kg of chemical fertilizers, pesticides and herbicides per year (Tourism Concern)

— Spain's 12 million visitors a year leave behind 100,000 tonnes of rubbish (Tourism Concern)

— Of the 109 countries with coral reefs, 90 countries have experienced damage from cruise ship anchors, commercial harvesting for tourism and careless water-sports activities. (Ocean Planet)

If the natural beauty that first attracted visitors is polluted, or coral reefs and mangrove swamps are destroyed along with their ability to form part of the natural coastal protection system, the impact on future business could be severe, leading to the decline of certain destinations and the erosion of business value. Similarly, if privatisation of beaches and the diversion of scarce water supplies to tend golf courses create social unrest in the countries, visitors will not enjoy warm a reception.

For companies in the tourism and leisure business, the sustainability challenge remains part of the success of destinations dependent on a healthy social and ecological environment. The challenge for the tourism and leisure industry therefore is to recognise the impact its operations have on finite natural resources and sensitive human and ecological issues in many parts of the world and balance these with the need to protect its long term return on capital. This calls for a more collaborative approach, particularly with a wider range of stakeholders.

The need for a different way of working, with the emphasis much more on partnership has influenced recent debate, including last year's World Summit on Sustainable Development in South Africa, and The Summit of the International Year of Ecotourism at Quebec. There are already excellent examples in South Africa and Egypt to confirm that a partnership approach can encourage a more sustainable type of development as well as longer-term economic benefits.

South African experience

South Africa enjoys worldwide recognition for its responsible tourism policies that attempt to incorporate the priorities and aspirations of all South African stakeholders. Rob O'Hanlon, Deloitte partner in South Africa believes converting these policies into a working reality calls for careful implementation and South Africa appears to be doing well, with numerous success stories. The Madikwe Game Reserve, for instance, in northern South Africa has conservation, bio-diversity and economic development through sustainable tourism as its main objectives. Twelve years ago, the reserve was nothing more than 75,000 hectares of grazing land. But with the government funding and the largest game translocation program ever undertaken, it has been transformed into one of South Africa's largest reserves.

This would not have been possible without the private sector financing lodge developments or community involvement in all aspects of the planning and decisionmaking processes. Madikwe authorities have already granted 21 concessions for commercial and corporate sector tourist lodges and Madikwe was a highly recommended destination in the 1998 British Airways Tourism for Tomorrow awards. The Government benefits through concessions income, and the community benefits from both the employment created and a community trust fund that receives a contribution from the lodge operators for each visitor to the reserve.

The success of Madikwe and other similar ventures has been the catalyst for the Government's current development strategies for several new major integrated tourist destinations. These ventures endorse and facilitate responsible tourism by acting as one-stop shops for investors. This means all the preliminary work such as environmental impact assessments, identifying the tourism products required, and securing and providing finance for local black empowerment partners is completed before the investment opportunities are marketed.

Flagship of these initiatives is the Greater St Lucia Wetlands Park, a recently declared world heritage site spanning 280,000 hectares along 280km of the South African East coast. Deloitte is proud of its involvement with the new government agency established to administer the park. This has exclusive responsibility for all zoning and related planning activities, followed by the granting of concessions on a tender basis. The initiative has attracted scores of potential foreign investors, and is set to create over 1,200 direct and sustainable jobs.

Rise of Red Sea tourism

The managed development of tourism in the southern Sinai peninsular in Egypt is another example of a successful working partnership between the public and private sectors. This is an area with a sensitive ecology that includes spectacular coral reefs, mangroves, wetland and desert. These natural attributes, combined with the cultural attractions and affordability of resorts continue to attract international tourism. Hotel capacity in the region has increased from 1,000 beds in 1989 to 52,000 in 2003. This staggering growth in tourist numbers could have had devastating impacts on the surrounding environment. However through protection and planning, made possible by public and private partnerships, this has been limited and the carrying capacity of the area has been successfully expanded.

The development of the first National Park of Ras Mohamed in 1989 has been followed by the creation of other protection zones, now covering 11,000km2 including interior, coast and marine areas. Through public private partnerships, these areas are, on the whole being effectively managed and protected. The Egyptian Department of Natural Protection, a specialised department in the Egyptian Environmental Affairs Agency (EEAA) works with new investors in the region, ensuring for example, that new developments have minimal environmental impact and that vehicle movements in the deserts are controlled through a network of tracks. The EEAA also has an ambitious programme of training and raising awareness among both the hotel staff and tourists on the fragility of the local environment, ensuring that every stakeholder plays their part in making the programmes successful.

The area is also home to the Bedouin people, many of whom choose to live in traditional nomadic ways in the deserts of northern Africa and the Middle East. The EEAA is careful to include Bedouin representatives into the management decision-making process of protected areas and tourism resort development, recognising that the long-term sustainability and success of these developments is significantly impacted by their attitudes towards them. Consultation has led to rules that tourists should not disturb known Bedouin sites and additionally efforts to ensure that they are not negatively impacted by the environmental conservation activities and reap real benefits from tourism revenue. Such benefits include, the provision of tourist experiences such as horse riding and buggy treks into their desert lands, organised tours of their homes and the sale of traditionally-crafted jewellery and clothes.

The South African and Egyptian partnerships are undoubtedly successful because of the high level of political support and the co-operation of the private sector. Tough legislation is critical as are the taxes paid by the hotels to benefit national park development and maintenance. However, beyond legislative enforcement, there has been a broad consensus on the actions needed amongst those operating in the area, and this consensus has ensured that actions are undertaken and the environment protected. In the Sinai example, the ongoing programme of education is pivotal in the effective protection of the region, and has substantially increased the tourist carrying capacity of the area.

Partnerships between public and private sectors therefore seem to be an excellent basis to help the industry square up to the challenges of sustainable development. But these partnerships won't necessarily be successful if the main players hold unequal reserves of resources, knowledge and power. An imbalance would not allow the objectives of sustainable development to be deeply embedded into actions.

ELECTRONIC EQUIPMENTS IN HOTELS

The hotel should employ any technology it acquires to its full capacity. The reason for this is, that by purchasing it, the hotel is both acknowledging the need for the system, and advising the guests that they are under the protection of the equipment in place. In the event of loss or injury, that might have been prevented if the installed equipment had been working to its full capacity, the hotel-owner has more claim to defend against. Close circuit television can be an effective security tool when installed and used properly.

It should be placed in areas with the greatest likelihood of effective use. Generally remote areas, such as parking lots need coverage, because other eyes and ears are not available for security purposes. Electronic door locks are useful to gain better control over room access problems. Maintaining adequate key control has long been a vexing problem. Mini-safes have become useful because theft from guest-rooms are responsible for the greatest percentage of reported hotel-related crimes.

Maintaining adequate insurance against claims of negligent security is essential both to defend against claims and to pay damages if awarded. Not utilising an investment in security equipment can be as bad or worse than not making the investment at all. The development of a clearly defined procedural manual is the backbone of the security programme. The procedures manual not only directs the security effort, but also serves as evidence that security considerations have been carefully and logically thought out.

Good lighting is an important crime deterrent and prevention tool. In an environment of increasing all-round crime, increased crime in hotel-related matters is not a matter of surprise. Hotels in particular are looked at as targets for local criminals, who see a fertile source of victims carrying cash and valuables. It is common to find criminal elements from adjacent neighbourhoods or those who are even willing to travel relatively long distances for the promise of a good haul from unsuspecting victims. Among the leading causes of hotel-related crime are:

— employee dishonesty;
— failure to recognise and respond;
— inadequate maintenance;
— absence of effective security procedures;
— lack of training;
— ignorance and carelessness;
— purchase of inferior hardware and security apparatus; and
— inadequate supervision.

Certain categories of guests require special security consideration because of behaviour-patterns, special needs, cultural differences or other characteristics that cause security problems to develop. These individuals and groups require special attention to ensure that their stays do not result in preventable losses or injuries to themselves or others. Foreign visitors are often victimised by criminals because they are tricked or misled into placing trust in dangerous individuals or bad advice. Convention guests or large groups are frequently targeted by burglars, prostitutes and con artists because of the ease of penetrating the group and learning about patterns of movement and conduct.

Convention groups should receive special reminders about security hazards, should be encouraged to practise stringent requirements concerning the use of deadbolts, chains and peepholes, and encouraged to cooperate with overall hotel rules and security personnel. Women travelling on business now represent 40 per cent of business travellers. These women often travelling alone, and have in recent years become the victims of especially brutal crimes including assault, rape and murder. Care should be given with room assignments, and every effort should be made to place women on notice of foreseeable risks. Airline flight crews, and particularly female members of these crews, have been identified by criminals as targets because the regular patterns of their stay is so easy to identify. Room thefts and personal assaults are higher than average for these crews.

Student groups, especially those attending proms or other school functions, often lack adequate supervision to ensure that they conform to rules and procedures. Trade shows, especially catering to industries involved in valuables such as jewellery, furs and electronics, attract thieves from all over the world. Group tours, because of their scheduled departures and the practice of leaving luggage and purchase in lobbies, storage rooms and unattended guest-rooms, suffer a high incidence of loss.

Celebrity guests, especially entertainment groups or sports teams, regularly suffer attempts by fans, curious, and persons with criminal intent, to accost them in public spaces, on sidewalks around the hotel, and even in their rooms. Always make reservations ahead of time and secure them with your credit card. Otherwise, if area facilities are overcrowded, you may find yourself stranded in unfamiliar surroundings or in an unsafe room.

If your room is not ready, ask to store your luggage in a locked room. Many hotels have a "dry room" where you can put your luggage and freshen up. If the hotel has more than one building, request a room in or near the main building. Request a room that faces inward towards other rooms or towards the lobby. Request a room that does not have easy access to the window, such as from the roof or street. Request a room on the second floor, but not higher than the seventh floor, near a fire exit, away from stairwells, elevators, ice machines, basements or garbage/refuse rooms. A room near the elevator helps avoid long walks down stairways.

If you have valuables or important documents, e.g., passport or airline ticket, store them in the safety deposit box at the front office and get a receipt. Use a room safe to store only items of moderate value. Large sums of jewellery or money should be placed in the safe at the front desk. If there is no room safe, put valuables in a money belt that you may wear, or bring along a "portable safe". These come in many forms: hollow books, shows with hollow heels, suitcases with hollow compartments, etc. Always use the deadbolt lock when in your room. Always use the chain lock which should be securely fastened to the wall and a solid core door. Windows should open and close easily from the inside. Use the extra lock or stick on windows, sliding or patio doors so that they do not lift out of their tracks.

If someone comes to the door, use the peep hole and ask the visitor to identify himself/herself. Call the front desk to confirm the identity of the visitors, even if they reply they are with room service, janitorial, etc. If you are expecting someone, pre-arrange an exact time of arrival, as well as some form of introduction or identification: a secret knock, business card under the door, or a phone call from the lobby. Completely close the curtains, especially in the evening or if you will be away from the room for sometime.

Public announcements are a means to disseminate information about terrorist threats and other relatively short-term and/or transnational conditions posing significant risks to the security of American travellers. They are made any time there is a perceived threat and usually have Americans as a particular target group. In the past, public announcements have been issued to deal with short-term coups, bomb threats to airlines, violence by terrorists and anniversary dates of specific terrorist events. There are generally, no established and specific 'security' standards within the lodging industry. Each property is unique unto itself—each has different threats and different assets.

A property protection programme should be developed so that the selected countermeasures can be appropriate to protect these unique assets against the unique threats. Access control is that countermeasure designed to limit, monitor, control or otherwise influence the movement of persons and vehicles onto, from, and within a property. Access control is designed to limit access. A locked or otherwise secured door to a storage shed limits access. Ease of access is lessened while not absolutely preventing the unauthorised entry into that building or room. Access control is designed to monitor access. A log-in sheet at a food-storage area monitors the unauthorised entry into that room. The controlling quality access control is designed to control access.

An electronic access code used in conjunction with a touch pad to a restricted area controls the unauthorised entry into that area. Access control is designed to otherwise influence access and the movement of people or vehicles. Perhaps the most obvious example of such successful influencing is the simple use of gender signs on restroom doors. It is obvious then from these and other examples that access control is a relative countermeasure. It is also complementary. That is to say, its effectiveness can be enhanced by its use in concert with other countermeasures and by adjusting the control features with the countermeasure itself.

While locking or otherwise securing the door of a storage shed provides a certain level of protection, the requirement that a roving protection officer intermittently check the building increases the access control protection level. While the requirement that a person entering a restricted food storage area sign in and out, the addition of a time-lapse camera which records such entries obviously makes the access control stronger. The protective features of having an electronic touch pad access to a severely restricted area can be further increased, for instance, by frequent and well-monitored changes to the access code.

The example of the gender signs on restrooms is an excellent illustration of how specific access control techniques can overtly influence those whom we are trying to affect. Access control attempts to limit, monitor, control and otherwise influence the movement onto, from and within a property of pedestrian and vehicular traffic. Many techniques and methods may be utilised successfully in this endeavour. Again, as is the case of all countermeasures, access control is property-specific and the methods and techniques utilised must be similarly individualised. Access control of vehicular traffic begins at the entrance or entrances to the property.

In the case of those properties which are located away from and out of sight of the main thoroughfares, access control sometimes begins off the property. In most instances, with the exception of exclusive resort properties, the entrances to the property are unmonitored. Signs are the most used access control devices at these points. Many properties post signs at the perimeter vehicular access points which enthusiastically welcome guests, and direct vendors. At the same time, these signs discourage unauthorised entrance.

Guests driving onto the property often require directions to the registration area. Clear, readable and attractive signs provide that needed service. Vendors and suppliers, likewise, require direction to their authorised destination. If the hours which property can accommodate vendors and suppliers are restricted or limited, this information, too, will assist in the orderly conduct of business. Speed must be controlled, and the normal method of such control is speed limit signs. Attention should be given to specific areas of greatest concern—pedestrian crossings, playground areas and areas of possible traffic obstruction or danger. Particular attention should be given to the lighting or reflective quality of speed limit signs.

Additional vehicular-control limiting signs include signs which announce traffic direction limitation on turns and signs which announce destination limitations. Motorists should be warned of possible dangers and situations which require their special attention. Sudden turns in the driveway, dangerous cross traffic, heavy equipment or truck traffic and pedestrian crossings are but a few of the examples which should be addressed. Special attractions, times of operation and events are often highlighted by the use of both permanent and temporary signs. Designated parking, especially for employees, is a major access control consideration.

Developing, using and enforcing employee parking has several advantages: it maximises available designated space for guest parking, it allows for better attention to employee personal protection, it reduces the likelihood of employee theft, and it allows for better control and safety of employee vehicles. Speeded bumps, when strategically placed, carefully and prominently announced, are often very effective in controlling speed in designated areas such as long, uninterrupted driveways or pedestrian crossings. Devices designed to allow only one-way designated travel of vehicles are effective but should be used sparingly and carefully. Not only are the diagonally-positioned teeth a hazard in and of themselves, but inadvertent damage to tyres is not uncommon.

Card access devices used most often for selected parking areas are less common in the lodging industry than in others. They are useful, however when circumstances dictate, but their expense should be considered. The most common and useful technique of pedestrian access control is that of alarms and other electronic and mechanical deterrent devices. When such devices are used or considered, appropriate safeguards are essential. The maintenance department should assure appropriate factory mutual approval and proper code compliance. Perimeter and broad area protection devices, while common in many industry groups, are less so in the lodging industry. Some applications exist, however, including the alarming of perimeter gates, usually installed with a central station annunciating capacity.

Application is also not uncommon in protecting pool areas during off-hours. Point of entry devices are more commonly used in protecting window and door access points which cannot be otherwise monitored. Such devices are often hard wired to a central annunciation point and allow response when intrusion is attempted. In other circumstances, simple local alarm devices sound at the point of attempted intrusion. Several versions and approaches are possible depending on the circumstance—glass breakage devices; contact devices; heat sensor and movement devices are examples.

The sophistication and capability of these devices increase consistent with their cost. Restricting exit pedestrian traffic at designated doors is another example of access control and provides an effective and relatively inexpensive way of restricting access to designated doors which cannot otherwise be monitored. Some are simple local alarms which annunciate when unauthorised access is attempted, but this approach is often inappropriate because of the effect which such noise has on guests. Another softer approach, although more expensive, is hard wiring such alarms to a central annunciation point from which appropriate response can be dispatched. Obviously the decision regarding the type and placement of door alarms will be steeped in circumstances.

Surveillance cameras are not an uncommon approach to access control. They can be useful but their use and appropriateness depends on the circumstance for which they were designed. For instance, surveillance cameras are not usually an effective access control tool when immediate response is required. There are several reasons for this limitation in effectiveness. Not only must a constant and alert capability be maintained at the monitoring point, but also situation diagnosis is often difficult to accomplish. Additionally, response capability and time are often inadequate. Better uses of surveillance cameras are in those instances when a recording backup exists and can later be appropriately viewed and diagnosed. Vendor and contractor badging procedures either in conjunction with their sign-in/sign-out requirements or used independently are often appropriate.

Not only do they provide a retainable documentation of visits, they act in and of themselves as a deterrent to unauthorised entry. The decision to utilise employee badges is a major one. As a rule-of-thumb it is encouraged for several reasons. It provides a method for guests to easily identify employees. Badges can be used for time and attendance purposes as well as for identification. If badges are issued on a daily basis, the system provides for a quick check on attendance levels. Different coded or coloured badges are useful for department and/or area access authorisation. Badges provide ease of access control when a discharge or termination situation takes place.

Badges are available in a great variety of designs, materials and uses. Management is well advised to plan carefully prior to selecting a badging system. The issues for consideration include initial and replacement cost, the use for which the proposed system is anticipated, and the appearance of the badge itself. The use of employee entrances can be an effective access control method. It offers several advantages:

— If properly designed and enforced, employee entrances can channel and restrict employees to desired designated areas.
— It can facilitate and strengthen time and attendance procedures.
— It can minimise exposure of employees to hazards.
— It can reduce employee theft.

In guest-room situations, particularly, employees should be encouraged and directed to encounter or report any person who has the appearance and mannerisms of being "out of the ordinary" or whose movements and body language suggest being lost, confused, or "suspicious". Obviously, if such a situation in any way suggests danger, the employee must be trained to call a predetermined person or department. When the employee is comfortable in a direct encounter, such should be encouraged. By reporting to predesignated persons or departments the appearance of persons who appear to be unauthorised, crime can often be deterred. In the event that a person or group is encountered who turns out to be authorised, the mere fact of having encountered them tends to "put them on notice" and the likelihood of subsequent in appropriate behaviour is decreased.

Every professional crime prevention authority agrees on the value of lighting as a deterrent. Studies performed in rural and urban centres, in industrial and residential districts, in virtually any and all settings, showed beyond a reasonable doubt that lighting is a deterrent to crime. This fact is no less true in the lodging industry. Lighting decreases the likelihood of crime in parking lots, hallways and corridors, storage areas, and access points to buildings. The advantages of the presence of lighting are not limited to a protection standpoint or to the deterrence of crime.

— Proper lighting is unquestionably a factor in accident reduction as well.
— Slip-and-fall incidents decrease with proper lighting.
— In the maintenance and engineering areas, accidents decrease with proper lighting.

— Sufficient lighting can have a positive effect on guest safety and satisfaction with guest-rooms.

Given these favourable aspects of lighting, one would think lighting would be an indispensable and widely-used countermeasure in every lodging setting. Perhaps it should be, but very practical problems exist. Lighting is often extremely expensive. Not only can the uncontrolled use of lighting greatly affect the profitability of a property, but the initial installation can be a major undertaking and the maintenance required to insure continuing proper application also can be a burden. Another inherent problem with lighting often presents itself. Managers at the property level usually find themselves faced with a lighting situation over which they had little or no initial input.

The property may have been several years or decades old when the managers began employment. The initial style, type, placement, design, and intensity are conditions with which the manager must deal and over which they have little control. The dual challenges, therefore, of this countermeasure being both costly and difficult to manage sometimes cause the lodging manager to shy away from it as an effective crime-control measure. This propensity to overlook or ignore this very useful countermeasure should be avoided. While the manager may have limited ability to influence the placement, illuminating capabilities and style of lighting on the property, he does have the obligation to address the subject with whatever latitude he possesses.

A written policy regarding lighting should be considered. This policy might describe required maintenance, including preventive maintenance. It should include inspection schedules and an intermittent audit of the documented work order trail from the time a malfunction originally occurred until the problem is expeditiously rectified. The areas of most common concern include:

— the perimeter,

— access points,

— broad open areas,

— parking lots and garages, and

— driveways and commonly-used walkways.

The perimeter of the property, depending again on the particular configuration, should be examined from a lighting standpoint. Diagnostically, the existence and effectiveness of such lighting will be determined during the property survey. However, the effectiveness of the lighting and its proper balance in concert with other appropriate countermeasures such as access control will be developed during the examination and analysis by the protection management committee. Access points, both pedestrian and vehicular, at the perimeter and at the exterior of commonly used buildings should receive appropriate lighting attention.

Crime deterrence is of particular concern in such settings. Often less concentrated lighting is appropriate in broad open areas, but aesthetics and limited places where criminals could easily hide are considerations in these lighting decisions.

Parking areas present classic challenges in so far as guest protection is concerned and lighting is normally required. Again, the decision on lighting should be made only after the diagnostic survey has been completed and the findings can be reviewed in conjunction with other appropriate countermeasures. Commonly used entry ways, the use of appropriate amounts of lighting is important. Crime as well as accidents can be deterred when lighting efforts illuminate such otherwise dark and dangerous areas. Normally the maintenance department conducts or directs the installation, maintenance and adjustment of lighting. Maintenance and adjustment should be accomplished on a scheduled basis and such maintenance should be documented. Work orders for lighting maintenance, like all guest protection-related work order requests, should be addressed in a timely manner.

In many cases preventive maintenance has been found to be both operationally and economically effective. By replacing, for instance, entire banks or section of lights on a carefully timed and scheduled basis, labour cost savings may surpass the replacement cost of the lights even if they have not yet burned out. If protection officers are utilised, lighting inspections should be an expected part of their scheduled or random rounds. Discovery of lighting malfunctions should appear on their patrol log and an appropriate work order submitted. Verification should be made that the work order has been received by maintenance and the work is being accomplished expeditiously.

Employees in any and all departments who, in the course of their work, are in a position to view lighting, should be responsible for reporting instances of lighting malfunctions. This responsibility should obviously include instances of inoperative lighting but it should not end there. Instances of "troublesome" areas (e.g., pockets of darkness) should likewise be reported and the appropriate work order request submitted. Follow-up and verification should be accomplished. Depending on the configuration of the property hallway lighting can be used effectively not only as a crime deterrence measure but additionally as a safety and aesthetic consideration.

Emergency lighting is often covered by regulation or code and compliance with such directives is, of course, an absolute requirement. Beyond or in addition to whatever code requirements exist, emergency lighting considerations should be given to placement, capability, intensity, inspections and repair. The control of keys within the lodging industry is essential. For no reason other than the sheer volume of keys with which a hotel manager must deal, the problem of key control may be seen as overwhelming.

In the face of this perception, however, two facts emerge which should mitigate temptations to ignore or mismanage key control. There are countless hoteliers active today who well remember the common use of the term "pass key". In today's lodging technological environment, such a word seems archaic, but even today, the use of such devices as key-in-knob locking systems and simple interior guest-room door hooks are not unheard of. It is true that a vast number of smaller properties do not have the means to upgrade guest-room locking systems to a level many larger properties accept as a given.

What must be stressed, however, is that regardless of the inherent level of effectiveness of a guest-room locking system, the requirement for key control within that system remains firm. The process of key control, while perhaps not perfectly circular, has no specific beginning and certainly no specific end. It involves a continuous series of actions, controls, requirements, and validations. It involves virtually every department on the property. And finally, it is multi-layered. The lodging industry is well aware that locking and keying technology has grown at a staggering pace over the past few decades. Such advance continues and it is a rare lodging magazine which does not advertise yet another newer and more advanced level of locking and key technology.

Of further significance is the fact that virtually without exception the training in and maintenance of the key control aspect of such systems is a part of the offering. As such, the buyer receives not only a state-of-the-art system, but also instruction and training in its use. Those vast numbers of properties still relying on mechanical systems have no such advantage. It is for the reader associated with those properties, that this chapter is particularly appropriate and specifically aimed. Most hoteliers agree that there are three distinct and identifiable levels of guest-room keys, ranging both in criticality and the need for protection and control. These levels include:

— the emergency key (E key),

— the master key, and

— the guest-room keys.

Each key is vital to the successful operation of the property. Each should be examined and understood in terms of its place on the key hierarchy and each must be afforded specific protection. The emergency key is defined as "that key which can both unlock a double locked door and double lock an unlocked door". Consider that a guest, following advice given him on a guest-room posting, double locks his door by depressing the button located in the center of the inside guest-room doorknob. His belief is that he is virtually as secure within that double-locked room as a guest can become. What he may not realise, however, and what highlights the importance of protection for the emergency (E) key is the fact that anyone with that E key can bypass the double lock and enter that otherwise secure room. There are several approaches to E key protection.

Limiting the number of E keys is, in and of itself, a protective measure. There are properties which limit themselves to one and only one E key. The production of the E key should be under the highest of controlled circumstances. Production authorisation should be limited to a minimum of senior management personnel and such production stringently monitored and documented. Issuance, like production, should be highly controlled and permitted only by the signature of the same limited number of senior management personnel.

Unfortunately, possession of the E key often becomes a status symbol, being in the mind of the holder tangible proof of his elevated and important position and functions. Control and availability of the E key are both vital and inherent in its designed use. The E key must provide access to all locked guest-room doors. Additionally, some properties and indeed some political jurisdictions operate in modes whereby the E key also provides access to all emergency-related doors such as electrical and boiler rooms, elevator access, and fire-alarm panels. While the E key must be maintained in the safest and most secure manner possible, it also must be available for obvious reasons at a moment's notice.

Normally such availability is made to front desk personnel, on a controlled and recorded basis. The E key should be safely stored, ideally in a locked but accessible mode. When use is necessary, a record should be made of the date, time, circumstance of the use as well as the identity of all personnel having access during that emergency. Some properties, even though they maintain an absolute minimum number off keys have found that a second E key securely maintained in the property safe and inventoried on a regular basis provides effective and sufficient back-up. Other than legitimate emergencies, no other use of the E key should be permitted.

There is no known justification for an E key ever being permitted to leave a property. When the issue of guest protection and reasonable care is raised in a civil law suit, there is perhaps no more damning evidence suggesting the absence of such levels than that of' having given insufficient protection to this most vital tool. The master key is defined as "that key which can open all rooms which are not double locked". As shown earlier, a master key is designed to allow access to guest-room doors which have not been double locked, as well as to selected other locked rooms within a given area. There are levels of master keys, depending on the size and configuration of the property.

Grand Masters are designed to open all doors on the property except double-locked guest-room doors. The use of these masters is becoming less and less common because of their vulnerability and the increased use of sub- or section- or building masters. Sub-masters, as the name implies, are subordinate to grand master keys and are designed to access all doors, except guest-room double locked doors in a given area.

Building masters, for instance, may access all such doors within a given building, floor masters may access such doors on a given floor, etc. Like the E key, strict controls and accountability are required for master keys. Whenever possible, masters should be subdivided into sub-masters. The loss or compromise of a sub-master is less serious or expensive to counteract than that of a master key. Assignment and accountability, too, support the division of masters into sub-masters. Sub-mastering and related appropriate issues and control procedures take into account this uneven access reality and allow for area as well as personnel departmental issuance.

Master keys should be accessible from limited sources. Often, they should be accessible, as is the E key, only from the front desk. On some properties masters have been permanently issued to key senior management personnel, such as the executive housekeeper. Even in these cases, however, the overnight or off-duty storage and control of the master is usually best assigned to the front desk. Irrespective of the location chosen for such a control point, the masters should be securely locked in a key cabinet or some other equally secure device and access/accountability carefully maintained. Issuance of the master keys from the central control point should be in conformance with a system carefully designed and constantly monitored.

Periodic review of persons authorised to issue as well as receive such keys is important. And issuance should be on a signature basis, limited to persons specifically identified by senior management. The key return likewise should be authenticated and inventory taken, ideally on a daily basis. The procedure should be in effect to immediately react when the inventory discloses a discrepancy. The documentation which verifies the issuance, return and inventory of master keys should be maintained and stored for an appropriate period of time. Coding is often successfully employed by hotels in their master key control system. For example, by using a colour code tag system, one colour may indicate departmental sub-masters and another colour might indicate floor or building or section sub-masters.

Such a tagging system aids in inventory control, issuance, and storage. The guest-room key is defined as "the key designed to open a specific guest-room which is not double locked". Like the E key and the master keys, centralised control of the guest-room keys is normally maintained at a central location, usually the front desk. A key "par" should be established and the number of keys below par should trigger appropriate re-coring, re-keying, hardware rotation and/or production of replacement keys. The number of keys which constitute "par" is a matter of individual management decision but the adage that less is usually better is certainly apropos.

Markings or fobs or engravings on the guest-room key should not identify the property. Room identification is best handled by eliminating the room identification from the key and supplying the key to the guest in a packet, card, or envelope on which is written the room number. Storage of the guest-room keys at the front desk should be in a secured drawer or cabinet, out of the view and access of everyone other than authorised personnel. The front desk, housekeeping and maintenance are the three departments most involved in the key control process.

The "beginning" of the circular route is the front desk. This department, generally speaking, is the focal point of the circular path which the guest-room keys will take throughout the property. Training of the front desk staff in the key control policies and procedures is essential if success is to be realised. This training should be a continuing process. Inventory of guest-room keys should be a matter of course and on a regular and scheduled basis, at least once daily. The ideal time for such inventory is often immediately after check-out time and appropriate inventory forms should be completed promptly.

Housekeeping, then should be placed into the inventory loop so that keys recovered by that department are considered. If re-keying, recording or rotation is appropriate, the affected guest-rooms absolutely should be placed out of service by management until this is accomplished. Guest-room keys are to be issued to registered guests only, normally at the time of registration. A method of recording the number of keys issued should be adopted and additional authorised issuance, should also be noted so that reconciliation can be made upon check-out. Both positive identification and authority must be obtained prior to issuing additional keys.

Additionally, guest-room numbers should never be audibly announced by the issuing front desk clerk. If the departing guest indicates his key or keys have been left at the guest-room, he should be assured that is perfectly acceptable and that housekeeping will retrieve the key during cleaning. On the other hand, often the guest has his key in his pocket and a simple courteous comment will serve as a reminder. When the front desk is alerted that a situation has occurred which might impact from a protection standpoint on the key control process, corrective action is called for immediately. Such procedures would be a part of the overall key control procedure and a continuing part of the training. Front desk responsibility normally extends beyond guest-room key control into both master key and E key control.

Both these types of keys should he inventoried on a regular basis, at least once daily. The ideal time for this inventory is often late afternoon when most of the master and sub-master keys have been returned to inventory. This recurring inventory, like the guest-room key inventory, should be appropriately recorded on an inventory form and properly stored according to established policy. The housekeeping staff normally is the next department to become involved in the key control process. During the daily process of cleaning guest-rooms, room attendants will normally retrieve several keys which have been left, inadvertently or by design, by departing guests. Ideally a locked box securely attached to the housekeeping cart should be utilised to store these retrieved keys until delivery at the end of the shift.

A responsible person should be assigned to transport all retrieved keys shortly after the end of the shift, back to the front desk so that they can be entered into the inventory. Strict rules prohibiting the access of anyone to locked guest-room doors should be established and rigidly enforced. Room attendants should be instructed that requests from anyone to enter a locked guest-room door should be referred to the front desk or to senior management. Master keys should be secured on the room attendant's person at all times. Chains which allow both such security and required access are usually successful. The maintenance department could be labelled as that point on the "circular" key-control route where all things begin. While from the guest's standpoint the front desk is where the process begins, in actuality, it is in the maintenance department that the process has its roots.

This is normally where the initial production occurs with the cutting of guest-room keys from the stored key blanks. This awesome responsibility, the ability to duplicate virtually any guest-room key at any moment, causes special attention to be focused on the maintenance department. Key-cutting machinery should be well stored, controlled, and access limited. This machinery should be stored in a secure area, either in a room to which access can be rigidly controlled or if this is not feasible, then sub-compartmentalised in a secured cabinet.

Access to the controlled room or the secure storage location should be by designated persons only. Key blanks should be controlled by a designated level of management—often the chief engineer or maintenance department manager. Storing these blanks and securing them independently from the key-cutting device and limiting access to them by designated management personnel allows for an effective audit method for security purposes. A running inventory of these blanks provides for assurance of control.

Normally guest-room key duplication requests come exclusively from the front desk and are printed in multiples allowing copies to be maintained at specific locations along the production and issuance path. The procedure as well as the format of the key request should provide and insure control at all locations along the circular route. The request form should indicate the reason for the request. Master and sub-master key reproduction requires special controls. Obviously a misplaced master or sub-master requires immediate attention, not only to replace the key but more importantly to re-key effected doors to which the misplaced master allowed access.

Authority for such duplication and the adherence to quick and reliable re-keying should be vested in a predetermined level of management. Adherence to the required rapid re-keying in this situation is essential and should be audited on a frequent basis. When a bellperson escorts a guest to his room, he should be certain that the guest-room key is functioning properly and that the guest understands how the key operates. If a bellperson assists a guest during check-out, the bellperson would remind the guest that the key is to be returned and that he can assist if that is desired. The retrieved key is then obviously returned to the front desk. Issuance of keys to the bell and valet staff should normally be controlled at the front desk. Van and courtesy drivers should remind departing guests of the necessity of returning keys and offer to accept from them any guest-room key which might have been forgotten. A locked box, not unlike that suggested for the room attendant's cart, is useful on vans and courtesy vehicles.

All employees, irrespective of position or department, should be trained in the importance of key control. They should be aware of key control discrepancies and proper response. Such events might include such circumstances as discovering misplaced keys or becoming aware of inappropriate issuance or "borrowing" of keys. Some properties employ a guest-room key deposit system. In such an approach, a nominal deposit is collected or announced during the registration process and then returned or eliminated from the billing process when the key is returned. There are at least two distinct advantages to this process:

— a reminder to the guest to return his key as well as an incentive to do so, and
— the system also provides a money stream to offset the cost of key replacement.

The principal disadvantage is the danger of poor guest relations. There is little doubt that this danger exists—guests often feel "put upon" when a deposit is required, feeling either that they are being mistrusted or that the property is taking unacceptable advantage of them. It is important, therefore, if a key deposit system is employed, that the front desk personnel be careful and thoroughly trained and scripted in the way the system is to be presented and carried out. At check-out time, a soft approach should be used—courteously accepting the guest's explanation, for instance, that he "left his key in the room". Obviously, if a key deposit system is employed, it must be universally applied. Intermittent use, for example, when a "suspicious" guest is being processed is unacceptable.

Finally, managers must understand that a key deposit system in no way is meant to replace a comprehensive and effective guest-room key control system. The security manager's first task is to assess the hotel's assets, determine which of these assets are vulnerable to theft, and then devise a programme that will reduce the risk. One helpful tool is to instruct the human resources department, while conducting employee exit interviews, to ask questions regarding employee theft, use of drugs, and so on. This technique usually will assist you with information to narrow down areas needing further investigation. The usual approach is to conduct a risk analysis of the property and its assets. This entails identifying the risk of loss and determining what measures may be employed to reduce or eliminate that risk. In addition to the actual physical survey, the security manager should review all reports of loss for the previous year to assess where and possibly how items were stolen. This approach will help identify the most vulnerable areas of the hotel.

Continue to conduct this survey as often as possible. This is done annually in most hotels; however, conducting a quarterly or even monthly survey would lead to the best results. The key to protecting assets is to obtain cooperation and assistance from all hotel employees. Security managers who think they can do the job by themselves are making a dreadful mistake. Security is everyone's job. In fact, this slogan should be emphasised during an employee's initial orientation programme as well as in monthly departmental meetings. Successful prevention measures depend on a well-designed programme that involves input from all employees.

The security manager can work with employees in a variety of ways. First, he or she should educate employees about the seriousness of theft and how it affects them.

Second, she or he should attempt to develop employees' understanding of the problem in terms that they as members of the organisation can relate to and appreciate. For example, if it is made clear that all losses cut into the profitability of the property and that reduced profits, if severe enough, may result in lower wages or even laying off employees, the employees may realise that they too have a financial stake in the prevention of losses.

Third, assistance from employees may be elicited by encouraging them to call and report suspicious people or circumstances and at least make an extra effort to secure valuables when leaving a work area (for example, securing tools in storage rooms).

Fourth, it is essential that the security department maintain a good working relationship with all employees, avoiding morale problems created by poor communications and a lack of understanding. Employees suffering from poor morale are not going to be very concerned about protecting the assets of the employer.

Finally, the security manager must work with all other department managers to get their input on solutions to the problem of losses. Some security personnel may think that the solution to the loss problem is locking up and limiting access to the hotel's assets, but if a measure interferes with the normal operation of a hotel, it will be resisted and is a guaranteed failure.

In fact, the security function will be viewed as less effective unless the solution recommended includes input from the departments affected by it. Programme design is only half of the crime prevention task. The other half, which is equally important, is continuous improvement. The security manager should repeat the risk survey at least quarterly, if possible, to ensure compliance with the programme, and to discover any changes in the physical structure or the hotel operation that may negate the original plan. The programme must always remain flexible to meet the needs of the business. New and better methods should always be sought for improved preventive measures. When losses do occur, as they will, evaluate the loss and adjust the programme accordingly.

One reason why hotel managers are concerned about the theft of guest property is the potential impact on future business. Legal issues, most states have limited an innkeeper's liability to a fixed amount and generally that amount is not very high. A history of serious guest losses may, however, drastically affect the hotel's reputation and may also be indicative of other weaknesses in the security programme which could lead to more serious crimes. Investigation of such losses should include, first, an examination of the locking hardware on the room to ensure that it is working properly. This could be a problem because guests frequently may not close their door tightly when leaving or when running down the hall for ice or soda. Second, determine which employees have access to the room under investigation and note them for further follow-up.

If good records are kept, after a short while the same employee's name will begin to appear regularly. Once that is discovered, the investigation could focus more on that individual. Third, find out when the locks were last changed or rekeyed. There may be an overall problem with key control. Finally, check for missing room or master keys that anyone could use to gain access to guest rooms. Prevention of guest room theft depends primarily on employee and guest cooperation. Employee cooperation and assistance were discussed above and apply to guest losses as well.

Guest cooperation is more difficult to obtain because of guests' transient nature, but can be achieved to a reasonable extent. The type of cooperation sought is generally limited to two areas: use of existing risk-reducing equipment such as safe deposit boxes and in-room safes, and making sure guests close and properly lock their room doors either when they leave or go to sleep. Some hotels put small signs or fliers in guest rooms advertising the availability of safe deposit boxes and in-room safes, as well as directions on how to properly secure the door. Other hotels use the cable system on the room television to promote safety and security measures. An employee's personal property, uniforms, and hotel equipment are subject to theft in locker rooms and work areas.

Although the theft of such property is not generally seen as a liability problem, it should be of concern from the standpoint of employee morale. It is a well-known fact that poor employee morale will reduce productivity and will fail to promote the kind of cooperation needed by the security department to prevent other losses. The theft of any employee valuable should be treated with the same level of concern and priority as any other loss. The two most common areas for losses to occur are locker rooms and office areas. In locker rooms, the lockers must be equipped with adequate locks and a sound key control system. Security also should check locker rooms frequently during their patrols.

This should be done randomly whenever security personnel are in the immediate area or intentionally as part of the routine patrol. When time permits, each locker should be checked to ensure it is secured, in addition to seeing that it has regular maintenance and bringing problems of abuse to the security manager's attention. Such inspections also reveal health problems (e.g., pest control) and problems such as stockpiling of uniforms or other hotel equipment. Consistent with this approach is the need for a hotel policy on what may be kept in employees' lockers and the hotel's right to search them periodically (a two-person integrity search is recommended). In office areas, the most frequent loss occurs when employees leave their handbags, wallets, backpacks, briefcases, or gym bags unattended in unlocked desk drawers or on top of desks.

The security manager needs to be sure that desks can be locked, and encourage employees to use those locks to protect their personal property. Another common practice is for employees to leave an office door wide open to give a false impression that they are still working, when in fact they have left for the day. Yet in doing this, they may leave their personal effects in plain view for anyone to take easily. Anytime someone is injured in the hotel or property is lost, security should conduct some form of an investigation. There are at least three advantages of a thorough investigation. First, the root cause of the problem hopefully will be discovered. If, for example, a guest became injured as a result of falling down a stairway, it is important to investigate the root cause of the fall. In such a case, the fall could b e caused by torn or worn carpeting, poor lighting, lack of handrails, wet or slippery surfaces, or some factor inherent to the guest.

Some possible reasons for the guest to fall include intoxication, improper footwear, bifocals, or other mobility problems. The same issues are present when an employee is injured on the job. The second reason for a thorough investigation is prevention. By analysing the cause of a theft, for example, security can determine how the article was stolen and then develop preventive measures to avoid similar losses in the future. The theft of food from kitchen storage areas is common to hotels and restaurants of all sizes. If investigation of this indicates that methods of inventory control are deficient, recommendations can be generated to implement better control and reduce further losses. The security manager who analyses all incidents and implements proactive procedures will prevent incidents of theft.

However, employees are constantly developing new methods to steal which, when discovered, should be used as learning tools for security. New methods of theft are usually brought into a facility by a new employee who introduces that method to other employees. The third benefit gained from an investigation also is related to future loss prevention. In a case of stolen property or drug dealing, for example, the simple process of questioning witnesses and suspects will create a deterrent to future crime. Routinely interviewing potential suspects will help establish an atmosphere of non-tolerance for crime.

Employees who may be guilty of wrongdoing, or who may have considered it, hopefully will be deterred from future activity if the impression is given that the hotel management will not tolerate misconduct. A timely and thorough investigation of every incident, requiring more than just an initial incident report, will enhance the department's image and will help develop an effective security programme. Chasing suspects, making arrests, and testifying in court are also job responsibilities of a hotel's security staff.

For many hotels, though, these activities often are ones of last resort when attempting to address the problem of crime and its associated losses. Although arrests may not be the preferred option of many hotels, they may be necessary and will occur in even the safest properties. Security managers, therefore, need to be prepared to deal with the problems generated by making arrests and prosecuting offenders. If the hotel security staff will use special police powers or licences, it is essential that they receive at least minimal training in arrest, use of force, and civil and criminal law—including the limits of their authority, use of weapons, and the rights of the accused. In addition to training, security personnel need directions in the form of written policies and procedures.

7

Allied Hospitality Provisions

More than ever hotels are looking for creative approaches to extend budgets and multi-task investments when it comes to guest service. Now with the introduction of new in-room refreshment design strategies like upgradeable and combination minibars, hotels have alternatives that to extend their budget and build brand loyalty. Traditionally, hotels have been limited to a few choices for in-room refreshment. It was pretty simple – minibar or refrigerator, manual or automatic. These decisions were often driven by budget as much as customer requirements.

Directions for Minibar Design

Today two new design strategies are allowing hotels to extend their in-room refreshment dollar. These alternatives allow hotels to pack more functionality – current and future – into their investments and serve the guest better as well:

— *Upgradeable minibars* – provide the economy of manual operations with the option to upgrade to fully automatic.

— *Combination minibar and guest refrigerator* – offer high-profit functionality of automatic minibar on one side and the convenience of a refrigerator on the other side.

Upgradeable Minibar Options

Typically, when a hotel determined that it required the control and efficiency of an automated minibar, the hotel would have to do a complete minibar system replacement. Each manual minibar would be removed and replaced by an automated bar. Costs included new hardware, new software, and installation. However, if you can anticipate a future move to automated, it is easy to install a manual system that is pre-wired for an upgrade to fully automatic. Hotel operators eliminate the cost of the new automated hardware or cabinetry and save on implementation. Following are the benefits of upgradeable system:

— Flexibility to transition to fully automatic minibar in the future

— Keeping the door open for automatic on a manual minibar budget

— Apply your manual or semi-automatic hardware investment to automatic in the future

— Use the same minibar unit or cabinetry for automatic

With this option, a minibar is pre-wired for easy transition in the future to automatic operations. A manual or semiautomatic minibar can be converted to a fully automatic system when its internal shelves are swapped out for sensor-equipped shelves and Bartech's server and software are installed. Designed for hotels that want the flexibility to have automatic minibars in the future but do not have the funds available today, the upgradeable option provides a cost effective solution.

Combination Minibar and Guest Refrigerator

The Combination Minibar offers one solution for two guest needs — a combination fully automatic minibar on one side and guest refrigerator on the other side. This patent-pending design provides added convenience for all guest types and added value for traveling families. Its functionality enables hotels to be more flexible in marketing to business travelers that may add a vacation weekend stay onto a business trip or have their family join them. The guest refrigerator is a necessary amenity for hotels and extended stay properties that market to family or combination business/leisure travelers. Followig are the benefits of a minibar-refrigerator combination:

— Opportunity to sell profitable in-room refreshments with automatic control and efficiency

— Convenience for hotel guests to store personal food and beverage items

— No need to swap out minibar with small refrigerator when season/guest profile changes

— Value-added amenity to travelers combining business and leisure

— Required in room amenity for traveling families requiring refrigeration

The combination unit provides flexibility and economy for the hotel and much needed convenience for the guest. Minibars are evolving with the changing nature of travelers and their needs. The industry is developing new minibar designs that fit the changing requirements of cross-profile guests, the uncertainty of dynamic hotel budgets, and the overall need to increase efficiency and grow profitability.

Design Factors for Minibar Selection

Following are the five top design factors for ninibar selection:

What is my guest profile and what do they expect?

Know your guest and what they are looking for.... Business or leisure; male or female; single or family traveler? All of these factors can help determine what type of system you need and how you should stock it. For example, recent studies indicate that an in room refreshment center is a strong requirement for female business travelers. They like the security and convenience of not having to leave their room if they are working late. Also, a business traveler minibar will be stocked with different items than say a family resort – alcohol, power bars, and mixers compared to juices, cereals, and sodas.

Does my guest profile change or do we have a cross-profile (one that changes within the stay)?

More and more, guest are combining business trips with leisure add on trips – staying the weekend or having the family join them after a business trip. So if your property has this type of changing guest profile or "cross-profile" you need to accommodate for that in your minibar. For example, in these cases you will want to see how different dry section configurations can provide help maximize additional merchandising opportunity by promoting leisure items such as disposable camera or suntan lotion. Also, a cross-profile is a good fit for a combination minibar and guest refrigerator. For this profile, you may have a parent traveling on business who is later joined by the rest of the family. The combination bar provides a convenient place of unfinished drinks, milk, and other family necessities.

What is my budget?

A traditional manual minibar is in the $200/unit range, semi-automatic at $300, and fully automatic in the $800-900 range. If you do not have the budget for an automatic today, consider an upgradeable manual or semi-automatic for just $100-200 more. This investment in future transition to automatic will leverage your hardware investment and extend the minibar lifecycle.

What are my style and dimension requirements?

It is important to define how you want to present the minibar in your guest room. You have many options – stand alone, inside a cabinet or armoire; clear glass front, customized promo front, high-tech brushed steel door or traditional wood front; right or left opening, dual door. It is important to understand all the options you have to customize your unit together with the restrictions of your room. Finally, you can have your minibar custom designed in terms of size, cabinetry, and functionality.

How do I want to streamline processes?

In selecting a minibar solution, you need to understand the potential impact to your minibar and front desk operations of the new system. How will rebates be handled – manually or automatically posting? (Some automatic systems can apply rebates automatically to the guest folio, without manual intervention.) Will refill report be printed on hard copy or accessed via a PDA? How many minibar attendants are recommend to service the new system? (An automatic system free up labor up to 75%, since an attendant can service 400 rooms per day compared to 100 per attendant with a manual system.)

Some hotels enjoy the revenue these special events provide to their properties with little or no concerns about disruption in operations. Others dread the thought of large groups of young people gathering in their lobby without any regard for the damage a can of silly string can do to a chandelier. Many hotel and motel managers are not aware of the laws that govern minor guests while on, in or about your property. The likelihood of loud disturbing noise, drug use and underage drinking should be on your high priority list. There are steps you can take to meet the needs of your underage guests while protecting your employees, other guests and your property.

Must you accept minor guests in your property? Generally speaking, the answer is yes. Innkeepers have a general duty to admit all persons who seek accommodations, unless the innkeeper has "just cause" to refuse accommodations. Just cause may include lack of available guestrooms, failure of the guest to pay for the charges and a reasonable belief that the guest may harm employees, other guests or your property. Failure to allow a minor as a registered guest in your property may be grounds for an unfair discrimination charge against the innkeeper. Since state and local laws differ, it is prudent for you to confirm your legal rights and obligations in your particular area with a qualified and competent attorney.

You can, however, implement clear and reasonable rules and regulations as preconditions to accepting minors in your hotel. You must be consistent with your implementation and enforcement of these rules and you cannot discriminate. Below is a checklist to review with your staff to make sure you are ready to receive these memory-seeking guests.

— As soon as possible, contact all the local junior high schools, high schools and colleges to learn about all upcoming dates for spring formal dances, proms, graduation, sorority and fraternity parties.

— If you are fairly new to your property, find out all you can about the history of these types of events occurring at your property and surrounding hotels and motels. Does your property have a reputation that you would like to change? Perhaps tighter rules are in order or consistent compliance efforts are needed. Review the areas that need improvement and address the situation before your underage guests arrive.

— Train your front desk in the proper procedures for admitting minor guests. Ask for photo identification. If the identification looks suspicious, ask for secondary identification. The Internet makes it very easy to obtain fraudulent identification cards.

— All states prohibit underage drinking. An innkeeper can lose his/her liquor license and may be subject to liability for accidents that occur as a result of guests driving while intoxicated. Do not allow front desk personnel to give honor bar keys to underage guests. If your honor bars are not key controlled but are accessed through an easily breakable plastic ring, have all alcohol removed from the honor bar when minor guests rent the room. In addition, make sure alcohol is not delivered to guestrooms used exclusively by minor guests either through room service or as part of a frequent guest amenity program.

— Anticipate the needs of small and large groups. Make it clear that guestrooms cannot sleep more than four people (if that is your policy depending on guestroom dimensions). Make sure you comply with your local fire codes on the number of occupants in the guestrooms at one time. Offer a hospitality suite or other meeting room space to minor guests late in the evening to lessen the chances of disturbing other guests.

— Add additional security measures on the evenings when your hotel hosts these types of events. For every group of fifty attendees, you might want to consider requiring the group to provide a security officer at their own expense. In addition, you may want to provide favorable room rates to parents in order to encourage the parents to stay the evening and chaperone the event. You may also want to provide, at your expense, additional security officers to walk the premises, including the parking lots, during these events. Make it known to all minors checking in to your property that security has been increased for their protection. Make sure security is visible to the minor guests and that they know they will be observed. Providing notice in advance of what is unacceptable conduct or behavior on your property, coupled with a visible security team, will confirm to your minor guests that you mean business and intend to uphold the law.

— As an innkeeper you need to protect yourself from the risks imposed by a minor's legal status since a minor may revoke a contract and refuse to pay for room charges. Request that payment be made in advance either with cash or a valid credit card. Verify authorization of the credit cards used by minor guests. Verify ownership of the card and the right of the minor child to use the credit card.

— Remind minor guests that disturbing noise, illegal drugs and underage drinking will not be permitted anywhere on the hotel property. As for intolerable noise levels, your rules may provide for an initial warning prior to any unregistered guests being escorted off property. Subsequent warnings will be grounds for the removal of the registered guests without a refund of the advance payment for room charges.

— Upon check in, a minor guest should be asked to provide parental contact information in the event the rules and regulations are not complied with during their stay and a call to the parents becomes necessary. Alternatively, you may request that the parent register the minor child or children so that the parents become aware of the rules and accept all responsibility for damage or injury during their children's stay.

— Your rules may require that minor guests be required to sign a form upon check in acknowledging that they are familiar with the house rules and regulations and agree to comply with them during their stay. When you must take appropriate action to remove the guest, having a minor guest's signature on this type of form will help defeat the guest's claim that they didn't know the rules.

— Training your employees on these rules and regulations is also essential. Each and every employee needs to know the rules to ensure consistent enforcement throughout your property.

— If you remove a minor guest from your property for failure to comply with the rules and regulations, you must exercise reasonable care. Depending on the specific circumstances, you may want to consider calling the parents or the police. Treat the guest as you would any other guest. For your guests protection and yours, don't let a guest who is noticeably intoxicated or under the influence of drugs to get behind the wheel of an automobile.

Providing a safe, memorable evening for a young adult can create long term customer loyalty and possibly result in future revenues for other life changing events such as weddings, anniversaries, and the like. Make sure the rules you create are enforced consistently, provided uniformly and are non-discriminatory.

Technology in Hospitality - Clash and Collaboration

Technologists and Hoteliers have very different personalities, yet both are critical to successful hotel technology decisions. Members of any IT department, from programmers to engineers, tend to be significantly different from the rest of their organization. Their strong technical skills, focus on logic, reason and order, as well as their discomfort with social interactions, places them at odds with the business world.

Yet the general business world, where the approach is more fluid and subjective, is not as adept at solving complex technical problems. Nowhere are these differences more apparent than the in hospitality industry, where virtually all of the employees are "people people". People who excel in hospitality possess very strong social skills and a perspective that perception is reality, "satisfaction" is subject to various opinions, and they don't necessarily follow an orderly set of rules.

Bridging this gap is often left to one of two groups: those who provide IT products and services to hospitality organizations, and more technically adept staff who are often "on the fringes" of guest relationships, such as those in finance and engineering. As the importance of technology increases, an inevitable conflict arises between hospitality organizations and the people responsible for technology. This has consequences that range from more costly, less optimal solutions - to true disasters with large financial ramifications.

There are techniques of increasing the success of this team effort, beyond simply recognizing the two very different worlds in which each "side" lives. The answers lie not in increasing the separation between these two groups, but by bringing them together in greater collaboration and by having each contribute their own expertise and knowledge. In particular, each work effort must be looked at closely, step by step, to determine which steps are "business related" and which are "technology related". One mistake to be avoided at all costs is excluding technologists from the early part of a project/effort with a significant technology component, on the belief that the technology component does not play a key role until the solution phase.

Technologists must be included in the problem identification or strategic planning phase. The following is a breakdown of the steps in most projects or improvement efforts which include significant technology components. The beginning of any project or improvement effort is planning. This includes deciding broadly what is to be done, establishing measurements and goals, and budgeting time and money. Businesspeople are the main contributors to this phase, with technologists perhaps weighing in on potential costs and their own involvement.

The next step is selecting a potential set of solutions. This may require more detailed analysis and information gathering around the problem, or it may simply need a detailed description of the problem, goals and measurements and a list of those who have solutions readily available. This step is likely to be split between businesspeople and technologists. Businesspeople will contribute much of the problem detail and desired solution, as well as their knowledge of those who may have the answers.

Technologists will contribute information about technologies or solution providers who may be helpful, but from a broader and "new technology" point of view. At this point a "tried and true" solution may be most effective or a "new way of doing things" may be best, it's impossible to tell and all potential answers should be explored in the next phase.

The third step is gathering detailed information about the potential solutions and their providers. Once again, this is a joint effort, with a high degree of collaboration between businesspeople and technologists. It involves providing a problem definition and receiving proposed solutions (often a proposal) along with details about cost, timing and approach. The temptation at this step is to have one group or the other act for both. Problems arise when there is no technologist available to the organization or when the technologist is handed the entire problem by the businesspeople, told what "needs to be done", and left to find the solution. Either is guaranteed to lead to a less-than-perfect outcome and in some cases, a disaster.

Technologists making business decisions with little input from those using the technology can lead to solutions which are great from a "latest and greatest" perspective, but are impractical or less than ideal solutions to the true business problems. Conversely, in a situation where the only technology expertise is provided by the product seller or another customer, there is a high risk of getting incomplete, or even misleading, information.

The fourth step is analyzing the proposed solutions, asking for refinements, more detailed proposals where required, and selecting the solution provider. In addition, all the terms and conditions, additional costs and guarantees and commitments should be spelled out by each potential supplier. Once again, a joint effort, with each group providing an analysis of the solution's desirability from their areas of expertise is ideal. As in the prior step, the temptation here can be to say "Mary can do this by herself now", with an equally high chance of a disappointing outcome.

Once a solution is selected and contracted for, the final step is implementation of the project or product. And once again, there is a temptation to draw lines between technology and business and assign each step in the implementation to one group or the other. Big mistake. This does not mean that businesspeople need to know how to configure a server for the new application, but that the businesspeople must play a key role in defining the security on that server and have a basic understanding of what it does. This is particularly key if the technologist is not on staff full-time, because bringing that person back in for each problem or question may not be possible, let alone cost effective. Similarly, delegating technical decisions and actions to businesspeople and the seller can result in decisions that are not in the buyer's best interests.

As a group of business-minded technologists, we are surprised by how often businesspeople in a hospitality organization are called upon to single-handedly solve problems that require technological expertise and perspective. Statements like "The GM has been working with that PMS software for 10 years, she really knows her way around it" or "Our controller is a whiz at computer backups" only serve to highlight the shaky technology foundation on which so many operations are built. And just as you didn't ask the GM to ensure that the structural foundation was properly cured and the roof shingles affixed to withstand a strong wind, don't ask him to ensure that your guest data is being adequately managed without some assistance. Even if he is a whiz at computers.

WHAT VALUE QUALITY?

Most Hospitality Operators use the term "Quality" somewhere in their advertising and promotion. What exactly does that mean? One would compile multiple responses, as Management tried to define "Quality". The same would be said for their Staff, and, just as importantly, the Guest. We all have different perspectives. Hospitality invites a Quality Experience, but, if expectations are not met, you have a disappointed Guest, reduced Revenue, unhappy employees and a deteriorating reputation. So, what is the Value of Quality: the Concept, the Experience and Reward, and how does this relate to your Hospitality Business?

The Basics

Quality is a Process: There are Performance Standards created, communicated and implemented. The Standards are reviewed constantly to stress Continual Improvement. Success Stories are heralded. Problem Areas are immediately addressed. Steady "feed back" is required. This is not a one day exercise. Quality must become integral to your Business Performance.

The Bottom Line: Does your definition of Quality translate to the Guest's expectations? Hospitality Operations are boldly diverse. We present to the Consumer various locations, architecture, ambiance, price, amenity, and activity. When they make a reservation – book a room, a table, or a ticket – the Guest has an Expectation.

The Assignment: How do we create a "common ground" to meet these expectations and avoid the false steps in fully serving our Guest? The Quality Process begins with recognized, reasonable Hospitality Performance Standards. ALL parties understand cleanliness. The environment you represent must be clean and not assault the five senses. These Performance Standards are the foundation, and the Guest needs to know you are serious and sincere. Particularly for those Destinations which are Family oriented, recognize that the greatest influence on where the Family will stay, dine and recreate is the Mother, and she holds Quality Standards dearly.

The Report Card: The success of a Process needs to be measured – a Performance Evaluation. Where do you rate with these Hospitality Standards? Do you deliver, and, just as importantly, does your Staff? Your Quality message must be communicated daily. Your Staff must abide by your Message. Clear guidelines, need to be in place, practiced and assessed. Attention to detail and meeting the Guest's needs are the Mantra. There are many means to evaluate your Performance: the personal relationship you have with your Guests; in-house mechanisms, like Comment Cards; Mystery Shop Services; Assessment Companies; and formal Guest Satisfaction Systems. They are all meaningful.

Managing partnerships – the good and the bad...

Unfortunately, most business partnerships don't work...but a lot of the problems can be avoided with planning and discussion. Here's a complete checklist to help you avoid the pitfalls. Partnerships are often seen as an easy or convenient way to overcome a lack of capital or skills – you have cash but don't know the business. The degree of intimacy and personal involvement can be surprising and challenging for many new business partners, who may wake up the next morning wondering who in fact they have 'married'! Below is a list of personal, legal and financial issues that should be considered.

Give everyone a copy of the list, then go through them one by one...together! Working with friends and family – issues in working with wives, husbands, lovers, sons, daughters, brothers and sisters.

— Are family members really the best person for the job, or are you just giving them a shortcut? Eg does your partner think her son is the best person to be head chef, and using what criteria was this decided? In many hospitality businesses, family members are understandably the only ones trusted with cash.

— Do family members have any extra privileges when they work in the business eg meals or avoidance of the worst shifts? Whatever you say, staff will see them as 'special' and may resent extra privileges or slack they are given. There are many professional people who will not work for a small family business because of the compromises and frustrations involved.

— Some business partnerships specify that spouses/partners or children of the business owners cannot work in the business. Is that appropriate for your business?

— Privacy and time apart from your family is an issue – husband and wife who have worked in different jobs suddenly share a business and may end up at each others throat when they have to spend 24/7 with each other. Teens and their parents may have had quite enough of each other at home without another shift together at work.

MONEY IN – RAISING THE CAPITAL

— Is there a requirement for partners to contribute extra capital at any time?

— In what proportion will capital be contributed and relate to their share of the business?

— If a loan from a partner or a related friend or family member is contemplated, what will be the terms of the loan? Normal bank interest or a special rate?

Money out – sharing the profits and repaying loans

— In what proportion will profits and losses (including capital and losses) be shared.

— Can partners draw money as an advance on profits?

— If work is not performed of equal hours, how will this be 'balanced' so both parties feel there has been a fair exchange?

— If a partner leaves, how and when are they paid out

Managing the partnership – who's the boss?

— There can only be one person in charge – who will it be? Often partnerships are formed by two or more people who are used to having their own way – watch out for problems!

— Will majority decisions of partners cover all decisions, and if there are only two equal partners, is there a way that deadlocks can be overcome?

— If there is real estate involved, how will it be held - by the partners or in trust for the partners or will a lease be granted to the partners?

— What cheque signing arrangements are there?

— How can this partnership agreement be changed? For how long does it last?

— Ownership by the business of any patents, designs, copyright or 'know-how' that is the original work of one of the directors.

— What right does each director have to do outside work?

— Is it understood that all partners are jointly and severally liable to the full extent of their private assets for the debts of the partnership (if a company structure is not used)?

— Accountants and solicitors should be appointed by the partnership, but it is preferable that they are not the same as those used by the partners privately.

Leaving the partnership – when you don't want to play anymore

— How long does the partnership last – is it up for review every few years with a let-out clause? Are there terms and options similar to a lease?

— Is there any prohibition on partners assigning or changing their interest in the partnership?

— Can a share be sold to someone else? This is usually undesirable in a small partnership given the high degree of trust and intimacy between partners.

— What insurance is taken out for the protection of the remaining partner in the event of death of the other partner? Specific insurance policies are available to finance the purchase of the deceased partner's equity from their estate and avoid these complications.

— If one partner leaves the business or sells their share, what restriction will there be on any other business they may want to carry out? Also restrictions on their use of confidential information.

Valuing the business if one partner wants out

A detailed method of valuing the business should be drawn up, especially looking at how the value of goodwill is determined and if extra value is put on assets beyond that in the balance sheet. Valuation will usually be based on previous profit performance but other methods may be chosen, based on the present profit performance. The future value of the goodwill will go up or down in line with the profit eg if profit next year increases by 50%, so does the value of the goodwill. Add to this the value of equipment and this will give the total agreed value of the business at any future date.

CHOOSING THE RIGHT DESTINATION

Choosing the right destination for a conference is a major decision for an association, corporation or agency. It is not easy, but the right choice is a determining factor for the success of an event. As a long-term partner for a growing number of (international) associations, corporations and other agencies, Congrex is often asked to help and advise in the selection of a conference destination and location. This selection process is often undertaken many years in advance of the meeting actually taking place - in general, the larger the event, the more years in advance this is done. Following are the steps in the selection process:

1. *Parameters of Choice*

The first step in the selection process is determining the parameters for choice. The association sets these parameters together with us as meeting consultants. It is important to be very clear on what the association's expectations for the destination are, right from the beginning. Broad questions such as "what does the association expect of the conference destination" and "where has the association been before, was that successful - what worked and what did not?" will allow us to help determine which location or venue will be right for the client.

2. *Consult your stakeholders*

We certainly always recommend that the association consults with the stakeholders in the conference regarding the upcoming choice of venue - stakeholders such as a representation of the members in a conference committee, but certainly also sponsors and (or) exhibitors. This is particularly important for those events that depend to a greater or lesser extent on the support that sponsors and exhibitors give to the event in question. Organising a conference is a partnership effort that needs as much collaboration as possible. All stakeholders should feel as comfortable as possible about the choice(s) made.

Of course, making the choice for a destination is different for each client - the process and questions asked will certainly be different. But "politics" should play as little a role as possible.

The decision on a destination should be made on sound reasoning - whatever that reasoning may be. It is of ultimate importance that the selection process is clear to everyone and as transparant as possible. The outside world, but also the membership and other stakeholders need to understand why certain choices have been made.

3. Physical Requirements

The physical meeting capacity requirements for the destination and location are determined based on key historical data going back a number of years. The questions and requirements are drawn up in a checklist which includes items regarding the venue, the meeting room requirements (size, etc), exhibition requirements, registration requirements etc. The second set of physical requirements are the questions regarding the hotels, their capacity and other such practical questions. It is of key significance that the requirements list(s) are based on as much historical data of past events as possible - it will make sure that the right questions are asked.

4. How the City Convention and Visitors Bureau can help

Questions regarding the destination infrastructure, specific location questions such as ease of access (train, plane, etc) and questions on what the city might offer in terms of marketing and other (financial) support also form an important component in the formal request for bids (or whichever other form the request may be issued in). The City Convention and Visitors Bureau should play a key role in this part of the bid. In fact, the CVB should be the one to help us, on behalf of the client, in finding all the components that are important to make a choice.

5. Value for money

It goes without saying that another set of questions relates to cost and money - but even more importantly - value for money for the association. In this day and age the value package that a city has to offer is just as important as the actual prices that are being charged by the conference centre where the conference might be held or the price of the individual hotel rooms in the city. The indication of price is a factor when determining a location, but the value offering is certainly another factor which should be taken into consideration. As an example, a city which is able to offer something special for the conference goer - one could think of the reduced public transportation pass, a museum pass, or in general something that could bind the participant to the city is certainly a plus.

Those cities that have their "act together" are those most likely to be successful in bidding for an event. The cities and Convention and Visitor Bureaus that have an integrated approach are the ones that are able to make the best value offering to the client. Organising a conference requires teamwork from all parties concerned - and this teamwork already starts with the choice of destination. As an example, it means that hotels need to be aware of the importance of a conference to the city - certainly a message that the Convention Bureau needs to put across. A conference is of importance to the whole of the city, not only the individual hotel and location.

When advising to an association or any other type of client for a choice of destination, the components mentioned above all are part of the recommendations. Of course, the physical requirements need to be met, but also the "soft" requirements form part of the recommendation. It is also important that the site is visited before a final choice is made. Often there are more locations that can house a conference than initially thought.

The right location and destination often make an event, the wrong choice can certainly break an event and therefore have an impact on the future success of that event and have even further reaching consequences for the organisation itself. Selecting a destination requires thought and reflection, close cooperation between the parties, mutual understanding - and certainly some hard work.

FURNITURE, FIXTURES, AND EQUIPMENT (FF&E)

The economy is solid and travel is on the increase, both for business and pleasure. As a result, hoteliers are proceeding at the strongest levels since September 11, 2001 with construction of new properties and with refurbishment of existing properties. That means decisions need to be made about furniture, fixtures, and equipment (FF&E), so here are some tips and trends to keep in mind. These are the things which will help turn a "good" look into the "best" look – and which will build customer buzz, satisfaction, and repeat business. The most important thing to remember is that guests want their hotel room to be a "home away from home" – and the next most important thing to remember is that you can give them what they want without breaking your budget.

In the guest room

If a hotel is trying to gain market share, linens can be used in marketing materials to promote a competitive advantage. First, determine the right specifications for your property. These levels may or may not be the same as franchise specifications, which tend to be minimum requirements. Then invest money in products that are used most often by guests, which typically are sheets, pillowcases, and bath towels. Next come bath mats, then finally come wash cloths and hand towels. Work with your FF&E partner to evaluate various linens buying decisions, such as product turns, usage, and inventory. Because inventory is cash, be sure your supplier can provide linens frequently and promptly – without large minimums or freight charges.

Bedspreads are more homey if you move beyond the traditional "throw" style. Select covers with more down fill and with unusual trim such as dust ruffles. Bedding adds to the residential feel when mattresses, box springs, and pillow tops are thicker.

Sound expensive? It doesn't have to be because there are literally hundreds of manufacturers in the United States, Canada, Mexico, and even Europe, Asia, and South America.

All this competition means attractive pricing – but be sure your FF&E supplier can compare "hard" costs with "soft" costs such as quality. Window treatments give still another "finishing touch" of home when you select styles such as cornices, valences, shutters, or Roman shades.

In the bathroom

Few parts of a hotel can make a guest feel more comfortable or special than the bathroom. It's almost always the first area that guests visit when they arrive in their room and it's the place that guests spend most of their time while in the room, second only to the bed. So clearly, investing in a few little extras in the bathroom can pay big dividends with your guests. Consider these ways to create a bathroom look that's both cozy and elegant:

— vanities and tub surrounds in granite or solid surface

— amenities such as mirrors encased in frames and built-in shelves

— softer lighting with wall sconces rather than traditional fluorescent tubes

— cabinets that have the feel of custom furniture

In lobbies and corridors

Studies show that among the most important impressions guests remember about a hotel stay is the look of the lobby, so this area should capture the attention of everyone who walks through it. Your FF&E supplier's in-house designer can carefully and creatively combine furniture with available space to create distinctive public areas that best match your geographical location, as well as to your mix of clientele. For example:

— develop depth and interest by using several different materials and finishes, including but not limited to marble, wood, metal, and cloth

— develop warmth, intimacy, and richness by using dark woods, natural fiber fabrics, textured glass, and granite

— develop food service areas, especially for breakfast, with an unmistakable look of home

Seven Deadly Sins of Hospitality Venue Design

In recent years club architects and interior designers have created some of the most dramatic and stunning clubhouses ever built. Often these structures are perfectly integrated with their surroundings, have spectacular views of the golf course, lake, or other natural feature, and are a great source of pride for developers and members alike. Often, though, these magnificent structures contain within them the unfortunate seeds of everlastingly higher operating costs. In many cases these problems could be easily and creatively rectified by input from knowledgeable operators. The following constitutes one list of club design issues:

1. Food service access across a hallway

Food service requires repeated trips by service staff back and forth from the kitchen to the dining space. Each course of a meal must be served and cleared, drinks must be replenished, special requests accommodated. When these service areas are separated from the kitchen by member-accessible hallways, service is continually hindered and periodic disasters are a certainty. The ideal design is for a central kitchen with direct access to each dining or multi-function space. Members and guests enter and exit from hallways dedicated for their use. Recognizing that this ideal is not always possible, architects should make every effort to limit member/service cross traffic as much as possible.

2. Seperation of employee entrance from loading dock/ receiving area.

Food service operations contain many attractive and easily pilfered items. When deliveries are received, boxes must be inspected and broken down; items counted, weighed, and properly put away; and inventory records updated. All of this takes time and is often the responsibility of one person. As a result, stock is often left unattended in the receiving area. When the loading dock/receiving area doubles as the employee entrance, it is just too tempting and too easy to come up short.

3. Inadequate dishwash station/breakdown area

Poorly designed dishwash stations have a direct bearing on the amount of china and glassware breakage. When servers bring dirty dishes and glasses from the dining room there must be an adequate space to set down their loaded trays to sort china, glassware, tableware, linen, food scraps, and trash. If this space is not provided, tray after tray of table detritus accumulates, often piled precariously one on top of another. Inevitably it all comes crashing down. All this costs the club in broken china and glassware, impedes the continuing efficiency of the operation, requires time-consuming cleanup at the busiest of times, and creates a safety hazard. While the problem is a challenge on any busy night, when you add to it the breakdown and clearing of a busy ballroom after a wedding for 350, you have nothing short of chaos.

4. Noise from the kitchen

Kitchens are inherently noisy operations. Nothing is more distracting to a quiet dinner for two, a family celebration, or a business meeting than the normal sounds of pots and pans, exuberant kitchen staff, and the clink and clank of dishwashers. Walls between the kitchen, or for that matter any noisy back-of-house area, must have adequate sound insulation. Special attention must be paid to doors leading from these areas to the front-of-house. Pantries make good transition spaces, but doors must be well-insulated and direct transition of noise dampened by masking walls.

5. Inadequate and poorly located storage spaces

Food service operations require many items that must be

properly and securely stored. This is particularly true for multi-function spaces that require tables, chairs, screens, linen, china, tableware, buffet service, band set up, audio-visual equipment, and decorations that must be moved in an out, often with back to back set ups with little time to spare. Beyond these immediate needs, clubs need storage for uniforms, food and beverage stocks, portable bars, hot and cold food carts, maintenance and housekeeping equipment and supplies, accounting records, and pro shop inventories. The location and size of the various storage areas is critically important to efficient operations. For instance, a bulk storage area for banquet tables and chairs located in the basement of a clubhouse will require extra hours of set up time for each function. Over the life of the building this could amount to hundreds of thousands of dollars in additional labor.

6. Multi-level food service operation

As much as possible foodservice operations should be on one level allowing for the most efficient production and service of food to various areas of the club. While multi-level food service is often dictated by the building footprint or topographical siting, such an operation will require an elevator of adequate size to accommodate rolling food carts and certain equipment must be available on all floors, such as refrigeration, ice machines, coffee makers, and tables for plating meals.

7. Inefficient design drives higher payroll costs

Like other businesses clubs have posted hours of operation and members expect the facility to be open during those posted hours. Given that labor cost is the single largest club expense, it makes sense to design spaces and facilities so only one employee is necessary to staff the area at the slowest time. As an example, if the dining room closes at 9 p.m., but the lounge stays open till eleven with a limited sandwich menu, it makes more sense to design a deli counter into the bar. This way the kitchen can close with the dining room and the bartender can make and serve fresh deli sandwiches till closing. The same concept might apply by having the pool entry and snack bar located contiguously.

On the slowest pool day, one employee can check in members and guests and also provide snack bar services. While such design is not always feasible, given the high cost of labor and the expected life of the facility, it makes sense to apply this principle whenever possible. The perfect club design is an operationally functional and timeless work of art; one whose beauty will be appreciated by members and guest for years to come and whose operation will be characterized by the built-in efficiencies of intelligent design.

Maintenance and Repairs

Maintenance is something that never ends in a hotel and just when one thinks it is under control either something expensive breaks or it is time to remodel or upgrade! Maintenance seems to fall into four categories:

1. Preventive room maintenance
2. Preventive equipment maintenance
3. Routine repairs based on work-orders
4. Emergencies.

Each has its distinct time element, relative priority and level of interest from management and the maintenance staff. Clearly everything stops for emergencies. A burst hot water pipe on an upper floor or a dead washer when occupancy is high will get everyone's attention. No one but a neighboring guest seems to care about squeaky hinges on guest room doors. How to keep all this balanced is a challenge to managers and owners alike.

Maintenance Saves Effort

The first thing that should be obvious is that routine repairs and, to a lesser degree, emergencies will be reduced significantly if preventive room and equipment maintenance is taking place.

The problem for many managers and maintenance people is how to get out from under the ongoing repairs and emergencies in order to conceive and implement preventive maintenance programs.

Preventive maintenance as a tax which is payable weekly in hours. No matter what, the tax must be paid. Even three hours, three days a week in an 80 to 100 room hotel is a significant start. In a smaller property its more than enough, in the long run. In a larger hotel one is dealing with a different scale, sometimes one or more persons spend full time on it, but the principal is the same. Two of those three days can be spent in guest rooms while the other can be spent on equipment and public spaces.

Guest room preventive maintenance is very straight forward. The place to start is not by being delayed coming up with the ideal checklist, but rather by coming up with a work cart for the maintenance staff. The cart can be an old maid's cart cleaned up and painted or something developed from a two wheel dolly with tool kits bolted to it and some shelves built for common spare parts. Just start with something inexpensive; one can replace it or improve it next month.

The key thing: get started. Go to the lowest numbered room in the hotel and start anywhere. Maybe the maintenance person likes to fix lamps and light fixtures so s/he starts there and checks all the fixtures in the room by tightening switches, adjusting harps, checking the security of the plugs and outlets (while down there) and making notes of any that need new shades. Next the maintenance person might cheek for dripping in the bathroom and replace or clean faucet aerators, and tighten knobs.

While in the bathroom, tighten the toilet seat and shower rod. Look for grouting that needs repair and make a note so that several rooms can have their grouting and tile worked on at once. Continue this process for an hour, then go to the next room and repeat exactly the same checks. In a small hotel, three or four rooms is a great start for the first day. Out of the effort several work orders will have been written for subsequent follow-up. The key to guest room preventive maintenance is in actually getting some things in the room fixed or adjusted, not in making big lists and certainly not in undertaking on a big project.

Equipment and Public Spaces

Along with the guest room preventive maintenance tax, add in a schedule of maybe four hours, two days a week for equipment and public space preventive maintenance. The total tax at this point is only 17 hours. With the remainder of the maintenance work week, work orders and emergencies are dealt with. Equipment and public space preventive maintenance is a little different than the guest room program. Most pieces of equipment come with maintenance instructions. These should be researched and organized on to cards or into a notebook. If the manuals have been lost, a vendor can usually help get them or at least a photocopy of very old equipment manuals.

Start with simple but important things, like keeping the machinery and equipment clean followed by servicing anything with moving parts. Get back to the machinery every two or three months or according to the manufacturers directions, if they are located. Some equipment needs more frequent servicing. A good example are older circulating pumps for domestic hot water. Some used to need their bearings oiled weekly. Modern equipment needs less and less servicing, but anything with air circulating through it needs filters and coils cleaned just as much as they ever did. Failing to do so causes them to overheat and breakdown prematurely.

Public spaces such as lobbies, halls, stairwells, restaurants and meeting rooms need continuous attention. Chairs, tables, doors, carpet and wall coverings all get heavy use and abuse. Without regular attention these items can cause a hotel to start looking shabby and unkempt. More importantly, some items become a safety hazard. By getting around to these areas weekly and inspecting them the person or persons working on maintenance can correct unsightly tears, fix loose legs and keep all the parts of the doors properly adjusted.

Work Orders and Organization

Work orders are a great tool for examining where preventive maintenance is failing by looking at the frequency, location or type of items that appear on the work orders. Except for damage caused by a guest or employee, many work orders are a result of poor preventive maintenance. Many maintenance people do not organize their work orders. Organizing them might include batching work orders together by location, similar projects requiring the same tools and supplies, etc. It is also appropriate to put low priority work orders off until s/he is going to that location for an additional reason. Time is money and time spent walking to and from different jobs, getting supplies and tools and just checking things out is wasted money.

The maintenance staff simply stops by the reception desk to note completed work orders on the permanent copy. Problem work orders are discussed at staff meetings or with the appropriate department head. Most hotels use a three part slip where one comes back to the originator when the repair is completed.

Emergencies Caused by Inattention

Emergencies have been defined by someone unknown to me as, "your poor planning becoming my crisis." A lack of preventive maintenance and attention to detail lie as the root cause of many emergencies. The definition of emergency in a hotel is subject to frequent changes of interpretation. The owner coming and the front door closer that s/he has complained about for three months still not being fixed is not really an emergency, but will be treated as such. Anything that is a safety hazard, or is causing further damage, or is going to impact revenue now is truly an emergency. You might think of some others, but this covers most emergencies.

After each emergency situation is resolved take a few minutes to examine it. Was it really an emergency? What could have been done to prevent or at least mitigate it? Finally, what are we going to do to keep it from happening again?

TRAVELERS WANT, AND WILL PAY MORE FOR HEIGHTENED SECURITY

Security solutions specifically designed for hospitality are easy to afford and operate, and built to provide the perfect blend of technology with design. Security systems of all types and for all applications are being embraced by hotels for their proven ability to deter and document crime.

Times have changed. Safety is paramount, and security solutions, such as electronic door locks, in-room safes and Closed Circuit TeleVision (CCTV) surveillance cameras, have become a critical component of hotel operations. *The Chicago Tribune, USA* recently released information from a survey conducted by John Portman & Associates, an Atlanta-based hospitality architect group, that stated: "Travelers welcome and are willing to pay more for heightened security."

Hotels need to step up security efforts

After Sept. 11th, travelers heard the worldwide wake-up call. Today they demand that their personal safety and security at hotels no longer take a back seat to profitability. Unfortunately, not as many hoteliers were listening when the wake-up call rang out. What the study found was that in contrast to media reports that hotels had enhanced their safety and security measures, hotels, in fact, made a modest effort to alter procedures and systems.

According to the CHR report: "Among the many outcomes of the terrible events of Sept. 11th is a renewed interest in the safety and security of hotels. The mere presence of security equipment, such as electronic locks or security cameras does not guarantee guests' security in the absence of personnel who are well trained to implement a fully developed security plan. On the other hand, a hotel would be hard pressed to implement an effective security plan in the absence of appropriate security equipment."

No price on security

While many believe that the majority of hotels have adopted electronic locks and CCTV, the CHR study found that there still is room for improvement. For those hotels in the limited service and economy segments that have not adopted these technologies, cost is generally the factor. Unpredictable revenues are running rampant within the industry. Capital investment for new technology can be difficult to secure, and it's sometimes risky to make big technology investments in an uncertain economy. The good news is that programs already exist to help properties that want to install safety and security solutions—namely e-locks, CCTV, in-room safes and other control solutions—with no upfront, out-of-pocket expense.

With specific programs, the monthly charge for security equipment is in direct correlation with a hotel's occupancy rates. By using a credit card, the cash outlay for the system comes after payment is received for the room. This "no guest, no cost" program is an ideal solution for new construction hotels and those undergoing retrofits and renovations; properties still using mechanical keys; and properties that were early adopters of electronic card locks 10 to 15 years ago and have not made an upgrade investment. It is also ideal for hotels looking to add on CCTV or in-room safes to their existing electronic locks offering.

Hoteliers Hail CCTV

With a capital assistance program in place, hoteliers from all segments no longer have an excuse not to upgrade their safety and security procedures and systems. According to The Chicago Tribune, USA report, and testimonials from hoteliers, CCTV in particular is in big demand by hoteliers, in addition to guests.

"There's no doubt that today's guest perception is that properties that don't have CCTV cameras lack fundamental security measures," said Dan Quam, vice president of Eastern Hospitality Management Inc. "If you don't have cameras, you run the risk of losing once-loyal guests to your close competitors 'who have seen the CCTV light' so to speak — not to mention insurance and legal liabilities with regard to taking reasonable steps to protect your property's people (both guests and employees) and assets."

Technology Meets Design

According to research recently conducted by the Bresslergroup of Philadelphia, more than 10,000 travelers, hoteliers, designers and architects agree: "The hotel corridor is the introduction to the guestroom, and the guestroom door lock is one place where manufacturers need to improve their designs." What Bresslergroup found was that today's electronic door locks are not aesthetically pleasing and actually are confusing to hotel guests. The current units on the market, while providing a vital security service, are actually "aesthetically challenged" in appearance to many.

Although electronic locks have become the rule rather than the exception, their key-card entry process is inconsistent. Bresslergroup found there are actually 14 different ways to open the various electronic door locks in the hotel market: Horizontal insertion/open in and open out, vertical insertion/open in, vertical insertion/open out, swipe magstripe right, swipe magstripe left, bottom-up/open in, bottom-up/open out, magstripe up, magstripe down, smart chip up, smart chip down, smart chip right and smart chip left.

Before selecting an electronic lock or safe, hoteliers and their designers/architects need to consider the physical and psychological interaction between guests and the hardware, as well as the system's intuitiveness on the guest's overall comfort. The hardware also must be aesthetically pleasing and user friendly. Decision makers at more than 15 global branded hotel chains, along with a focus group of designers and architects, told Bresslergroup that they welcome a new electronic lock that improves aesthetics and ease of use, without compromising security.

Changing the physical appearance of an electronic lock or in-room safe to blend in with the hotel's overall design is just the first step. Bresslergroup's research tells that technology design also needs to mirror the hotel's segmentation. For example, an electronic lock on the door of a luxury hotel should not be the same lock as one installed on the door of an economy hotel.

One-Stop Security Shopping

Obviously, one size technology, and one design, does not fit all ? not in overall hotel design and not in technology design. As travelers begin to demand more from hotels in the security arena, manufacturers must work closely with hotels and end-user guests to develop and incorporate design trends and travelers' preferences into their products for technology to be truly successful in 2003 and beyond.

Hoteliers looking to provide their guests with improved safety and security features should be pleased to know that there are companies out there that provide a one-stop-shop resource for purchasing electronic locks, electronic safes and CCTV systems. Leading industry experts such as Greg Plank, former president of Suburban Lodges of America and current president of Atlanta-based Worldwide Travel Marketing Inc., commend companies that offer a one-stop-shop, customer-centric approach to developing and delivering security solutions.

Plank said one-stop-shopping in the lodging industry has been around for sometime with supplies and consumable items. While the concept is not new to hospitality, the ability to purchase security systems and integrated facilities management solutions in a one-stop-shop environment is new – and it's BIG news. "In the security arena, a one-stop-shop concept centralizes the service and sales process for the customer creating efficiency and time savings," Plank said. "The customer has one point of contact and can work in partnership with the company to develop new solutions in different areas instead of having to work with several entities that don't communicate effectively."

There's a heightened sense of security knowing that we can purchase our e-locks, safes and CCTV from a proven hospitality technology provider, and that in the rare event that an issue should arise, all we need to do is make one call to one person and we're covered," Patel said. "Working with a company that offers one-stop-shop electronic security solutions saves us considerable time and monies on the front end, and will continue to do so for years." For all hoteliers, the challenge lies in making careful choices. Working hand in hand with the right security solution

Busting the Key Loggers...

Key logging is one of the most disturbing ways currently being used to illegally obtain customer's sign-in details for e-commerce enabled sites, ultimately leading to financial loss either to the customer or the vendor. A product released and that was developed in Korea, where online crime is among the highest in the world, offers online providers, and bankers in particular, the closest to "full-proof" protection yet. As simple in its design as the very problem it is there to solve, K-Defense, goes to the lowest level of a computer's basic architecture to intercept and effectively mask keystrokes from anyone other than their intended recipient.

When you consider how simple the concept is, its surprising so little attention has been given to the development of preventative measures, or indeed adoption of the few products that are available by the vendors themselves. Currently most forms of protection rely on firewalls and anti-virus software to intercept and delete malicious programs that can be used to record and then forward keystrokes to an unknown assailant. However, the degree of protection is only as good as the last update and even then, that assumes the customer has actually bothered to install some form of Internet security on their PC in the first place.

And this is where K-Defense really stands out as it can be made a mandatory and integral part of the vendor's own online channel, and best of all at a realistic cost. The small piece of code is downloaded to the customer's PC each time they arrive at the vendor's online channel. This is obviously far more attractive than relying on the customer to install, and maintain, software or hardware based security products. In this way, a customer is unable to login or use the vendor's Internet channels unless K-Defense is physically present in the customers PC. When this is coupled with digital certificates used by the vendor, the effective protection against key logging, using a conventional keyboard, is near enough 100%.

Key logging works on the premise that the fundamental design of computers relies on keystrokes passing a standard route from the keyboard through a hardware interface and on to the operating system, and then, the application. As a result, most keystroke protection systems rely on encryption that is carried out in the operating system of the PC, using 128 bit based algorithms embedded in the software. Unfortunately encrypting at this level is normally too late, as most malicious programs run below the operating system and therefore well ahead of the protection.

K-Defense, on the other hand operates at an even lower level, creating a barrier between the operating system and the physical hardware components. It does this by creating a random routing path that takes the input directly to the application program level, making the need for encryption unnecessary and making it near impossible for the malicious code to track. Once at the application the vendors existing security takes over, transmitting the data over its secure lines directly to its server.

This simple but effective solution is further enhanced by the nature of it being page based as opposed to field based Meaning that the protection offered can be activated by the vendor on any page, instead of, activated at each and every input field. Some other similar systems necessitate the rewriting of applications to embed coding at each point of data input, which can become a costly and time intensive project.

Finally, when the customer leaves the vendors online channel, or closes their browser, the K-Defense system quietly deactivates until the customer next visits the vendor. Taking almost 2 years and involving a number of their 2,700 strong development team, the IT division of Hyundai developed K-Defense. It was first put to use late last year at the country's Ministry of Information and Communications, with a number of financial institutions in Korea looking to deploy the system in the coming months.

Although K-Defense addresses the conventional keyboard, which is physically connected to the PC, it does not yet offer protection for wireless devices. While the popularity of wireless keyboards is still not that high, some tests carried out in the US have found that with the correct conditions it is possible to "eavesdrop" on transmissions and effectively play them back in real-time on another PC. However, as more incidents of online theft from banks are pushing many country's financial regulators to impose greater responsibility for customer security back on to the bank's themselves, cost effective solutions such as K-Defense are likely to become considerably more widely adopted, rather than wait for the next development.

One-stop shopping, Accountability and Cost control

Project managers and purchasing agents offer a new advantage when planning renovations. The world of project management has come full circle. Today, a hotel owner wanting a renovation can work with a project manager/ purchasing agent (PM/PA) who provides the advantage of single-source responsibility for the renovation's quality, schedule and cost. Once, hotel owners performed all their own renovation project management and purchasing duties.

Then, seeking a cost-effective way to streamline the process, they turned to legions of specialized consultants — an architect/designer, project manager and purchasing agent. Now, hotel owners are seeking out a handful of companies that provide one-stop shopping — with project management and purchasing abilities combined into a single entity.

In the early days of franchising, the franchisor continued to provide technical services to its franchisees. Often, the franchisee was required by contract to use the flag's technical services department. Fees were high, product cost expensive and the service so-so at best. It worked great for the flag, but not so great for the franchisee. Franchisees revolted and insisted on going their own way. They agreed to adhere to the flag's standards, but refused to accept the flag's large overhead cost, high fees and mediocre service. The franchisees believed they could do it faster, better and cheaper — with equal or better quality.

An industry of designers, purchasing agents and project managers sprang up to meet their needs. The owner was then managing a team of consultants, whereas previously, the flag provided one-stop shopping. REITs also grew by developing a new type of client, the "asset manager." These institutional owners were strictly owners with little or no in-house technical support. The asset manager, often with solely a financial or operations background, was responsible for managing capital projects.

The asset manager was concerned with bottom line — not only income. Capital projects that drive revenue (but provide little or no return) may benefit the manager, but not the owner. Thus, the asset manager needed technical expertise working for his best interest. All these changes in hotel economics — franchising, REITs, corporate layoffs — led to the creation of an industry of architects, interior designers, project managers and procurement agents servicing independent and institutional hotel owners.

8

Professional Hygiene for Customer Satisfaction

The development of the Institutional and Industrial (I&I) cleaning and hygiene business has occurred during the second half of the 20century. In the early part of the 20century, cleaning products were largely soap-based, and disinfectants were limited to a few basic types. The industries which used such products were still relatively small in scale. Food manufacture, distribution and catering were more locally based and the chain from farm to fork was short because of the limited preserving properties of the principal foodstuffs. Even hospitals were relatively independent. During the 1950s and 60s, all this began to change.

Sustained economic growth, increasing scale and geographic spread of customer operations and the introduction of new technologies and processes, in the food business as well as in healthcare, increased the need for good hygiene. This in turn dramatically increased the volume and sophistication of the demands placed on I&I suppliers. The I&I industry responded not only with the development of improved products and manufacturing technologies, but by deepening understanding of the risks that could be posed by microbes and how best to manage them. Specialist I&I companies developed and began to extend their service to providing training to customer organisations.

More recently, the emphasis of innovation by the Industry has moved on to developing computerised and automated systems, which deliver hygiene in a highly cost-efficient way. The environmental impact of I&I hygiene has been reduced by improved, higher performance, ingredients and by controlled dosing systems which, as well as ensuring consistent hygiene results, help eliminate overdosing and the consequent waste.

Hygiene procedures and techniques of application have been integrated, through use of systematic hazard analysis systems such as HACCP, into packages comprising products, training and customised hygiene schedules. This approach more completely delivers the end benefit that customers really seek - the positive assurance of microbial safety for their operations. This has made close working partnerships between customer and supplier an increasing feature of the I&I sector. Today, fast growing I&I markets in convenience food, tourism, healthcare and the accommodation industry are again creating new needs. Meeting these, while adapting to changing legislative frameworks, and continuing to build true long-term sustainability, represents a significant challenge for the I&I industry.

PRINCIPLES OF HYGENE

Hygiene can generally refer to a whole range of measures, which protect health and well-being and improve the quality of life. The main role of hygiene in the I&I sector is to protect people and animals from disease caused by infectious or toxigenic micro-organisms: bacteria, fungi, viruses and sometimes protozoa and prions. A second role is to prevent spoilage of perishable goods, such as food and cosmetics, through contamination with bacteria and fungi, which can grow in them.

Hygiene is concerned only with preventative measures, so it does not deal with the treatment and cure of established diseases. Modern hygiene protects people, animals and products not by obliterating all microorganisms, but by interrupting routes of transmission and contamination, and by controlling harmful microbes below safe levels. Every year, in every country, there are outbreaks and mishaps that show the consequences of failing hygiene - disease, discomfort and financial losses.

Inadequate Hygiene- A Growing Risks

Contrary to the prediction of the US Surgeon General in 1967 that it would soon be time to close the book on infectious disease, the risks and impacts of infections on mankind in 21st century Europe are in reality still increasing. The world is rapidly changing in so many ways that new opportunities for microbes to transmit disease are appearing faster than hygiene and infection control systems are adapting to control them. Increasing case numbers of foodborne infections are reported all over the world. Trends towards industrialisation of the food chain, mass catering and centralised food processing increase the potential impact of hygiene failures.

Improving worldwide logistics now daily deliver foods from around the globe, and people travel faster, further and more frequently. Both bring Europeans into contact with a wider range of microbes and allow diseases to spread more widely and more rapidly than ever before. To add to these increased risks, emerging foodborne pathogens, such as enterohaemorrhagic E. coli (EHEC) or Listeria, have a higher pathogenic potential (in terms of severity of infection) than the classical foodborne pathogens.

While modern medicine is improving and extending the lives of millions, many new techniques make the patient temporarily more vulnerable to infection. Highly invasive procedures from heart surgery to hip replacements, and therapies for cancer and other diseases involving suppression of the immune system, were impossible years ago. They depend absolutely on excellent hygiene to prevent infection during treatment and recuperation.

As the average age increases, the proportion of the general population who are more susceptible to infection is also continuously increasing. These 'vulnerable groups', including the very young, pregnant women, the elderly and those who are ill, now account for around 20% of the population. The evolution and spread of microbes that are resistant to antibiotics is making infections more difficult to treat and threatening our ability to cure infectious disease.

Medical and public health experts are emphasising the importance of improved hygiene as a response to this threat. Better prevention of infection reduces the number of cases to be treated and also reduces the use of antibiotics that drives the resistance problem. Note that because disinfectants used in hygiene, in contrast to antibiotics, are used at higher microbicidal concentrations, and work by multiple and unspecific mechanisms, there is no trend despite decades of use towards resistance to disinfectants.

Outside the field of infectious disease, today's larger-scale industrial processes (e.g. paper production, cooling systems) are also more vulnerable to problems caused by the growth of microbes than are smaller operations. While the hazards posed by microbes may have changed little from the past, the risks (the probability of the occurrence of the hazard and the consequences of that occurrence) are steadily rising as the complexity of our world increases.

Hygiene and Disinfection

Hygiene is a highly flexible concept. Modern hygiene systems tailor packages of measures for each specific application that will work together to minimise the risks of transmission of infection, or of other adverse effects of microbes Hygiene in the I&I sector begins with the identification of the potential risk factors for each situation. Using tools like HACCPand RABC for example, the relative importance of each hazard is assessed, and the critical steps to control the risks are identified.

Hygiene systems are built upon sound working practices that seek to avoid opportunities for cross-contamination wherever possible. Cleaning and disinfection steps are then selectively built into this framework in a systematic and targeted way to control the remaining risks at critical places and times, and provide appropriate margins of reliability and safety. Hygiene is thus no synonym for abundant use of chemicals.

Cleaning and disinfection are only a part of hygiene, and products can only deliver their benefits within a properly managed framework of good practice. The foundation of good hygiene, which seeks to minimise opportunities for microbial cross-contamination throughout a process, is the physical separation of clean and dirty (contaminated) items and processes. During food preparation, for example, raw and cooked food must be kept and handled separately. If they must sometimes occupy the same space, they should only be there at different times, with a suitable cleaning and disinfection process in between.

The same principle applies in other areas, such as operating theatres. There are either separate rooms for septic and aseptic surgery, or septic surgery is done at the end of the day followed by thorough disinfection of the whole theatre. Any item that is used in two consecutive processes, such as an endoscope, must be thoroughly decontaminated before the second use to avoid the transfer of microbes, in this case from one patient to another. While separation of clean and dirty processes achieves a great deal, the risks of casual contamination of clean processes can be further minimised by regular cleaning and/or disinfection of the sources of that contamination - surrounding surfaces, items, equipment and instruments for example - and by frequent washing or disinfection of the most common means of transfer, the hands.

Cleaning and disinfection are distinct but complementary processes. Cleaning is the physical removal of dirt, and a thorough cleaning step can also remove up to 99% of microbes from a surface. The microbes removed by cleaning are not usually killed, however, and unless they are efficiently rinsed away with clean water, they can contaminate the cleaning equipment and solution and be spread again when cleaning the next area.

When followed by thorough rinsing and drying, which also removes nutrients and moisture and inhibits survival and regrowth, thorough cleaning can make many low-risk surfaces and items sufficiently free from microbes to pose little risk. But in many higher-risk situations, even a 99.9% reduction is not at all enough to be safe. When initial microbe numbers are often measured in millions, thousands of organisms could remain. This is more than enough for some organisms to cause infection directly, and only a small number of organisms contaminating and growing in food, or entering the bloodstream, can cause major problems.

In such situations, microbial numbers must be further reduced by disinfection. This involves the destruction of microbes, and it can be achieved by chemical or by physical processes (e.g. using heat or UV light). It is vital that cleaning precedes or accompanies the use of a disinfectant: it makes the microbes accessible to the disinfectant and prevents dirt interfering with the process and undermining reliability. Disinfection does not, however, constitute sterilisation, in which all microbes are destroyed. This is only required in special situations, such as for surgical instruments. Disinfection seeks only to ensure that microbes are reduced to an acceptable level. This level has to be defined for each field of application.

National and international standards have been developed to assess whether a disinfectant has the appropriate efficacy for a particular application. Scientific studies increasingly illustrate and quantify the ability of improved hygiene in the I&I sector to reduce the burden of infections in practical situations in the face of increasing risks. For example:

— Hands of staff have been shown to transport microbes from patient to patient in hospitals. Improvement in the application of hand disinfectants by a training programme significantly reduced the rate of hospital infections.

— An epidemic of vancomycin resistant Enterococci (VRE) in a German hospital could only be terminated by rigorous disinfection measures: "Implementation of stringent hand disinfection and environmental disinfection policies, as well as measures for patient isolation contained this...outbreak of VRE..., which emphasizes the importance of hygienic measures for the control of nosocomial spread of these organisms.

— Hygiene interventions reduced the level of respiratory and gastrointestinal infections in a pre-school day care centre, indicating that cross contamination had been an important factor in their spread.

— Cross contamination was reported to be a contributing factor in 39% of general outbreaks of foodborne disease in the UK in 1995 and 1996. Most of these outbreaks occurred in catering or institutional settings.

— Listeria is a pathogen that is frequently found on smoked fish. Raw fish however rarely contains Listeriaand the strains found on the smoked fish correlate with those found in the processing environment. Disinfection is thus critical in minimising contamination.

— A recent study in which US Navy recruits were ordered to wash their hands five times a day, showed that respiratory infections such as coughs were 45% lower than for a control group.

— A review of 64 interventional or observational studies involving hygiene education and handwashingconcluded that by improving standards of personal and environmental hygiene in these situations it is possible to reduce the transmission of infection by over 20%. This is in accordance with earlier reviews of hygiene impact.

— Cleaning and disinfection play a central role in hygiene, but they can only be effective in the prevention of infection and contamination if they are conducted within a framework of sound hygiene practice.

Delivering Hygiene

The following section provides some examples of the practical systems and procedures that are used to deliver hygiene, often to meet specific legal requirements. While these examples cover some of the more important application areas, similarly, detailed procedures tailored to specific needs and practices are applied across many other specialist fields, including veterinary medicine, animal husbandry and pharmaceutical production for example

Food hygiene

EC Directive 93/43/EEC requires the proprietor of any food business to identify any steps of the activities of the food business which are critical to ensuring food safety and to ensure that adequate safety procedures are identified, implemented and reviewed. This covers every activity from food production (post-harvest) and processing to storage, distribution and catering. This requirement can be met by the use of hazard analysis systems, the most common being HACCP(Hazard Analysis and Critical Control Point). A hazard is anything that could cause harm to the consumer. The three main hazards that may arise with food are its contamination by:

— Bacteria or other micro-organisms that cause food poisoning.

— Chemicals, for example by cleaning materials or pest baits.

— Foreign materials such as glass, metal, plastic etc.

Of these, the most important hazard in terms of risks and consequences is likely to be harmful bacteria or other microorganisms that may contaminate and/or grow in food. On its way from farm to fork, food passes through many steps - delivery, storage, preparation, cooking, cooling and so on. Hazards can occur at any or all of these steps. Each business must identify, for each type of food, the hazards that may occur at each step in the process.

Critical control points are steps that are systematically identified at which the hazards must be controlled to ensure that the specific risks that might arise from the hazard are either eliminated or reduced to an acceptable level. Some of the cornerstones of the risk management system are, for example, that:

— Any cooking or re-heating step should be able to kill harmful micro-organisms. Cooking is normally the most important control step in most food preparation. Chemical disinfection of equipment is another control point designed to kill micro-organisms.

— Any step where food may become contaminated should be controlled. Controls will include personal hygiene of staff as well as cleaning and/or disinfection of equipment to kill harmful germs.

Cleaning

Even in the most highly automated food business, operating under the most controlled conditions, soiling of both surfaces and equipment is unavoidable. The type and extent of soiling will vary considerably, but, whatever the operations, it is essential that such residues are not allowed to accumulate to levels which expose food to the risk of contamination sufficient to present a hazard. Closely defined cleaning schedules and routines are designed, implemented and monitored to ensure soiling is adequately controlled.

Disinfection

Cleaning may remove large numbers of micro-organisms it does not usually kill them and therefore may not be sufficient on its own to reduce contamination at certain critical points to levels which are low enough to be safe. An unsatisfactory cleaning operation can itself be a major vehicle of contamination within food premises. In such cases, disinfection is required. Normally disinfection is carried out after cleaning although in some cases the two processes are combined, sometimes referred to as sanitisation.

Disinfection does not need to be used for all surfaces and situations. It is only needed where the presence of micro-organisms at the levels that may otherwise be found would jeopardise the safety or quality of the food handled. If disinfection is considered necessary it will normally be restricted to: Direct food contact surfaces, including;

— Chopping boards, preparation tables /work surfaces.
— Food processing machinery and plant such as slicers, mixers and mincers, knives, tongs and other utensils.
— Containers.
— Production belts.

Hand contact surfaces, including:

— Handles - doors, refrigerators, freezers, cupboards, and drawers.
— Taps.
— Switches.
— Food workers hands.

Contamination and bacterial multiplication hazards such as;

— Cloths and mops.
— Waste bins and their lids.
— Floors and walls, where unpackaged food is handled.

Cleaning Schedules

Good practice requires systematic cleaning schedules for all surfaces and equipment. There should be a separate cleaning schedule for every piece of equipment and every area of the premises. A cleaning schedule should identify: -

— The task to be done, including where necessary the need to disinfect.
— The responsible person.
— Frequency.
— Cleaning materials and products t o be used.
— The method (including details of strip-down and re-assembly of the equipment).

— Safety precautions.

— End-result standard expected.

Organisations served by I&I suppliers of cleaning and hygiene products and ancilliaries frequently rely on the supplier's expertise to design an integrated package of cleaning schedules, methods and products that will guarantee the necessary hygiene results for their specific circumstances. The service is complemented by on-site training.

Cleaning in Place (CIP) is a highly specialised and sophisticated technique for cleaning and disinfection of large-scale plants, particularly in the food and beverage industries. Food factories, dairies and breweries for example have large plants including vessels and complex pipework that need to be kept scrupulously hygienic. This requires frequent and precise cleaning and disinfection that must be accomplished without dismantling the equipment.

In the largest operations, the costs of lost production time must be reduced to a minimum and the process must be highly reliable as any hygiene failure would affect large quantities of product and, if undetected, could affect many consumers. Cleaning and disinfection in CIP installations relies not only on the chemical action of the products but also on mechanical forces from spraying or turbulent flow under pressure to ensure efficient and complete decontamination. Flow rates of between 1.5 and 2m/sec are generally employed.

CIP systems were originally developed to operate on a single use of the cleaning or disinfecting solution. The flow of the solution must be precisely directed and controlled. Tanks can be cleaned, for example, by spraying solution via spray balls onto the inside of the dome at the top of the tank. The spray must be arranged to ensure the liquid forms a closed, even film that completely covers the tank walls as it runs down them. The correct pressure must be chosen to avoid "fogging" - atomisation of the cleaning solution that disrupts film formation.

Rotating spray balls can reduce the volumes of solution needed by up to a half, and enable use of higher pressures without fogging. Operation of these CIP systems is often straightforward, opening and closing valves in strict sequences to provide, for example, successive pre-rinsing with water, cleaning for a fixed time and a final water rinse.

Single use CIP systems have been developed into more advanced systems which recover and re-use the cleaning solution many times. 'Multiple-use' systems have obvious economic and environmental benefits in terms of both resource use and waste disposal. Multiple use systems have been continuously developed into a whole range of highly sophisticated, and increasingly automated, computer-controlled systems. Precise control of the levels of solutions in tanks and vessels is essential not just to ensure smooth operation and effective cleaning but also, for example, to avoid foam formation as solutions remix or the damage of pumps if they run dry.

Increasingly, the concentrations of the cleaning solutions, which determine their efficacy, are automatically controlled. By monitoring the conductivity of the solutions during use, when concentrations fall, products concentrate can automatically be dosed to the store tank to bring them back to the required level. The consequences of a failure in a large CIP system, if undetected, would be proportionately large. Adequate hygiene performance is routinely monitored by microbiologists, but since large volumes can be produced by the time a hygiene failure is detected, the most advanced systems are adopting advanced computer software to provide real-time monitoring and fault isolation.

Like many highly automated systems, such advanced CIP installations are strictly regulated to guarantee safe operation. Automated systems have many benefits in terms of cleaning efficiency, reliability and economy of operation and also environmentally because they minimise the use of ingredients and energy and minimise waste. To achieve optimum results the operation of CIP plants requires a close working partnership between user, equipment supplier and cleaning product supplier;

the I&I industry has invested heavily in developing these little known, but vital, systems to their full potential.

Retailing and Catering

'n the later stages of the food chain, for example in food retailing and catering operations, cleaning and disinfection procedures comprise five basic stages that are similar whatever the field of application, soiling type or circumstances:

— Pre-cleaning to remove any loose and heavy soiling.

— Main clean - wash with warm water and detergent.

— Rinse to remove any traces of detergent and soil with clean hot water.

— Disinfection, allowing sufficient contact time.

— Final Rinse in clean hot water.

The following examples illustrate procedures employed in specific circumstances.

Cleaning a surface manually

— Remove loose soiling.

— Wash surface with warm water and appropriate detergent, using cloth scourer or mop.

— Rinse with hot water and a clean cloth.

— Apply a chemical disinfectant, following the manufacturers' instructions.

— Rinse with clean water.

— Let dry in air or use a disposable paper towel.

'Ware-washing' - cleaning dishes and food-related equipment - by machine.

A machine can automatically perform all the necessary tasks, apart from the removal of gross soiling which needs to be done before loading. This depends, of course, on:

— the machine being loaded correctly.

— the correct dosage of chemicals being used (if not automated).

— the manufacturer's instructions being followed.

— the necessary routine maintenance being carried out.

A key part of the service provided by I&I suppliers is the expertise, training and automatic dosing equipment to ensure the effectiveness of the machines.

Manual 'Ware-washing'

— Wherever possible use two or three sinks side by side.

— Remove gross soiling - scrape and rinse if necessary.

— Wash the items, ideally in the first sink with luke-warm water and detergent, using a cloth or brush.

— Replace the warm water if it becomes cool or greasy.

— If the equipment is available the items can be rinsed and disinfected in hot water at 82°C for at least 30 seconds.

If this cannot be done safely then the items should be rinsed and then soaked in a chemical disinfectant following the manufacturer's instructions.

Disinfectants suitable for use in the Food industry are limited to those which, when used correctly, will not have deleterious effects on food, equipment or personnel. For example, they must not 'taint' food with any odour or taste, they must be compatible with all the various materials used in equipment and surfaces, and they must be safe for use in the sensitive applications for which they are employed.

In practice, different types of ingredients are used, each having its own strengths and weaknesses. Ingredients must be chosen and formulated for specific applications to guarantee results with maximum efficiency and minimum impact on personnel and the environment. The ingredients most commonly used in food hygiene include amongst others:

— sodium hypochlorite.

— peracetic acid.

— quaternary ammonium compounds.

— amphoterics.

Hospitals by their very nature contain many areas where bacteria and other micro-organisms need to be controlled. At the same time they bring together people with infectious diseases, who are potential sources of infection, and vulnerable people whose illness, therapy, surgical treatment, age or physical condition reduces their immunity and makes them highly susceptible to infection. Many micro-organisms that would be harmless to healthy adults can be very dangerous, even life-threatening, to such vulnerable groups.

A good hygiene regime to prevent cross-infection, or self-infection via open wounds is of the utmost importance. Responsibility for the hygiene regime, including an appropriate cleaning and disinfection policy, is normally allocated to an Infection Control Team or Committee, containing microbiologists, pharmacists, doctors and infection control nurses (hospital Hygienist). They may be sufficiently experienced to produce their own policy or may adopt the recommendations of Government Health Departments, Professional Societies or other official reference centres.

In some parts of hospitals and other healthcare institutions, hygiene needs and processes closely parallel those in non-medical settings. There are in addition, of course, many special hygiene needs and procedures that are very specific to the medical setting. For example, hygiene in medical areas such as operating theatres, for medical equipment and in response to medical events such as specific infections or spillages of body fluids, involves closely defined practice and procedure.

In areas such as the food and catering industries, and the medical arena, which must routinely manage a high risk of transmission of infections, there are many specific hygiene procedures closely tailored to control these risks. In contrast, more general hygiene procedures are applied wherever people go to minimise the likelihood of spread of disease. The I&I sector provides products to meet these general needs in all kinds of public places from schools and offices to hotels, retirement homes, leisure facilities and public transport.

Away from food preparation areas, bathrooms and toilets are among the most important areas in public places to be kept clean and hygienic. The risks of transmission of infection here are greater because of the presence of gastrointestinal organisms that transmit disease by the faecal-oral route, and because such areas are often moist which aids survival and transmission. As in many institutional situations, handwashing is the most important hygiene measure because hands are the vehicle on which organisms are most easily transported from a source of contamination into the body to cause infection.

Surfaces and items that are frequently touched by different people's hands, such as taps, handles and toilet seats, are thus also important points at which transmission can be interrupted. Other surfaces such as floors and walls which are infrequently touched are less important, and although they need to be kept clean, they need disinfection only in response to specific risks such as spills of hazardous material or the likely presence of infectious fungal organisms.

The I&I sector thus provides soaps, skin disinfectants and other products to maintain hand hygiene as well as a wide range of cleaning and disinfection products for surfaces, toilets, etc each formulated to combat the particular kinds of soils (e.g. soap scum and limescale) that need to be removed. Surface cleaning and disinfection products are also available for use as appropriate to keep lower risk areas such as office areas, schoolrooms and bedrooms clean and hygienic.

T1he cleaning and care of textiles is another field where there are hygiene needs to be met right across the institutional and industrial spectrum. Hospitals and nursing homes, food factories and shops, restaurants and canteens, hotels, leisure facilities and even prisons all must have clothing and other textiles that are clean, comfortable and hygienic. Textiles can harbour and allow the spread of micro-organisms that can transmit infection and affect the safety and/or quality of food. In all these settings where textiles are used and shared at different times, by patients and customers, or used by staff providing care or handling food, ensuring textiles are free from microbial contamination is of the utmost importance.

Depending on the field of use and the size of the organisation, textiles for such uses may be washed in large industrial washers with high throughput rates or sometimes in smaller units not very different from the domestic washing machine. Whichever is the case, washing processes must be designed to ensure the removal of the various soils with which clothing and textiles used in these fields come into contact, and the reliable disinfection of the item.

The process design must take care of factors such as the nature and extent of the soils to be washed away, of the microbes to be removed or inactivated, and of the nature and characteristics of the textile. It must take account of the size and design of the equipment, and of interfering factors such as water hardness. The process must specify a dose of product, a processing time and a temperature which, together with an appropriate input of mechanical action, can guarantee satisfactory cleaning and hygiene results with minimum use of product and energy.

Disinfection of textiles is achieved by a combination of physical removal (promoted by the combination of detergent, water, mechanical action and subsequent rinsing) and inactivation of microbes. This latter component may be achieved by thermal means (i.e. washing at higher temperatures) and/or by chemical inactivation by a biocidal ingredient, assisted in each case by final drying, which may also use elevated temperatures. It is important to ensure that microbes that are physically removed rather than inactivated are thoroughly rinsed away, and not redeposited elsewhere in the same, or a subsequent load.

Different countries specify different conditions in terms of times and temperatures for achieving disinfection by thermal means alone (thermal disinfection). Optimisation of the process is also helped by using a HACCPstyle approach. These will typically define adequate routines for:

— Identifying hazards
— Selecting 'critical control points'
— Defining control-measures
— Monitoring
— Taking corrective actions
— Documentation

Especially in larger machines, effective hygiene results with minimum use of product and energy are ensured by use of automatic, computer-controlled, dosing. Chemical inactivation of microbes in the laundry process is most often delivered by oxidising agents such as peroxygen or hypochlorite bleaches. These products release amongst others peracetic acid or hypochlorite respectively. Peracids bleaches (such as perborate or percarbonate) work most efficiently at higher temperatures (70°C and above), though peracetic acid can be used to help deliver disinfection at lower temperatures. Hypochlorite and similar bleaches are used in many countries for bleaching and desinfecting white textiles at low temperatures.

Factors for Hygiene Delivery

While the removal of visible dirt using normal cleaning products can easily be monitored by the user, micro-organisms are invisible and the efficacy of processes intended to leave a hygienically clean result needs to be ensured in other ways. Microbiological tests to measure any residual contamination are both complicated and take a long time to complete, so that routinely checking results is completely impracticable in most situations. In many cases, users do not have the expertise or resources to do such checks and consequently they rely on the

I&I product supplier to assure the efficacy and reliability of their hygiene process.

I&I product suppliers ensure good hygiene performance by thorough testing of products, before they are put on the market, in conditions that reflect the intended use, and by the development of detailed use instructions, perhaps with staff training and/or by automatic control. Even the best performing product cannot guarantee results if it is not properly and appropriately used. Developing a suitable combination of product and procedure to deliver the desired hygiene result must begin with choosing an ingredient that is effective against the relevant types of microbes.

The different kinds of microbes (such as bacteria, fungi, viruses), and their different subgroups (e.g. gram-positive and gram-negative bacteria, myco-bacteria, yeasts and moulds, naked and enveloped viruses) and species, have different susceptibilities to different anti-microbial ingredients. Few ingredients are effective against all kinds of microbes: a product may even be highly effective against one species and harmless against all others.

Proven efficacy against the important types of microbes must also be established for each different field of application under the specific practical conditions for that use, because many other factors can affect the performance of a product. For example, the presence and nature of dirt (soiling), including organic matter, can have a major effect. Moreover, so can the nature of the surface or material to which the product is applied - whether the surface is porous (wood, for example) or non-porous (tiles, metal etc). The temperature of the surface on which the product is applied can also be important, and must be taken into account for products to be used in cold-rooms or at higher temperatures for example.

Different types of anti-microbial ingredients are susceptible to such factors to different degrees. Over and above such factors, the efficacy of a disinfection process depends absolutely on using an adequate concentration of active ingredients and allowing an adequate time of contact between the product and the microbes to be inactivated. Proper procedures are thus of crucial importance. They must provide for adequate contact times and also allow, for example, for the dilution effect of use on wet surfaces. Using an otherwise effective product at the wrong concentration, or in the wrong way, can be dangerous as it creates a false sense of security.

In certain critical areas such as pharmaceutical production, complete hygiene processes need to be validated before implementation for routine use. In other areas the results of anti-microbial measures are verified retrospectively and their effectiveness documented after final control on site, e.g. via systems such as HACCP. While hygiene failures can be detected and corrected, the aim is always to identify, isolate and eliminate the cause to avoid the possibility of financial loss or risks to consumers.

Developing and applying tests to establish the efficacy of biocidal products has been a constant preoccupation for manufacturers, users and regulators since disinfectant use began. Even when disinfectant use was in its infancy, efforts were made to standardise tests so that they could be widely applied. Historically, a variety of national and industry test standards have arisen in different countries, as each has tended to develop its own methods for the most frequent and most important application fields.

Passing specified tests has often become a legal requirement for the sale and use of products, particularly in critical fields such as health-care and food production. Such methods define all the important variables that must be taken into account for the specified use - the nature and degree of soiling, surface composition, water hardness and temperature for example. Even where not legally prescribed, manufacturers use the same principles to support their individual claims to their customers. Standard tests also define the relevant strains of micro-organisms against which the tests must be performed.

Strains of microbes are specified which have a relatively low susceptibility to disinfectants compared to others of their type. They must also behave consistently under test conditions so that test results are reliable and reproducible. By selecting such representative species, efficacy against broad groups of microbes for defined product concentrations and contact times used in defined conditions can confidently be established. National and Industry standards thus give vital guidance to manufacturers in developing products, establish a basis for comparison of products and formulations, and can provide assurance of efficacy at affordable costs.

Sometimes, new uses, or new ways of using products, arise where standard tests are not available, or efficacy against different organisms may need to be established. In such circumstances manufacturers need to develop ad-hoc tests, often by modifying standard ones. Such tests need to be scientifically substantiated for the intended use, and their results, including proper use conditions and limitations in efficacy must be clearly and appropriately communicated.

Whilst national standards have provided the framework for biocidal product use for most of the 20th century, as Europe has evolved towards today's single market where international trade and harmonisation are the norm, the need for more widely accepted standards has become clear. Otherwise, products to be sold across Europe may need to be tested repetitively against many similar criteria, which all broadly establish the same thing.

Another difficulty is that the details of national test procedures, especially from smaller countries, are not sufficiently known in other countries and their results not necessarily acknowledged by foreign authorities or users. This inhibits trade and reduces choice. Besides this, many national standard methods have not been sufficiently validated to be consistently reproducible in different laboratories and use situations. To address this need, the European standards organisation CEN has been working since 1989 to harmonise available national standards such as AFNOR, DGHM, DVG and BSI into a coherent set of European standards (EN-norms). This work is being conducted within its specialist committee CEN/TC216, by expert representatives from many European Countries.

The aim is to develop a hierarchy of standards, firstly based on suspension test methods, followed as appropriate by laboratory methods more directly reflecting the conditions of practical use, and/or by field tests, as follows:

— Phase 1: basic suspension test methods to establish that a product has biocidal activity without regard to specified conditions or intended use.

— Phase 2/step1: suspension tests methods to establish that a product has biocidal activity under laboratory conditions appropriate to its intended use.

— Phase 2/step2: application test methods (e.g. surface tests), including hand-wash and hand-rub tests simulating practical use conditions.

— Phase 3: field test methods under practical use conditions.

Over the last few years more and more of these harmonised standards have been agreed upon and are now being published by each of the National Standard Bodies for use to support biocidal claims in different applications. Currently, however, passing national test standards is often still mandatory for the application of biocidal products in certain cases. Through A.I.S.E., the industry is strongly supporting the development and use of these CEN standards as internationally accepted methods for demonstrating the efficacy of biocidal products for use in hygiene throughout Europe.

A.I.S.E. member companies serving the I&I sector pay the greatest attention to ensuring the safety of their products for their own and their customers' staff as well as for the environment, during manufacture, storage, transport, use and disposal.

Occupational Safety

Compared to consumers, for whom cleaning is an occasional task, some professional cleaning staff allocate a much greater part of their day using I&I products. As with any industrial operation, customer organisations develop procedures and routines that guarantee a safe and healthy working environment for their employees, and monitor employee health to make sure there are no adverse effects. A.I.S.E. I&I companies support their customers in taking care of the occupational safety of their staff in a variety of ways.

First and foremost, though some products or ingredients inevitably have certain hazardous properties, such as irritancy, flammability or toxicity if ingested, suppliers design and develop formulations, processes and procedures for using them that avoid these giving rise to significant risks during use. For products with volatile ingredients, for example, formulations and use conditions are designed to keep concentrations in the air, and hence any amounts inhaled, well within recognised safety limits for whole day exposure as expressed by measures such as the Threshold Limiting Volume (TLV) or "Maximale Arbeitsplatz Konzentration" (maximum workplace concentration, MAK).

Some of these steps are enshrined as legal requirements. For example, the formulation, packaging and labelling of any hazardous I&I products, as with any chemical formulations, are regulated by EU Law, including the Dangerous Substances Directive (DSD) and the Dangerous Preparations Directive (DPD) and their counterparts in national legislation. Safe design is supplemented by detailed information provided to customers about products, about any hazardous properties, and about the procedures and precautions necessary to avoid risks.

Central to this are the comprehensive Material Safety Data Sheets-MSDS's that must be drawn up by suppliers for each and every product, and provided to every customer using the product. These sheets detail the key properties of the product, including a listing of any hazardous ingredients. They spell out toxicological information on the products and list standard safety information that must appear on labels. These 'R- and S-phrases' highlight in clear, succinct terms, specific hazards such as 'R38 Irritating to skin; R41 Risk of serious damage to eyes'.

MSDSs also help avoid risks by describing conditions of storage and transport, and conditions of use to control exposure, including specifying personal protection equipment such as gloves or goggles. Finally, in case of accidents, the MSDS describes the appropriate first aid measures, firefighting methods, and procedures for spill containment and disposal.

Future Trends

It is already clear that the early years of the 21st century are going to present an increasingly difficult challenge for I&I suppliers and their customers. The world is seeing an increased threat, from emerging infectious organisms, for example, as the opportunities for transmission of infections are also increasing because of more frequent, more wide-ranging travel and tourism, the progressive globalisation of food supplies, more frequent eating out, and greater consumption of centrally produced and convenience foods.

The population facing these threats is simultaneously becoming increasingly vulnerable to infection, through deterioration of immune competence through ageing and immune system diseases, and the ability to cure infection is being weakened by the emergence and spread of antibiotic-resistant organisms. The importance of preventing infection rather than relying on cure is now greater than at any time since the beginning of the antibiotic era. While societal trends such as these are increasing the need for hygiene, internal pressures and trends in many customer industries and institutions are making this task more demanding.

Increasing complexity of processes and machinery, the trend to automation to control labour costs, and the more intensive use of increasingly expensive equipment, will intensify and complicate hygiene needs and reduce the time available to clean and disinfect. To meet these increased needs, I&I suppliers will need to build upon close collaboration with customers and with machine manufacturers. Increasing use of automated cleaning and hygiene systems, with computerised Management Information Systems providing feedback to optimise performance will be vital. So, too, will working with manufacturers of machines and surface materials to improve design and construction to make cleaning and disinfection easier.

On the other hand, the ability of the I&I industry to meet the challenges is going to be increasingly constrained by new legislation. The Biocidal Products Directive, while bringing much needed harmonisation of standards for efficacy assurance and human and environmental safety, will severely restrict the availability of biocidal ingredients on which infection control often depends. The costs of registration of an individual biocidal ingredient will be prohibitive for the manufacturers of many small volume, specialised biocides, and they will disappear from the market.

Similarly, the procedures for testing and registration of new biocides, which may be more effective, more efficient, safer for people or safer for the environment, will be sufficiently complex and costly that innovation to find better products is going to be much more difficult and the supply of new, improved, biocides will be very limited indeed.

The provisions of the New Chemicals Strategy, now being discussed within the EU, while providing greater transparency and assurance of safety, may further restrict the ability of the industry to deliver its benefits. It is an uncomfortable paradox that the supply of biocidal ingredients is going to become more constrained just at the time when needs are increasing. Meeting hygiene needs, while optimising and improving products and processes to widen safety margins, to reduce environmental impacts, and to improve longterm sustainability, is clearly going to be a very difficult challenge for I&I suppliers and their customers in the coming years.

Index